THE
SHIP MODEL BUILDER'S ASSISTANT

THE
SHIP MODEL BUILDER'S ASSISTANT

By

CHARLES G. DAVIS

Illustrated by the Author

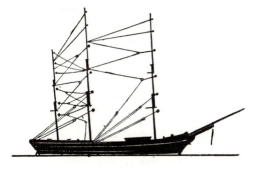

DOVER PUBLICATIONS, INC.
New York

Published in Canada by General Publishing Company, Ltd.,
30 Lesmill Road, Don Mills, Toronto, Ontario.
Published in the United Kingdom by Constable and Company,
Ltd., 10 Orange Street, London WC2H 7EG.

This Dover edition, first published in 1988, is an unabridged
republication of the work originally published as Publication
Number Twelve of the Marine Research Society, Salem,
Massachusetts, in 1926.

Manufactured in the United States of America
Dover Publications, Inc.
31 East 2nd Street
Mineola, N.Y. 11501

Library of Congress Cataloging-in-Publication Data

Davis, Charles G. (Charles Gerard), 1870–1959.
The ship model builder's assistant.

Reprint. Originally published: Salem, Mass. : Marine
Research Society, 1926. Originally published in series:
Publication no. 12 of the Marine Research Society.
Includes index.
1. Ship models.   I. Title.
VM298.D27   1988   745.592'8   87-30312
ISBN 0-486-25584-0 (pbk.)

PREFACE

THE recent publication by this Society, of *Ship Models: How to Build Them*,* written by Charles G. Davis, a naval architect of unusual practical experience in the building of ships and also ship models, at once resulted in a demand for additional information on this fascinating subject. Not content with building a block model, a greater knowledge of ships developed a desire for information on the framing of the "built-up" model. Ship model builders in all parts of the country required details on the deck furniture of various types of vessels at different periods and also on the thousand and one things that the ship builder and rigger must know in order to practice his craft.

Desiring to supply the particular information required by model builders, a questionnaire was sent to everyone who had purchased, direct from the Society, a copy of *Ship Models,* and a large number of replies was received. In an attempt to meet this demand, in part, at least, Mr. Davis has written this book and made a large number of drawings which illustrate, in working detail, the construction of the more important fittings of the ship, its masting and rigging. The whole subject is so extensive that the critical expert is likely to persuade himself that he must collect a library of original source books, but it is believed that *The Ship Model Builder's Assistant* and its predecessor, *Ship Models: How to Build Them,* are useful working manuals that present, in practical form, comprehensive directions on building ship models correctly and in proper proportion.

*Reprinted by Dover Publications, Inc., in 1986, ISBN 0-486-25170-5.

The thanks of the Society are most heartily extended to the many friends who made suggestions concerning the subject-matter to be included in this volume, in several instances entailing considerable correspondence. Mr. Elmer F. Tanner, model builder, of Boston, on several occasions has supplied valuable advice. With a high appreciation of Mr. Davis' expert knowledge and ability, Mr. Malcolm B. Stone and Mr. William B. Northey have watched with enthusiasm the inception and growth of this volume and at every stage they have given advice and criticism. All model builders, using this book, will be under obligation to these three men.

CONTENTS

THE
SHIP MODEL BUILDER'S ASSISTANT

THE
SHIP MODEL BUILDER'S ASSISTANT

CHAPTER I

Types of Ship Models

PACKET ships and clipper ships had distinctive characteristics by which they could be recognized at a glance from that little heard of but more numerous type of plain, common, everyday merchantman that constituted the bulk of the American tonnage. Packets and clippers had a pedigree of their own, as it were, and the newspapers gave long, glowing descriptions of them and their records were given columns in the newspapers, while the rank-and-file would be dismissed in a line in the marine column, reading—"Ship *Betsy,* Sharp, from Madeira." But there were dozens of *Betsies* and *Sallies* to one clipper. They were the common wall-sided, flat-floored, bluff-bowed and heavy, square-transomed ships with which everyone was so familiar that they were just ships and nothing more.

Today, looking back and reviewing all the different types of ships, those little, three hundred ton ships, of about 1820, with their decks laid out with the same simplicity that characterized the schooners and brigs, are a novelty. They had one big, main-cargo hatch just forward of the mainmast. Fiferails, of course, were around each mast, at the deck, for belaying the gear. A fore-scuttle was forward of the foremast and a cuddy, aft, giving access to the after quarters. A log windlass lay across the decks, just abaft the foremast, with a pair of stout bitts at the heel of the bowsprit. Away aft was the steering wheel with its drum and tiller tackles exposed above decks. This constituted the visible deck furniture.

To appreciate what the smaller, single-decked ship really was, one should look at some of the old whalers, as many merchantmen, when worn out from carrying heavy cargoes, have been sold and used for whaling; to float around under topsails, as an ocean tramp, for the remainder of their days.

The shape of ship's hulls, in various decades, has gone through a gradual development that may be traced with some accuracy; but the way in which the decks and houses were built has varied so at all times that no one particular arrangement can be called a standard, for it depended on what trade she was built for or employed in and then, too, the size of the vessel always called for various layouts.

Small ships, single-decked ships, as they were called, because they had only one deck, laid dunnage boards over the top of their ballast on which to stow their cargo. As ships were built larger and deeper they needed another deck to stiffen the hull and also to avoid piling the cargo so deep as to crush the under part, so another deck was built and this was called the lower deck.

During the days of slavery, vessels that were only single-decked, used to carry

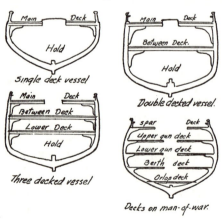

Fig. 1

a temporary deck, only three or four feet below the upper deck, into which low space hundreds of human beings were crowded. This was called a slave-deck and its presence in a vessel was one way by which the men-of-war's men could identify a slaver. Even the presence of lumber on board, with which to build such a deck, was considered sufficient evidence to convict. The female slaves were crowded into the after cabin or partitioned off in the after end of the craft. The officers and crew gave up their quarters below, to accommodate the slaves, and slept at night in what were called "sleeping boxes." The cooking was done on deck in sand-boxes, much the same way as the native small craft in the West Indies do to this day. It is said that the peanut, a native of South America, found its way into the United States by way of Africa, having been carried by the slavers as food for the slaves.

When the depth of hold increased, during the packet ship days, another deck became necessary and this, between the main and lower decks, was called the between deck, pronounced " 'tween decks," by sailors. Some large ships had another deck, away down in the bottom, and this fourth deck was called the orlop deck.

In building ship models, it is the upper decks that mainly concern us. Men-of-war called the main deck, the gun-deck, and the upper deck was called the spar deck. Between the forecastle and the quarter-deck, covering the gun-deck on frigates, were gangways, a narrow strip of deck along each side, just wide enough to cover the guns below and connecting the two so that the sail trimmers had free access fore and aft. Merchant ships built with a continuous upper deck, are said to have a spar deck. Ships with this spar deck, that had an open rail on turned stanchions instead of bulwarks, thereby permitting the water to flow off unobstructed, are said to have a hurricane deck.

The poop deck is the raised deck, aft, and the forecastle head is the raised deck, forward. The poop was usually built with full headroom, which might be between five and six feet, but when it was only three or four feet above the main deck, the ship was said to have a half-deck, and she became a half-deck ship. On this type of ship, the after cabin, with its floor on the same level as the main deck, stuck up through the half-deck far enough to give full headroom in the cabin.

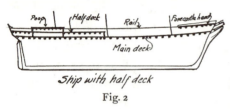

Ship with half deck

Fig. 2

The packet ships, the predecessors of the clippers, were heavy looking craft in their topsides, though under water, while they were big and burdensome for their dimensions, in a more modest way, they aimed for speed also. From 1816 to 1845, just after a long period of warfare on the seas, in their day they naturally followed the trend in design that had brought the American frigates into world-wide renown. They were high-sided, bluff-bowed and wide across the transoms. Everything about their construction had the massive appearance of the frigates from which they descended. Peaceful frigates they were, to carry freight, mail and passengers, for there were no steamers then and the later packets, that had to compete with the early, undeveloped steamships, could outsail the steamers and every trip west, across the Atlantic, found them loaded to capacity with European emigrants eager to come to the land of freedom and opportunity for a poor man.

The pioneer packets, the Black Ball Liners, of 1816,

were small ships of only four hundred to five hundred tons. Larger and larger ships replaced them until in 1843 they were of one thousand tons capacity. These packet ships had long poop decks extending from the stern forward just a little beyond the mainmast. A bulkhead crossed the ship at the forward end of the first-class cabin passengers' quarters which were built in the after part of the ship, below this poop deck. This bulkhead kept back some six or eight feet aft of the end of this deck which formed a covered shelter below. Access was had to the main deck by means of a steep ladder on each side, under two small, square hatchways in the poop deck. Aft, there was a roomy wheelhouse and smoking room with a stairway also leading down to the cabin passenger quarters below. Forward and aft of the mizzenmast were skylights and then came a broad open space to the mainmast, broken only by a capstan placed about midway between the main and mizzenmasts.

On top of the main hatch, down on the main deck, just in front of the mainmast, was a cow-house lashed fast to ringbolts in the deck. Forward of this was the ship's long boat, stowed in skids, also lashed down to ringbolts. The galley smokestack came up through the deck just forward of this boat and behind or aft of the foremast bitts.

Access to the quarters below was down a cuddy or slide just forward of the foremast, the crew's quarters being forward in the eyes of the ship and the steerage or second-class passengers lived under the main deck between the fore and mainmasts.

Some of the larger packets, such as the famous *Dreadnaught,* launched in 1853, a 1400 ton ship, 200 feet long, 39 feet beam and 26 feet depth of hold, had

a covered house clear across the stern. The wheelhouse
or helmsman's quarters, was in the middle, with toilet
rooms to starboard and bathing rooms to port. This
covered house or decked-over part was ten feet long,

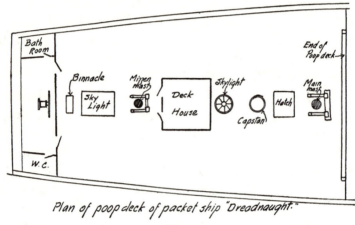

Plan of poop deck of packet ship "Dreadnaught."

Fig. 3

fore and aft. Out on the deck, just forward of this,
where it could be seen through the windows by the man
at the wheel, was the binnacle and forward of that, a
skylight just behind the mizzenmast. Just forward of
the mizzenmast was a large deck-house over the stairs
or companionway, as sailors term them, leading down
to the first-class cabin passengers' quarters,—passengers
who could afford to pay for comforts denied the steerage. The fare in 1830 was 35 guineas for the voyage,
which included beds, bedding, meals, wines, etc. In
this deck-house, with two doors opening aft, were fitted
chairs and settees as a lounging and smoking room.
Forward of this house was a round skylight, one of the
fancy kind with tapered panes of glass. Then came a
capstan, a hatchway and the mainmast.

The total length of this deck was fifty-five feet,

which, in fair weather, gave a fine promenade for the cabin passengers. None of the steerage were allowed off the main deck below.

The clipper ship era was from 1841 to 1860. It began with the little Webb-built ship *Helena,* of 135 feet length on deck, 30 feet 6 inches moulded beam and 20 feet depth of hold, with a tonnage (old measurement) of 856 tons. She was constructed for A. and N. Griswold, for the China tea trade. Following the *Helena* came the *Rainbow, Montauk, Houqua* and *Sea Witch* and after her many others, increasing in size from 500 to 800 tons burden to 2300 tons, in the last of the clippers.

The little *Helena,* following the custom of the packet ship, the clipper's predecessor, had much the look and model of a frigate; but once started in quest of speed, the American designers and shipbuilders soon dropped all preconceived ideals of ship's proportions and a comparison of the plans of the *Helena* and the *Sea Witch* will show to what extremes the changes in ship modeling went in the short time between 1841 and 1846.

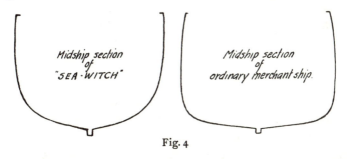

Fig. 4

The *Helena* was bluff-bowed at the water line, and the *Sea Witch* was hollow-bowed. No wonder the waterfront community said that the latter's bow was turned inside out. The midship section was cut away so fine and round, that by contrast with the square, box-like midship sections of former craft, the change was too sudden for the comprehension of waterfronts and all kinds of disaster was predicted for her. It was predicted that she was going to founder by running her bows clean under water. Instead of that she ran her bows up out of water. Other builders then began to sharpen up on their ship's bows but they did it very cautiously, each ship being a little finer. But none of them would concede to the easy midship section that Griffiths, who designed the *Sea Witch,* put on his ships. They clung to the flat-floored midship section as long as they could.

The changes more apparent to the casual observer, were the elimination of all the fancy work at the bow

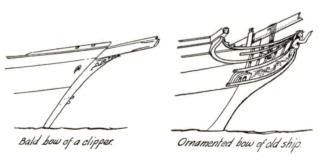

Bald bow of a clipper.   *Ornamented bow of old ship.*

Fig. 5

and stern. There was nothing left on the later clippers but a small carved image, close up under the bowsprit, on an otherwise naked bow, where formerly there were fiddle-boards, trail-boards, hair rails, hair brackets and ornaments galore. At the stern, the big, heavy, bay-window effect, with its overhanging galleries, carved pilasters and slanting windows, so dear to the hearts of the old-time seamen, were cleaned off as neat and clean as on a Whitehall boat's stern. The squat, lower transom disappeared, the rudder carrying up almost to the deck line, the after quarters were so lean and sharp.

The most astonishing thing, however, concerning these huge clippers, was the spaciousness of their broad decks and their great length. After climbing over such little ships as the *Rebecca Carnano,* the *G. D. Zaldo,* and others, whose decks from bow to stern were a continuous congestion of hatches and deck-houses, the large, open sweep of a clipper's deck struck one very forcibly—decks so wide that there was a capstan on either side of the poop deck and either side of the forward deck by the foremast with ample room to walk the bars around and have room to spare. Everything about the deck furniture seemed so small, due to the bigness of the ship, that it impressed one with the size of the craft. A man shrank into such insignificant proportions aboard one of these craft that it fairly awed him with respect for such of his fellowmen as dared attempt the mastery of such a hugh fabric of wood and iron. The topsail halliard blocks appeared small in the maze of spars, ropes and other blocks, but when you came to lift one you discovered what immense things they actually were.

A little south of Rio we sighted a sail astern, early one morning. At noon, one of these big Frisco-bound ships was abeam, as delicate-looking as a spider's web, with every stitch of canvas set including three skysails, and going through the water two feet to our one. Our bark carried a crew of eight men and the stranger probably stowed about thirty in her forecastle. Those immense blocks, that were all one man could lift, looked to us no bigger than beads and the heavy ropes rove through them, like threads. But a handsomer picture never was presented to the gaze of man than such a ship logging her twelve knots under full sail.

Such a ship is a different creature, when viewed at sea, clothed from deck to skysails in white canvas, cut and set as only a Yankee ship's sails were, from the same vessel lying inert and disheveled, alongside a wharf, while being loaded.

Deep-waisted bulwarks, around the naked-looking decks of these ships, gave an appearance of simplicity, in striking contrast to one of the two thousand ton, Bath-built ships of 1870 or thereabouts, with its many deck encumbrances. These later ships were built with a high quarter deck aft and a raised forecastle-head forward. They had fore, main and after hatchways for loading and unloading cargo. A long deck-house ran clear from the foremast, aft, almost to the main hatch, containing crew's quarters, carpenter shop and galley. Some ships fitted with a steam donkey-engine and boiler, had a room in the deck-house, called the "donkey room." On top of the deck-house, turned upside down on skids, were two ship's long boats, for these craft carried a crew of thirty-odd men.

The after house, raised some three feet above the quarter deck, was fitted with skylights and companion-ways and sometimes a couple of double-ended whale boats would be stowed on skids, one on either side, just forward of the mizzen rigging. This elevated poop deck was the sanctuary of the ship's officers and in tacking ship it gave the "old man" room enough to stomp about, wave his arms and cuss to his heart's content. A long, steep ladder led down from the forward end of this poop to the main deck and a short ladder led aft to the quarter deck, which ended near the after end of this after house with a ladder at each side in the alleyways.

There was a private companionway leading down to the captain's quarters, aft, and just aft of it was the steering wheel.

The little, flush-decked coaster had a single barrel lever pump abaft her mainmast, but this big, soft wood ship had a double-chambered, diaphragm flywheel pump mounted on the extended main fiferail.

To handle warps, there was a small capstan, away forward, on the forecastle head, and a heavier, double-acting capstan was near the after end, for hoisting and stowing the anchors and for heaving the windlass. There was another capstan, aft, between the mainmast and after-hatch and also winch heads at the fore and main bitts for emergency cases in getting out cargo. These were also used for mastheading the heavy main-topsail yard when reefing topsails down off Cape Horn where man-power becomes all but exhausted in the killing weather of those latitudes.

These big, Maine-built ships were beauties and represented the last word in ship construction. Many of them, nowadays, are referred to as clippers, but they are as different from the true clipper, as a brewery horse is from a trotting mare—well kept, but not speedy.

CHAPTER II

THE BUILT-UP MODEL

THE height of every ship model builder's ambition is to make a real built-up model of one of those old-time three-decked men-of-war that were the pride of European nations during the seventeenth century. They were round-sided ships with tumble-home top sides, beautifully adorned with carvings along the upper works, their sterns a blaze of colorful carvings and paintings, with windows and bal-

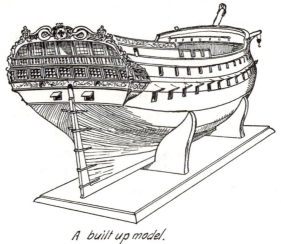

A built up model.

Fig. 6

conies, all harmoniously proportioned. The other end of the ship was also adorned with curved rails and an elaborately carved image for a figure-head that was generally symbolic of her name.

There is a lot of work connected with the making of one of these models and anyone undertaking to build one should first of all be very careful to get a design to work from that is correct. It is most exasperating to get well along with the construction of your model and then find that a grievous error has been made in the plans. It is far better to go carefully over the plans before you begin work. Only recently, a friend of mine undertook to build a three-decked French line-of-battleship, from a set of plans printed in an old book on shipbuilding. He had all these plans enlarged by the photostat process and naturally supposed they were accurate. He went ahead and did a lot of work; bought a whole log of boxwood and had it sawed up to the proper thickness for frames and keel and then, when he got stuck, called upon me for help. I found that the three plans did not agree; that they were unfair; that the heights in one plan did not coincide with the heights in the other. The result was that he had to scrap most of the work done, redraw and fair-up the set of lines and then begin over again.

Boxwood is preferable in several ways to use for the built-up model. It is close grained and holds fastenings well; does not split easily; lasts almost forever and will take on a beautifully polished finish with varnish to show the work. If the model is to be painted, other cheaper woods can be used. Maple, apple and black-walnut are good woods for the frames, and for the straight members, such as the keel and planking, use black-walnut, or mahogany, if it is not possible to get boxwood that is dry and well seasoned. Clear white pine or Spanish cedar also makes good planking but is so soft that it is necessary to use more fastenings to hold it to the frame; but on a painted model this will not show.

Cut the keel, stem, deadwood and stern-post out of separate pieces and fasten together with glue and nails.

This forms the backbone (Fig. 7), as it were, of the ship and on this you should mark the location of each frame. Then, referring to the body-plan, as the end view which shows the shape of each frame is called, determine how deep and at just what angle the plank-

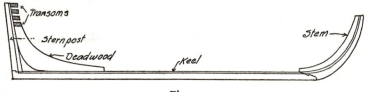

Fig. 7

ing comes off the frame into this keel and cut a continuous notch, termed the rabbet, in the keel to receive the planking. By referring to the body-plan you will notice that this varies in angle as the frames become more vertical towards the ends, than it is at the middle of the ship (Fig. 8).

If in doubt as to how thick the keel, deadwood, stem,

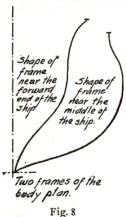

Fig. 8

etc., should be, use the rule laid down by the old-time builders of ships which was to make the keel's thickness equal to .04 of the ship's breadth of beam. The bottom plank should be .0185 of the half-breadth of the ship, and in cutting the rabbet, the depth was always regulated so as to take that thickness and no deeper. Yet, the lowest plank, the garboard (Fig. 9), as it was called, was one and one-half times as thick as the bottom planking, the back of it being cut off to fit the rabbet, which had to be wider up and down but cut in no deeper than the bottom plank

would require. The three planks next to the garboard
gradually diminish in thickness until they are the same
as the bottom planking.

The seam, where the edge of the
plank meets the keel, is called the
rabbet and is left, as it should be in
every seam on the outside of the
ship, slightly opened on the outer
edge so that caulking can be ham-

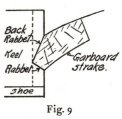

Fig. 9

mered in, wedging tighter and tighter to make the seam
watertight. The angle made by the rabbet should be

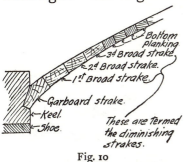

Fig. 10

neutral to both the face of
the plank and the face of
the keel so that in caulking the iron exerts an
equal pressure on both
(Fig. 11) and does not
act as a wedge to lift the
plank off.

Where the outer face
of the garboard, or side planks, and the keel meet is
called the *rabbet line;* where the inner corner of the
plank makes an angle in the keel is the *back-rabbet line;*

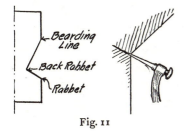

Fig. 11

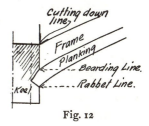

Fig. 12

and where the inner face of the plank and keel meet is
the *bearding line,* which is the line where the men adz-
ing away the wood start to cut or "beard" (Fig. 12).

There is another important line that should be carefully laid out on the plans before you even start to cut out the keel or deadwood and that is the *cutting-down line,* a line to show where the inner edge of the frames meets the side of the stem and deadwood (Fig. 13). It is the line that really determines the shape of the deadwood, for it shows to what height, at each frame, it is necessary to leave wood to have something to fasten the frames to in the ends of the ship, before she flattens out sufficiently to let the frames themselves go right across the keel when no more deadwood is required.

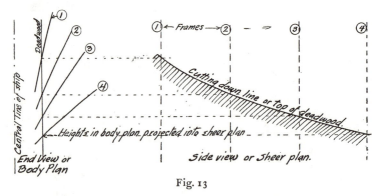

Fig. 13

This may seem dry and unimportant detail to go into, but it is the very foundation of your ship and its neglect has caused many failures in attempts at model ship-building. The rest will come easy if you only start right.

Get those three lines right—the rabbet, bearding and cutting-down or deadwood lines—before you try to put up the frames.

By building up only what can be seen on the outside, a model that looks like a real ship, unless carefully inspected, may be built by leaving out a lot of the really difficult interior construction. This is the way the ma-

jority of built-up ship models are made. Many of the
so-called Admiralty models were left incomplete inside
but on the outside, the highest class of skilled wood-
carvers and the men who spent their lives building
models, put forth great efforts to make the models look
attractive so as to curry favor with the "big-wigs" in
authority, who were to decide whether or no the ship
should be built.

One way of building what looks like a built-up ship
model is to carve out of a block of wood the shape of
the hull and then nail the narrow strips of planking to

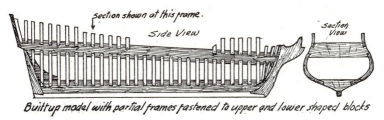

Builtup model with partial frames fastened to upper and lower shaped blocks

Fig. 14

this block. While this is an easy way of making a very
effective looking ship it does not show the construction,
as the real built-up ships do, where the planking is left
off showing the frames. But that can be done and even
now is being accomplished by carving out the bottom
part of the ship and also the topsides and connecting the
two by sawed frames to show the open, built-up effect
(Fig. 14). Enough planking is then put on to hide the
joints between the blocks and the frames.

It requires care and great accuracy to work closely
to the plans and there must be a temporary, but rigid,
and at the same time a removable connection between
the top and the bottom blocks to keep them from slew-
ing out of line and thereby making a crooked ship while
building. After a few frames, at wide intervals, are

fastened in and while there is yet room, the spacer chocks used inside can be removed and the framing completed.

This construction is recommended for several reasons. It is the easiest and simplest way, and by being cut from one block of wood, it gives a rigidity to the topsides and insures an accuracy, to obtain which, in a full built-up model, would drive most men to despair.

If you are going to construct a built-up model begin right. Don't try to build on too small a scale. One-quarter inch to the foot has been found to be as small a scale as it is practical to build to.

Amateur ship model builders always take great pains to get the outside of the frame fair but are not so careful on the inside. In ship-model building, the inside is faired up first and wood enough is left on the outside to dub, or cut it down fair, after the fore and aft clamps and stringers have been fastened inside. If care is not taken to cut the frames just the right thickness and bevel, these fore and aft members push and pull the frames until they are fair inside. The outside, thus pushed out in places, can be cut or filed off later to a fair surface, but it is awkward cutting down on the inside.

Frames are made in two thicknesses, one piece overlapping the joints in the other, and both are then glued and fastened together (Fig. 15). By so making them in sections, the grain of the wood can be made to run lengthwise. Cut out, fasten together and true-up each frame before setting it up in its place on the keel. By frame, we mean both sides of the ship, and while it is not so important in a model, in real shipbuilding it is of vital importance to shift the butts or joints, in no matter what part of the ship's

Fig. 15

structure they occur, so that they do not make a continuous row, which would be a structural weakness.

The spacing of the frames was always a percentage of the length of the ship, .027 in merchant ships; .0172 in a war-ship of about 400 tons; and this was termed the "room and space," or the distance between centers of the frames, the frames themselves being a little less (.47%) than half this distance. The wood required to saw the frames out of, therefore, should be half the thickness of the frames, and in sawing the shape of the end frames one-half of the frame will bevel under and the other half *over* from the

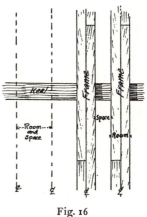

Fig. 16

line representing the shape of the frame where the two halves meet.

Mark off the distance represented by the room and space along the keel and set the center of each frame to those marks (Fig. 16). The space between frames should be

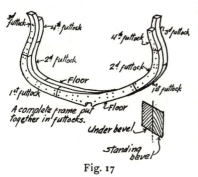

Fig. 17

about the same width as the room the frames themselves occupy. This, in some models, is left entirely too big.

Do not use screws, nails or bolts in putting together the futtocks, as the short lengths composing each frame are called, as they will interfere with more important fastenings when you come to fasten on the planking.

Buy at some drug store, a box of small, round, wooden "applicators," as they are called. They are about the diameter of a match, and about six inches long. Drill

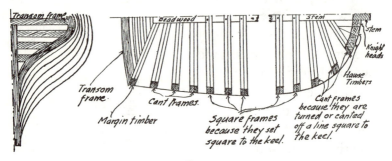

Fig. 18

holes so that they will just drive in snug and with a drop of glue, when driven through and cut off flush on each side, they will make a strong fastening yet one that may

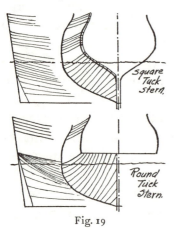

Fig. 19

be bored through when the outside planking is put on.

The frames in the middle of the ship are easy to make as there is very little bevel to them, but at the ends this bevel becomes very acute. The last six or eight frames are "cant frames," that is, they are canted or turned a little so that they fit more nearly square to the outside of the ship (Fig. 18). The corner between the forward cant frame and the stem is packed solid with timber, the two (one on each side) next to the stem being the knight-heads, the timbers that are carried up to steady the bowsprit, and the others the hawse-timbers, through which the hawser-holes are cut. At the stern, the last cant frame is termed the margin piece, it forming a corner piece on the old ships prior to 1610, as the planks all ended on this frame and the ship's stern was planked up so that she was flat across the stern, even down below the water line (Fig. 19).

Pett, an English naval authority, in 1610, abolished this cumbersome stern on English ships and carried the planking up rounding to the transom, to a horizonal cross seam at the wing transom.

The wing transom is a heavy horizontal beam fastened to the sternpost in the center and to the margin frame at the counter, or the outer ends. The space below the wing transom and the sternpost is filled with horizontal framing similar to transoms, moulded to the shape of the ship, the bevels being too rank, or acute, for any more vertical frames.

On modern sailing ships, with high-tucked sterns, the transom was built up of several heavy timbers, for a depth of three or four feet, and was, so far as strength went, the real ending, aft, of the ship. The stern was carried aft with counters enough to house the rudder head and form a short space aft which was used for the storage of ship's gear and termed the lazarette. This space was reached through hatches in the deck above. But on old timers, the stern frame was built up and up in a series of decks, with counters extending aft, each one a little more than the other, with a most elaborately carved, arching stern frame crowning all; and on each side, little castle-like galleries were built out overhanging the water and also covered with gilded and brightly painted carvings of figures, animals or floral designs.

If one is going to the trouble of building a built-up hull, he should frame up all this stern, as it is impossible to express its beauty in any kind of solid-block carving put on in one piece. This may be done if it is a faked built-up model, before mentioned, with bottom and top carved with partial frames between. In that case, the built effect can be nailed on outside of the solid piece which gives the shape, the finish being "plaster-work" stuck on the outside.

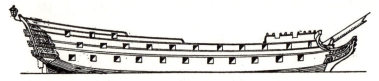

Fig. 20

What makes the old seventeenth century ships so difficult to build is the fact that the outside construction members of the hull, such as the wales, had nothing whatever in common with the inside decks and clamp strakes. The sweep of the rails was considerable, but the deck lines ran almost straight fore and aft. The line of gun ports, which has to be a certain fixed distance above the deck (see chapter on gun ports), did not follow the sweep of the outside plank, but cut promiscuously through it (Fig. 20). This looks so odd that many amateurs think it should not be and so make their ship's decks and gun ports follow the sweep of the outside lines. Aft, on such a built model, the deck would sweep up on an incline on which no human being could ever keep his footing in wet or slippery weather. Ships were not built in this way. It is a case of misinterpretation of plans by men who do not know.

If the top of your model is carved out of a solid block, the portholes can be bored and cut out square to a suf-

ficient depth so that when painted black they will look
like real portholes; but if the ship is really all framed
up it is quite a puzzle to leave all the ports, especially
on a three-decker, each row of ports being staggered,
between those below them and not all
one above the other. The frames,
also, are lighter and lighter as they go
up from the keel, each futtock being
a little thinner than the one below it;
so that the frames at the top are about
one-half the size they are at the floor
ends.

Fig. 21

Most built-up models do not have
their frames lightened up at the top,
but are all sawed out of one thickness of wood. It will
be found much easier to work in the gun ports (Fig.
21) if the frames are diminished in thickness at the
head, and if properly laid out, so that the futtocks end

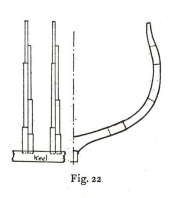

Fig. 22

Fig. 23

just below the gun ports, the ledge, made by the difference in thickness between the frame's futtocks, will
come just right for the chock to land on when put horizontally between the frames.

Personally, I always prefer the built-up sectional

frames (Fig. 22), but many men saw all the frames on each side, from rail to keel, out of one piece of wood, laying the frame out so that the grain of the wood runs diagonally across it and thus escapes being absolutely cross-grained at any one point (Fig. 23). They make the frame of only one thickness and lap the two pieces at the keel. Most of the Admiralty models are made this way; and all that one needs is the body plan of the ship, showing each frame, and then saw each of these out with a jig saw.

The previously described method is the way real ships are built and it is a complex undertaking for a

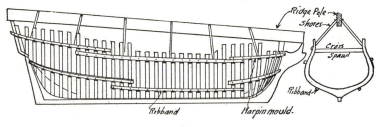

Fig. 24

novice to tackle, for the butts of the various futtocks, or pieces composing a frame, are confusing, yet, once understood, it saves a lot of wood as all small pieces can be used and a stronger frame results from not using any cross-grained wood. Be careful not to have one continuous line of butts from bow to stern. Stagger the butts.

There are a hundred and one little things to learn about keel and frame construction, such as the various kinds of scarfs or joints, coaks, used at every bolt to make it watertight; stopwaters, at every outside seam, to keep the water from seeping through; chocks, at each butt between frame futtocks; salt stops, etc., etc., but as all these are not really needed in making a good-looking ship model, we will have to eliminate such details.

When the frames are all up, each one braced securely from the top to a central fore and aft ridge piece, and with ribbands or thin battens bent lengthwise from frame to frame to keep them in proper alignment

Fig. 25

along in the middle of the ship (Fig. 24), and with sawed out curved pieces, called "harpin moulds," to fit around on the outside of the end frames, we are

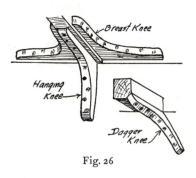

Fig. 26

ready to proceed with the deck-frame. If it were a real ship, the whole of the inside of the frame would have to be dubbed, that is, cut fair with adzes so that the inside ceiling would lie fair against the frames; but this is all left out in models. Some run a single clamp strake, at the level of each deck line, so that the deck beams may rest on it (Fig. 25), but many model builders don't even do that, but just fasten the deck beams to the side of the frames.

On real ships, all these deck beams butt against the frame and are further secured by great, wooden knees;—breast-knees, laid horizontally; hang-ing-knees, put vertically; and

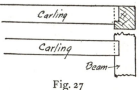

Fig. 27

dagger-knees, set off at an angle (Fig. 26). On account of its inaccessibility, all this work is generally omitted in models unless they are built to a large scale, ¼ of an inch to the foot or more. When the model is a three-decker, an occasional frame is fitted on the lower and upper gun-decks, but on the deck that is uppermost of all, the main deck, or spar deck, and the poop and forecastle decks, it is framed in full. The lower decks, such as the berth deck and orlop deck, are generally omitted entirely.

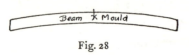

Fig. 28

Where there are hatch openings in the deck, and also on each side of the mast, forward and aft, the beams are usually made extra heavy and the fore and aft carlines that pick up the ends of the short beams are notched into them (Fig. 27).

All deck beams, on the real ship, must be sawed out with a crown or arch of about a quarter of an inch to the foot. Make a pattern, a beam mould, and shape all the beams by this, the mould being a true arc of a circle (Fig. 28).

Just how the deck beams are laid out depends upon the individual ship. The arrangement of hatches and decks, the size of the ship and the trade for which she is built, all govern this. Men - of - war required stronger deck frames than merchantmen, to withstand the weight and recoil of the cannon. That is why there are so many fore and aft car-

Fig. 29

lines, for, like the cross-braces or the bridging between the floor joists of a house, they stiffen the deck beams, which are supported, as well, by vertical stanchions. These stanchions go from deck to deck, clear down to the bottom of the ship where they rest on the keelson, one under each main beam, at each end of a hatchway, and forward and aft of the masts, etc., etc.

There is nothing very difficult about framing the deck. It is something almost anyone, with a plan, showing how it is laid out, can comprehend readily. All that it requires is careful cutting and fitting of joints. At each mast there is a solid packing of wood of the same thickness as the beams, and bracing it to the heavy beams are breast knees. This reinforcement is called the mast partners (Fig. 29). Similar knees are fitted at the corner of every hatchway or opening in the deck, and along each side where the beams join the side of the ship, tying the deck frame to the side frames.

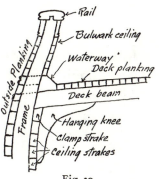

Fig. 30

When the deck frame is all in we come to a really difficult job, and that is the fitting in of the waterways, the heavy timber in the corner formed by the bulwarks and the deck (Fig. 30). On modern sailing ships, those of the 1850's, the sides of the ships were so straight that the waterway can be sprung in from a straight stick. But with the old style of tumble-home topsides on ships, with more curve to their side lines, it is safer to shape the waterways so that they fit in naturally. The hardest part of all is around the bows, where old-time ships were so blunt that they formed a half circle. There the waterways must be cut out in sections, scarfing, as the laps are termed, the ends of the pieces together (Fig. 31).

If great accuracy in detail is desired, fit hook scarfs

to all these joints instead of the more easily cut plain or flat scarfs (Fig. 32). The scarf should be in length four times the width of the timber and be fastened with four clinch bolts and with two spikes in each nib end.

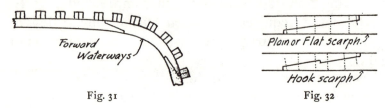

Forward Waterways

Plain or Flat scarph.

Hook scarph.

Fig. 31   Fig. 32

Most model builders do not carry the waterways clear through, from end to end, as much of it would be hidden under the poop and forecastle. They only carry out all the detail of construction where it shows on the upper deck. The same kind of waterways are carried out on each deck, but on men-of-war there is a distinct difference from the waterways on merchant ships. Merchant ships have raised waterways, but on men-of-war this would interfere with the wheels on the gun carriages, and the deck must be all on the same level (Fig. 33).

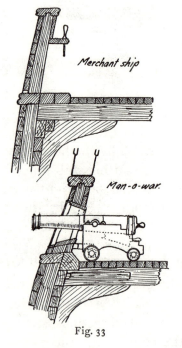

Merchant ship

Man-o-war.

Fig. 33

Merchant ships had only a single thickness of planking to their bulwarks, that on the outside, but men-of-war used the bulwarks as a breastwork and had inside plank as well.

The former is termed an open bulwarks, the latter, a solid bulwarks. The packet ships of 1830 and 1840, that followed on the heels of war, had the solid bulwarks; but while this style lasted in some ships into the 1850's, by 1860 the open bulwarks came into general use on American ships.

Do not attempt to ceil up the inside of your model's bulwarks with narrow strips, but cut out one wide piece to fit from waterways to rail and scratch the seams in to represent narrow planks. The greatest difficulty in connection with this light work is to get the proper fastenings. The wood is only about one thirty-second of an inch thick, so the pin or nail need be only about three sixteenths long. Take half-inch bank pins; cut them off and file a new point and then, holding the pin in a pair of pliers, file the oval-topped head down to a paper-thin flat head. I have not yet found where I can buy such small nails, but evidently someone makes them, for they are used on mouth-organs, one at each end, on each side, to nail the tin down, and are just $\frac{3}{16}$ inch long and about as thick as a No. 70 drill.

On account of the expansion and contraction in such a wide surface as the deck of a model, it is not advisable to attempt either to lay it all in strips or to put it on in wide sheets, creased to represent boards. The latter will buckle or crack. It is better to do as most of the old Admiralty model builders did, viz.: to lay a few strips of decking inside the waterways and a wide strip down the center of the deck and let the deck beams show the rest of the way. Crease the seams to represent the deck plank, if one wide board is used, and paint it with a rather thick mixture of black, mixed with just a little oil and plenty of turpentine and work it well into the seams. Then, before it dries, wipe it all off again and the seams will stay black. Then scrape the surface lightly and the deck will look like that on a real ship.

If the deck is to be planked up, each plank separately, use a straight edge to push the new plank snug up against its neighbor. If each plank has its upper edge bevelled slightly and a wiping is given of thin, black, marine glue along the edge, not only will the two pieces stick together, but the seams will be filled up with black. This glue can readily be scraped off when chilled, but not when it is warm, for it softens like rubber in hot weather.

The ends of the deck planks should never show a sharp, slim point. Ships were never built so. Just inside the waterways, a plank, the same thickness as the decking and about one and a half the width of the deck planks, is bent around against the waterways and jogs are cut into this "nib-strake," to take the squared-off nib ends of deck planking (Fig. 34). They were laid this way so that the ends could be caulked with a narrow caulking iron.

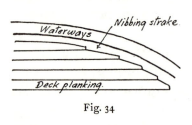

Fig. 34

At the forward edge of the poop and quarter decks and both forward and after edges of the forecastle, the waterways are carried across thicker than the deck, the same as at the sides, but projecting over the vertical bulkhead a foot or so. On old-time ships each stanchion of the vertical bulkhead was ornamented with the full-length figure of a Nubian slave, or something of that character. Sometimes the carving represented an animal or a floral design. It is the exquisite carving with which many of the old Admiralty models are decorated that appeals so strongly to many persons (Fig. 35).

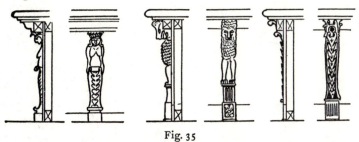

Fig. 35

The date at which many models were built may be traced by the heraldic design depicted in the elaborate stern ornamentation. This is also true of the ship's nationality, as English, French, Spanish, Dutch and Swedish ships of state were so ornamented and also the early American men-of-war.

In 1815, the square beak-head was abolished. Up to that time this had been the usual way of building ships; but prior to that, ships were built square across the front of the forecastle head, which set back from the point of the stem, so that the main deck formed a small platform forward of it and the whole space across, from head rail to head rail, under the bowsprit, was filled with gratings (Fig. 36).

The bulwarks carried through to the knight heads, on almost all of the ships, but the height of the bulwark and the sweep it was cut to, on top, depended on the relative height of the knee of the head, to the main deck. It generally coincided in height with the hair rail that swept in a curve from the cat-head to the back of the figure-head.

Aft, the decks went up like a pair of steps, their framing of beams and carlines being constructed the same as

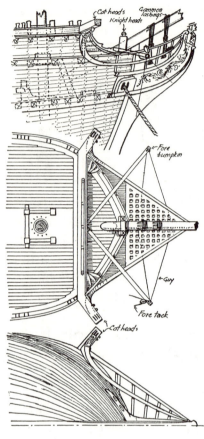

Fig. 36

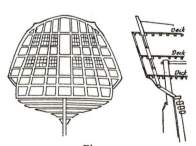

Fig. 37

the main deck except that smaller sized beams were used. Where these decks end, aft, at the transoms, the construction, on ships with two or three decks, is quite elaborate, as most of those big ships had glass windows or doors clear across the stern. The windows were of nine or twelve lights, and three or four feet farther aft, extended balconies with fancy turned balustrades, the deck above forming a sheltering roof. The sides and decks carried aft, farther than the transom, and were finished off with an arch-like stern frame, beautifully carved. This stern frame extended out wide enough to include the little quarter-galleries that were built out on each after quarter of the ship (Fig. 37).

In building your model, frame up the transom, with all its windows and doors, but leave off the stern frame until the model is all planked up.

If you are skilful at wood carving, you will have ample opportunity to display your skill on this stern frame, for on the old men-of-war it was one mass of carving.

There is now on the market a product called plastic-wood. It is very fine wood-dust mixed with some sort of glue and ether. It dries quickly and becomes as hard as wood; has no grain and can be modelled easily to the rough outline while it is being stuck on like so much putty, and the finer parts can be picked out after it has hardened. When finished off in various tints of color and gold leaf, this is as good as if carved out of solid wood and yet, if too much should be cut off, the work is not ruined, for more can be stuck on over the work and the carving tried again and again until it is satisfactory. I have modelled ship's small boats, out of this wet pulp, as thin as paper, and when thoroughly dry they were stronger than carved - out boats as there was no cross-

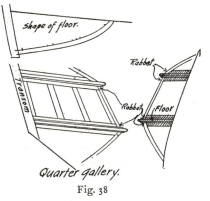

Fig. 38

grained wood and they can be finished off with a fine file to show small details of construction.

But to return to the stern of the model. One way of building out those little bay-windows, on each quarter of the ship, aft, is to carve them out of a solid block and put the stiles and rails on, plastered on to the outside with glue, using under them a thin, washed-off photographic film to represent window glass, with thin lines painted on to represent the window frames. This can be done or the galleries can be built on piece by piece.

First cut out thin pieces of wood, to the shape of each floor, putting on a band of celluloid, or film, where the glass windows show and then, after carving the outer rails, stiles, etc., fasten them on against the floor pieces. Be sure to make these floors thicker than the

finished edges that show a beaded edge on the outside, so there will be a ledge or rabbet to hold the windows and other outside finish parts (Fig. 38).

Above all, see that the stiles are symmetrical. All should radiate from a point above and if this is not strictly observed, the entire beauty of the architecture of the stern is

Fig. 39

destroyed (Fig. 39.) The same is also true in regard to the fore and aft sweep of the various rails, for they should carry out the lines of the sheer of the ship and conform strictly to them. If one of these rails is the least bit out of line, it will catch the eye instantly, but if all run true and fair they give a most pleasing impression.

The trouble with most models is that the carving is made entirely too clumsy, too massive, which was just the effect the ship builders and carvers of old strove to overcome. They put their ornamentation

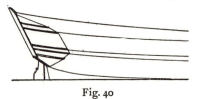

Fig. 40

on so as to give a light and delicate appearance to hide the massiveness of the structure behind it all.

It is astonishing how rigid the frame of one of these little models becomes, when the clamps and deck beams are all fastened in; but for all that, great care must be exercised when fairing up the outside of the frame so that the planking will lie true against it. It is a good plan to put small chocks of wood at the bilge and half-way up the side, to fit snugly between each two frames and steady them all, so that with a wide, flat file you can, by rubbing it fore and aft, cut down the high frames to fair up with the rest without fear of racking or breaking a frame.

Old ships had several strakes of heavy, square timbers, forming ridges fore and aft, with the thinner

Scribing To find the shape of a plank

Fig. 41

side planks forming belts or bands between. The plan will show the number and location, according to the type of ship, and when these are nailed fast, the frame will be tied together so there will be no further fear of their being knocked out of place.

The sweep of these, the main wales and channel wales, determines the beauty of the ship and when you put them on carefully sight them from all angles of view and see that they run true and fair in relation to the other sheer lines of the ship. Forward, the ends will have to be steamed and bent to get them around the bluff bow (or they can be sawed out to the shape required), but aft, they can probably be sprung on cold.

They need not be all in one piece, but when you join them make a scarf joint; don't just butt them together.

The belts of planking, in between, can be got out in one width or put on in narrow strakes, as one prefers. But in either case there will be some fitting around the bows. Take a very thin ($\frac{1}{16}$ inch or less) piece of wood or cardboard and bend it around and cut and fit it so that you can determine the shape the planks must be, edgeways (Fig. 41). It is not advisable to bend the plank edgeways, too much, in model work, as the

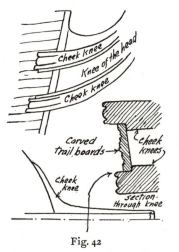

Cheek Knee
Knee of the head
Cheek knee

Carved
trail boards→
cheek
knees

cheek
knee

Section
through knee

Fig. 42

fastenings are so small they are apt to give way and let seams open. It is safer to shape the wood perfectly to the work rather than to force it.

After all the planks are on, take a smooth, flat file and file down flush with the planking all the button-like pin-heads or nail-heads. Then lay out the location of the cheeks and cheek-knees (Fig. 42). The latter are put each side of the knee of the head to steady it, with the sweep to match the cheeks and with their outer edge shaped to a moulding. The upper and lower cheek-knees are riveted to the bows of the ship and through the stem and knee of the head, being continued on, up, in an arc of a circle or section of a parabola, to the figure-head.

On a real ship there is a shoulder rabbeted out on the under side of the upper knee and the upper side of the lower and fastened from one to the other were the trail boards, the product of the ship carver who carved these boards into beautiful floral or scroll designs, working in at the same time some ideas symbolic of the ship's name or nationality (Fig. 43). These trail boards butt against the cheeks, with a thick padding of wood between the cheek knees, on the bow, and on top of these cheeks are fastened two or three hawse pieces or pads of hard wood to round out the hole (hawse-hole) that the rope cable leads through, so that the

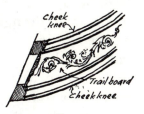

Fig. 43

cable will not be broken by being bent over too sharp a corner (Fig. 44).

The rails of the head are a delicate job and must be done just right or they will be a disappointment rather than an ornament.

Looking sideways at the bow, the rails of the head should all radiate from the scroll at the top of the figure-head, widening out as they go aft. Their relative positions will be easily remembered if one understands that they were intended to form seats of ease for the crew. The top rail is the back rail, the second the seating rail and the third the foot rail (Fig. 45). The top rail is termed the *hair rail,* as it ends forward at the very top in the hair of the figure-head. The second is called the

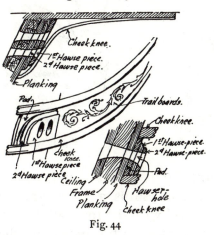

Fig. 44

middle rail and the third the *main rail,* by those too
modest to use ship yard expressions or terms.   Once
understood one cannot get these rails misplaced.   First
put on the hair rail, from the forward corner of the
beak-head, in a straight line, looking down on the ship
to the end of the figure-head.   In the sheer view this has
a sweep down in a parabolic curve, though, in the very
old ships, this curve was almost an arc of a circle.   With
this rail in place fit the five hair rail brackets that butt
against the stern and top of the upper cheek knee.   The
first one to fit is the one on the stern just forward of the
plank ends and on the same rake or slant as the rabbet
line.   Each successive knee, forward of this, should
have a slightly increasing rake or slant, all radiating
from a point down near the ship's fore foot (Fig. 46).

Fig. 45

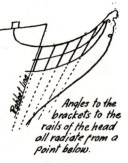

*Angles to the
brackets to the
rails of the head
all radiate from a
point below.*

Fig. 46

Don't set them vertically, for it makes a clumsy, un-
shiplike appearance.   On small ships, a slat or grating
floor was laid across on a level with the foot rail, but on
very large ships these rails were too far apart, and the
floor was laid across on a level with the hair-rails and
seats of ease were built in along the sides of the bowsprit
or in the after corner up against the ship's bows.

CHAPTER III

Wooden Sail Models

CASE oil or kerosene used to be shipped in wooden boxes, with a wood partition, that held two five gallon tin cans. Those empty tins would be found everywhere from Peru to China and from Cape Town to Scandinavia. They were used by the natives to carry water in, to cook in, and for a thousand and one other purposes. The wooden boxes were often made of a fine grade of white pine that cut like cheese and this was used by the sailors to carve out sets of wooden sails for all kinds of vessels from a schooner to a full-rigged ship. The full-rigged ship was generally preferred above all others and royals, skysails, moonsails, and star scrapers were put on regardless of accuracy, for sailors loved to brag of the ships they had sailed on as having unusual sails and lies (drawing the "long bow," as they expressed it) were indulged in promiscuously.

That is why those sailor-made models are of no historical value, as, with no pretense of being to scale, they were just whittled out to pass away time in watches below. A handy man, with his jack-knife, by the time the ship reached port, would often have several sets of these sails stowed away in his sea chest. Only half of each sail was made, that part from the mast out. They were cut on their inner edges to a bevel, and when nailed to a painted sky backboard they would stand out in quite a realistic manner. Half of the ship's hull was then added and a sea of putty completed the picture. Shallow sides were usually nailed around and a glass front was put on just like a picture in a shadow-box (Fig. 47).

Some men were more skilful carvers and instead of representing only half the sails, they carved the full sail which made a much better appearance, as the space

Fig. 47

between the ship's masts was filled up more with sails. The inner edges were bevelled in the same way. The front of each sail was carved as if it were full of wind and the outer edges were bevelled down to a very thin edge while the backs of the sails were left thick, as thick as the wood had to be, to allow carving the rounded surface.

Another trick the knowing ones always turned, was to cut the bevels on the back of the upper sail so that it stood out more square to the backboard. The next sail below was bevelled a little more, each one, going down from the top, being bevelled more and more (Fig. 48) just as a ship's sails were "checked in," as it is termed, so the light upper sails will give warning by backing when the ship comes

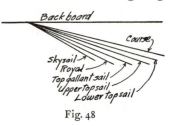

Fig. 48

up too close to the wind, before the lower sails come aback.

To carve these sails, you will need a soft, even-grained piece of wood, in which the grain runs cross-ways, that is, from the backboard out to the edge of the sail.

To make a full model is more difficult. Besides having to make the complete hull, from the waterline up, with the under side cut on a bevel so that the ship will set heeled over to one side, you will have to make a set of masts and then carve a full set of sails. The outside of the sail is rounded first, after having been cut to shape to fit between the yards, and then the inside or back of the sail is hollowed out with a very sharp, flat gouge. It is a very delicate job and only selected, even-grained white pine or mahogany is fit to use, for when the sail is thinned down to about $\frac{1}{16}$ of an inch it breaks very easily. The wood can be left thicker in the middle or belly of the sail, but the thinner you get it the better it will look. These sails when painted white are very realistic.

CHAPTER IV

THE MASTING OF SHIPS

BETWEEN the years 1750 and 1850 there were greater changes made in the development of the sailing ship than in any other century. From ships of three to four hundred tons burden they increased in size until the larger ones reached a tonnage of two thousand tons.

With this increase in size naturally occurred many changes, both in the shape of the hull of the ship, her modelling and also in the masting and sparring.

By masting of ships is meant the locating where her spars shall stand; how far from the bow, the first one, the foremast, shall stand, and how far apart the other two, the main and the mizzen shall be, to give the ship the greatest aid in pushing her through the water. The older ships being small, were naturally fuller-bodied craft than the longer, larger ships of later days, and being so full-bodied, the "apple-bowed craft" of the modern story writer, the foremast was much nearer the bow than in the sharp, lean-bowed clipper ships of later days.

It is by a knowledge of such peculiarities in design that one experienced in ship matters is able to tell at a glance if a model be a true representation of the type of ship she assumes to portray; and by noting the position and rake of her masts this can often be decided at a first glance. For those who care to make models that are correct in such details, a table is here given showing how the masts were located in ships during a long period of time.

In order to properly apply these measurements we must know just where to measure from. The figures given are all based on the length of the ship between perpendiculars (Fig. 49) and this coincides with the

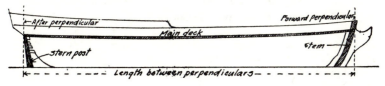

Fig. 49

length as measured for tonnage, which is the distance measured along the main deck from the forward side of the main stem, to the after side of the stern-post. Where the main deck line crosses the forward side of the main stem, not including the cut-water, is the forward perpendicular, and where the main deck line crosses the after edge of the stern-post, is the after perpendicular. The figures for placing the masts are given in percentages of this distance.

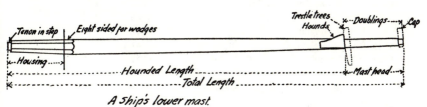

A Ship's lower mast.

Fig. 50

TABLE SHOWING LOCATION OF MASTS AT DIFFERENT PERIODS

Year	Ship or System Used	Percentage of length between perpendiculars from forward to:		
		Foremast	Mainmast	Mizzenmast
1747	Alfred: *Black Prince*, West Indiaman, 440 tons	.112	.6	.82
1765	East Indiaman, 630 tons	.097	.55	.824
1780	Hall: West Indiaman, 362 tons	.13	.61	.855
1800	French system	.29	.655	.865
1800	Swedish system	.128	.564	.817
1800	Danish system	.111	.506	.834
1812	Old 1-4-6 rule, American (⅐, ⁴⁄₇, ⁶⁄₇)	.142	.571	.857
1824	Packet ship, *Philadelphia*, New Orleans cotton-trade	.14	.512	.827
1839	Donald McKay, American shipbuilder	.166	.571	.857
1853	J. W. Griffiths, American shipbuilder	.189	.536	.813
1850	Sheppard-White, British shipbuilder	.21	.60	.85
1850	*Queen of the West*, American clipper, 1168 tons	.211	.586	.89
1854	*Lightning*, American clipper, 2000 tons	.22	.52	.8
1856	*Sweepstakes*, American clipper, 1737 tons	.162	.5	.76

System for Sparring Brigs

Year	Ship or System Used	Foremast	Mainmast	
1775	*Lexington*, American brig	.166	.66	
	Danish system	.166	.625	
	French system	.21	.65	
1839	McKay system, American shipbuilder	.222	.6	
1853	Griffith system, American shipbuilder	.189	.536	

System for Sparring Schooners

Year	Ship or System Used	Foremast	Mainmast	
1800	Pink, American fisherman	.16	.516	
1800	Baltimore clippers, American	.18	.58	
	Baltimore clippers, American	.19	.57	
	Baltimore clippers, American	.22	.56	
	Baltimore clippers, American	.20	.58	
	Baltimore clippers, American	.20	.62	
1826	Skiddy, American pilot	.23	.676	
1839	McKay, American shipbuilder	.2	.575	
1853	Griffiths, American shipbuilder	.253	.561	
	French shipbuilders	.25	.625	
	Danish shipbuilders	.25	.625	

A sloop's mast was ⅛ the length from forward perpendicular.

The fallacy that raking masts make a ship more weatherly has long since been disproven. There are some advantages obtained thereby, in the swinging of the yards, but it does not necessarily improve a vessel's windward-going qualities. In the famous Baltimore clippers this rake was carried to extremes and as that was the only visible difference between them and other craft, writers have attributed the wonderful speed of these craft to the fact that their spars were so raked.

Had they better understood the rudiments of naval architecture they would have known that this rake of the spars was the only means of preserving a proper balance or distribution of sail over a hull that was nearly twice as deep in the water aft as it was forward (Fig. 51). The speed of the

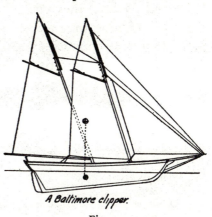

A Baltimore clipper.

Fig. 51

Baltimore clippers was due to the fine easy entrance into the water at the bow. Not necessarily a sharp, knife-like cutting edge, but it was a bow having an extreme rake which pushed the water down under, as well as easy water lines, pushing the water aside, which gave a diagonal line, a line closely approximating the flow of water around the hull and which was a hundred per cent sharper and easier than on any craft of its day.

Herreshoff of Bristol, R. I., in 1891, some eighty years later, applied the same principles to the bow of the famous sailing sloop yacht *Gloriana,* and she left every other sailing craft so far behind that his name will stand forever in the Hall of Fame among yachts-men the world over.

A small amount of rake to the masts naturally adapts itself to resisting the forward whipping of the spars as a ship fetches up against a head sea. It gives the back-stays a better chance, a certain amount of leverage, to hold the spars against this pitching strain. As a matter of appearance also, the three masts of a ship should open out, fan-like, as they go up from the ship's deck. If placed parallel they will appear to come together at the top. In fact, they were always spread apart at the top. Just how much they should spread may be seen by the figures given in the following table.

TABLE SHOWING THE RAKE OF SHIP'S MASTS

	Steeve of Bowsprit	Fore-mast	Main-mast	Mizzen-mast
Baltimore schooners	3°	7°	8°	
Baltimore schooners	4°	11°	12°	
Pink, American fish schooner	29°	10°	11°	
Danish ship	20° to 25°	1°	2°	5°
Swedish ship	30°	0°	2°	4°
French ship	23°	3°	4°	7°
1839 American ship	23°	⅛″ in 3′	¼″ in 3′	¾″ in 3′
1820 American frigate		0°	½″ to 3′	1¾″ to 3′
1776 English man-of-war	14″ in 3′	1⁄16″ in 3′	⅝″ in 3′	1″ in 3′
English man-of-war	63″ in 12′	2″ in 12′	6″ in 12′	10″ in 12′

The steeve of the bowsprit is the measure in feet and inches, or in degrees, that its outer end is above the level of the inner end at the stem.

One of the most common errors made in modelling ships is in getting the masts too tall. There was some leeway in this matter for some individual ships carried tall spars or longer yards than was the common rule. The ship *America,* owned by the Crowninshields of Salem, was noted for its immense spread of sail, her mainmast, from deck to truck, being greater than her

SPAR DIMENSIONS OF SHIPS IN THE UNITED STATES NAVY

Rate	120 guns		80 guns		74 guns		44 guns	
Ship's name	Pennsylvania		Delaware		Franklin		Potomac	
Length bet. perpendiculars	212' 11"		199' 2"		190' 10"		177' 10"	
Beam, extreme	75' 6"		54' 6"		54' 7½"		46' 2"	
Depth	24' 3"		21' 7"		19' 9"		21' 2"	
Tonnage	3104 66/95		2602 34/95		2243 34/95		1684 14/95	
	Mast	Yard	Mast	Yard	Mast	Yard	Mast	Yard
Fore	121'	100'	115'	96'	105'	90'	95'	84'
Foretop	63' 6"	75'	63'	71'	63'	67'	56'	62'
Foretopgallant	37' 6"	48'	32'	46'	37'	45'	29'	41'
Foreroyal	22'	23'	22'	33'	22'	30'	20'	27'
Forepole	17'		11'		6'		10'	
Main	132'	110'	124' 6"	107' 6"	117'	105'	105'	95'
Maintop	70'	82'	70'	78'	70'	77'	63'	71'
Maintopgallant	41'	52'	41'	52'	41'	51'	32'	30'
Mainroyal	24'	36'	24'	36'	24'	36'	22'	20'
Mainpole	18'		12'		6'		11'	
Mizzen	99' *	80'	97'	80'	98'	80'	84'	66'
Mizzentop	55'	52'	55'	52'	53'	49'	46'	45'
Mizzentopgallant	33'	33'	29'	33'	33'	32'	24'	30'
Mizzenroyal	20'	23'	20'	23'	20'	21' 9"	16'	19'
Mizzenpole	14'		10'		5'		8'	
Bowsprit outboard	54'		56'		48'		45' 9"	
Jibboom from cap	43'		40'		36'		32' 9"	
Flying jibboom	24'		21'		20'		21' 3"	
Spanker boom	61' 6"		60'		60'		50'	
Spanker gaff	38' 10"		38'		38'		30'	

* Steps on orlop deck.

SPAR DIMENSIONS OF SHIPS IN THE UNITED STATES NAVY

	Albany		Levant		Yorktown		Truxton	
Rate	22 guns		22 guns		16 guns		10 guns	
Ship's name	Albany		Levant		Yorktown		Truxton	
Length bet. perpendiculars	150' 7"		134' 7"		119' 7"		102' 6"	
Beam, extreme	39' 6"		36'		32' 11"		28' 2"	
Depth	18'		15'		15'		13'	
Tonnage	1041 90/95		770 3/95		569 30/95		329 89/95	
	Mast	Yard	Mast	Yard	Mast	Yard	Mast	Yard
Fore	84' 1"	77'	72'	65'	65' 6"	60' 9"	65' 6"	55'
Foretop	50'	57'	53'	49'	42'	45' 6"	37' 6"	42'
Foretopgallant	25' 3"	39'	23'	32'	21'	30' 6"	19'	28'
Foreroyal	16'	28'	15'	22'	13'	20' 6"	13'	20'
Forepole	8'		5'		6'		5'	
Main	89' 7"	77'	80'	75'	72'	67' 6"	63' 5"	55'
Maintop	50'	57'	47'	56'	45'	50' 6"	37' 6"	42'
Maintopgallant	25'	39'	24'	37'	22'	34'	19'	28'
Mainroyal	16'	28'	16'	25'	14'	22' 9"	13'	20'
Mainpole	8'		5'		7'		5'	
Mizzen	70' 3" *	47'	66'	53'	54' 6" †	52'		
Mizzentop	38'	39'	37'	36' 6"	32'	34'		
Mizzentopgallant	19'	25'	20'	29' 6"	16'	21'		
Mizzenroyal	13'	17'	13'	15'	12'	14'		
Mizzenpole	6'		4'		5'			
Bowsprit outboard	32' 8"		33'		30'		22'	
Jibboom from cap	29'		25' 6"		22' 9"		21'	
Flying jibboom	19'		14' 6"		13' 3"		15'	
Spanker boom	41'		35'		34'		50'	
Spanker gaff	35'		28'		28'		32'	

* Steps on berth deck. † Masthead in line with main trestle-trees.

SPAR DIMENSIONS OF AMERICAN MERCHANT SHIPS

	Packet *Patrick Henry*		Clipper *Queen of the West*		Packet *Courier*		Clipper *Sweepstakes*	
	Mast	Yard	Mast	Yard	Mast	Yard	Mast	Yard
Rate	Packet		Clipper		Packet		Clipper	
Length bet. perpendiculars	160' 0"		164' 6"		116'		216'	
Beam, extreme	34' 10"		37' 8"		27'		41' 6"	
Depth	21' 10"		21' 10½"		16' 10"		21' 6"	
Tonnage	881 38/95		1168 20/95		380		1737 23/95	
Fore	78'	65'	80'	68'	58'	49'	86'	78'
Foretop	44'	51'	48'	53' 6"	34'	39'	49'	62' 6"
Foretopgallant	24'	37'	25' 6"	39' 6"	18'	30'	32' 5"	43' 6"
Foreroyal	17'	28'	17' 6"	29'	12'	24'	20'	33'
Forepole	11'		14' 7"		9'	20'	12'	27'
Skysail pole			9' 11"				7' 6"	
Main	80'	69' 6"	82'	73' 6"	60'	52'	90'	83'
Maintop	46'	55'	48'	59'	36'	42'	51'	67'
Maintopgallant	26' 6"	41'	26' 6"	45'	19'	33'	34'	48'
Mainroyal	20'	32'	19' 6"	34' 6"	13'	26'	21'	38'
Mainpole	13'		15' 6"		10'	22'	13'	31'
Skysail pole			10' 6"				9'	
Mizzen	73'	55'	75'	57' 6"	54'	42'	82'	65'
Mizzentop	37' 6"	42'	39' 6"	44' 6"	27'	33'	42'	50' 3"
Mizzentopgallant	20'	30'	20' 6"	32'	15' 6"	26'	29'	35' 3"
Mizzenroyal	14' 6"	22'	14' 6"	23'	11'	22'	16'	26' 6"
Mizzenpole	10'		12'		8'		10'	21'
Skysail pole			8'				6'	
Bowsprit outboard	30'		29' 6"		20'		26'	
Jibboom from cap	25'		26' 6"		17'		16'	
							15' 3"	
Flying jibboom	16'		17'		11'		50'	
Spanker boom			46'		33'		56'	
Spanker gaff			43'		24'		47'	

length on deck. The 74-gun, line-of-battle ship *North Carolina,* of the United States Navy, was 209 feet long on her spar deck and from this deck to the truck, on her main skysail, measured 211 feet. But in most cases the ship's length exceeded the height of her masts as may be seen by referring to the several tables of spar dimensions of ships given in the appendix. The clipper ships were generally regarded as the greatest canvas carriers in the world, but they will be found to be less lofty than is supposed. This was due to the fact that their hulls were carried out, forward and aft, to long, sharp extremities which made the hull longer, in proportion to the height of the masts, than was the case with their predecessors, the stub-ended packets that carried immense rigs.

It is a crushing blow to some enthusiastic model makers who dote on lofty spars, but figures do not lie and the dimensions given are authentic. What confuses most men, in trying to lay down a plan from these figures, is in not knowing how far the lower masts step down inside the hull. For their guidance the depth of hold or inside depth of the ship is given.

Another difficulty is in trying to determine how long the doublings are, that is, how long the mastheads should be where one mast laps down in front of the other. On old-time ships, craft built prior to about the year 1800, the mastheads were quite short, being on the mainmast, only about one-sixth of the spar's length. The fore masthead was $\frac{9}{10}$ of the main and the mizzen head only $\frac{3}{4}$ the length of the main, if sparred according to the American or the Swedish custom. A ship with a sixty foot mainmast, accordingly, would have a ten foot masthead, a French ship, 8.57 and a Danish ship, 7.5 foot. This shows the proportional difference between the sparring practices of these various countries.

After 1800, the mastheads were lengthened. By the Wilson, American system, the same ship would have a masthead 13 feet long on the main, 11.7 feet on the fore, and 10.7 feet on the mizzen.

It was found that the extra stiffness given to the spars by the longer mastheads supplied so much more efficiency that it more than offset the extra weight added by the long masthead.

TABLE SHOWING LENGTH OF MASTHEADS IN PROPORTION TO THE LENGTH OF SPARS

	Swedish	French	Danish	American (clipper)	American ship before 1800
Main masthead	⁵⁄₃₆	⅐	⅛ to ⅑	⅙	⅛
Main topmast head	⅑	⅐	⅙	⅙	⅐

In 1843, the United States Navy's rule for length of lower mastheads was .29 times the length of the topmast; and the topmast head was .32 times the length of the topgallantmast.

The clipper ship *Sweepstakes,* of 1737 tons, designed and built by Daniel Westervelt, at New York, in 1850, was 228 feet long on deck. Her mainmast was ninety feet long and three feet in diameter and the masthead was fifteen feet long. Her topmast, fifty-one feet long, was headed nine feet with a diameter of 18½ inches and her topgallantmast, thirty-four feet long and thirteen inches in diameter, had five feet and six inches length of masthead.

These figures should be compared with the spars of the frigate *Essex,* built by Enos Briggs, at Salem, Mass., in 1797. She was 850²⁹⁄₉₅ tons measurement and 141 feet long on her gun deck. Her mainmast was 85 feet long and 27 inches in diameter and she had a 12-foot masthead. The main topmast was 55 feet long and 18½ inches in diameter, with 7 foot 6 inches at the masthead, and her topgallantmast was forty feet long, with a twelve inch diameter, and had a fifteen foot royalmast above it, in one stick.

We have evidence that in sparring the big clippers individual ideas and no set rule prevailed, for the clipper *Flying Cloud,* of 1851, a Donald McKay ship, had a mainmast sixty-five feet from rail to top, with a thirteen-foot masthead and a topmast forty-six feet long, with an 8½ foot head. The *Champion of the Seas,* with a seventy-one foot mainmast, had a seventeen-foot masthead, and a topmast fifty feet long, with a ten-foot masthead.

In the days of little ships, prior to 1800, their masts were small enough in diameter to shape them out of one tree. Before the American Revolution there were king's agents in America, who picked out all the largest and best trees and branded them with the "broad arrow" denoting the king's property. The agent up the Hudson River reported he could find trees to make masts thirty inches in diameter but that thirty-two inch trees would be difficult to find.

The *Essex,* with a mainmast eighty-five feet long and twenty-seven inches in diameter, no doubt had one solid stick for this spar, but clipper's masts, thirty-six inches in diameter, were built up of many pieces hooped together with iron bands. Old records show that the 44-gun U. S. frigate *President,* with a mainmast one hundred and four feet long, had forty-seven hoops about it; the foremast ninety-four feet long, had thirty-seven mast hoops and the eighty-one foot mizzenmast had twenty-five hoops. This gives a spacing for the hoops on the mainmast about every 2 feet 3 inches; the foremast, every 2 feet 6 inches; and the mizzenmast, 3 feet 3 inches.

The length of the hounds, the cheek-like projections built on the mast to support the trestle-trees and tops, should be one-half the length of the masthead. For American ships the mast should be eight-sided where it goes through the partners at the deck, for about a foot above the deck, then round up to the hounds, where the two cheeks are bolted on, and above that square (Fig. 50).

The shape of the mast and the amount it should taper, is as follows:—divide the length from the deck to the top of the hounds (which is the same as the lower side of the masthead) into four equal parts or quarters and their sizes can be proportioned by the following figures.

	1st Quarter	2d Quarter	3d Quarter	Heads Lower Part	Heads Upper Part	Heels
Masts that are cheeked	.9836	.9333	.8574	.8574	.625	.857
Masts that head themselves	.9836	.9333	.8574	.75	.66	.857
Topmasts and top-gallantmasts	.9756	.9287	.8333	.6923	.5454	
Yards	.9677	.875	.7	.428		
Bowsprits	.9756	.9166	.8	.555		
Jib-boom	.9836	.928	.8333	.66 end		

Length of the cheeks, $\frac{6}{20}$ the length of the mast.
Length of the head of main and foremasts, 5 inches for every 3 feet of length.
Length of the head of the mizzenmast, 4 inches for every 3 feet of length.
Length of the hounds of all masts, $\frac{2}{6}$ the length of heads.

This is an old rule for ships prior to 1800 and gives short mastheads; but the proportional taper to the spars would be the same for later ships up to about 1840 when parrel straps on the topsail yards gave way to sliding iron parrel bands on the topmasts.

Some may not understand the designation, masts that are *cheeked* and masts that *head* themselves. The older ships did not square the mastheads, but carried them up round, clear to the upper cap. Where cheeks were bolted on, to form a ledge for the trestle-trees, the mast was said to be cheeked. Where they were cut down to a square masthead, forming a decided shoulder, they were said to head themselves.

The trestle-trees are the two fore-and-aft pieces of wood that rest on the cheeks and support the cross-trees and the tops. Where the shrouds go over them, a rounded, hardwood piece, called a bolster, is fitted on top of the trestle-trees to take the crushing strain of the shrouds.

In making spars for models it is better practice to use clear, straight-grained white pine or similar soft wood, as they stay straight better than spars made of hard wood. I have seen expensive models that had been repaired by men who thought they were doing an extra fine job by turning the yards out of boxwood and the spars had warped and twisted like a cow's horn, because the grain was not straight. Be sure you have straight-grained wood. Split it out into strips and then you are certain to get suitable wood.

Plane the stick down square to the taper required. Then plane down the corners to an eight-sided stick and then round it off, finishing with sandpaper. If it is to represent a built-up mast and hooped, there is a lot more work in the making, but it is well worth the trouble for the finished appearance it gives the model. Space off the distance between the hoops and with the point of a penknife cut out the little V-shaped chapellings in the spar and when these are painted white and the mast stained and varnished a reddish tint, to imitate Oregon pine, the effect is very striking. But don't cut chapels down the front of the mast, as there was always a raised bib on the front quarter of the spar, clear from the hounds to the deck or, in some ships, only two-thirds the distance down. This smooth-surfaced bib took the chafe off the courses as those sails slatted against the mast in calm weather. Shape your mast so this bib will show a slightly raised surface on the mast. Don't try to put actual hoops on a small model. Just paint black bands around to represent them as they would hardly be any thicker than the paint.

Many model makers just guess at the sizes to make the tops, trestle-trees and cross-trees on masts and the results generally show it to one versed in such matters. The old-time shipbuilders found by experience the proper proportions for all these parts of the mast's outfit and if their rules are adhered to, models will look much more like the little ships they are supposed to portray.

In a book written by Mungo Murray, in 1765, this information is given in very concise form for ships of that period.

Proportions of Diameters of Masts and Yards

Main and foremasts, in all ships down to 60 guns, 1 inch diameter per yard in length (the whole length of the lower mast).

Main and foremasts, in all ships down to 50-40 guns, $2\frac{7}{28}$ inch diameter per yard in length.

Main and foremasts, in all ships down to 24 guns, $1\frac{2}{13}$ inch diameter per yard in length.

All topmasts, $\frac{9}{10}$ inches per yard in length.

All foretopmasts, as big as maintopmasts.

Topgallant mast, 1 inch per yard.
Mizzenmast, $15/_{22}$ inch per yard.
Mizzentopmast, $5/_6$ inch per yard.
Bowsprit, $1\frac{1}{2}$ inch per yard.
Jibboom, $7/_8$ inch per yard.
Main and fore yards, $5/_7$ inch per yard.
Topsail, cross-jack and sprit-sail yards, $9/_{14}$ inch per yard.
Topgallant, mizzentopsail, sprit-sail yards, $8/_{13}$ inch per yard.
Mizzen yard, $5/_9$ inch per yard.
All studding-sail booms and yards, $\frac{1}{2}$ inch per yard.

PROPORTION OF HEADS AND HOUNDS OF MASTS

Main and foremastheads, 5 inch per yard of length of mast.
Mizzenmasthead (if steps in hold), $4\frac{1}{8}$ inch per yard.
All top and topgallant mastheads, 4 inch per yard.
Length of hounds, $2/_5$ respective heads.

PROPORTIONS FOR TOPS

Breadth—$\frac{1}{3}$ length of topmast.
Mizzentop, by some, $9/_{13}$ of mizzentopmast.
All tops fore and aft length—$3/_4$ of breadth.
Square hole (lubber's hole), 5 inch to the foot.

PROPORTIONS FOR CAPS

All caps, except jib-boom, to be in breadth twice the diameter of
topmasts and in length twice their breadth.
Thickness of fore and main caps, $\frac{1}{2}$ their breadth.
Mizzen caps, $3/_7$, and topmast caps, $2/_5$ of their respective breadth.

PROPORTIONS FOR TRESTLE-TREES

In length, to reach within 3 inches of outer edge of top.
Depth of main and fore trestle-trees, $25/_{26}$ inch to foot in length.
Breadth, $5/_7$ of depth.
Depth of mizzen trestle-trees, $5/_7$ inch to foot in length.
Breadth, $11/_{16}$ of depth.
Main and foretopmast trestle-trees in length, $\frac{1}{5}$ length of topgallant-
mast; depth, $25/_{26}$ inch per foot in length; breadth, $18/_{25}$ of depth.
Mizzentopmast trestle-trees, $\frac{1}{2}$ maintopmast trestle-trees; depth, 1
inch per foot in length; breadth, $5/_{16}$ of depth.

PROPORTION OF CROSS-TREES

Length of main and fore cross-trees to reach within 3 inches of outer edge of top.

Mizzen cross-trees same as trestle-trees.

Cross-trees same breadth as trestle-trees and ½ their depth.

As some parts of these rules, such as the breadth of the tops, depend on knowing the length of the spars, we supply the same author's rules for finding these lengths.

Mainmast = beam of ship × 75 and ÷ 100 = length in yards.

Foremast = mainmast × 90 and ÷ 100 = length in yards.

Mizzenmast = mainmast × 86 and ÷ 100 = length in yards.

Bowsprit = mainmast × 61 and ÷ 100 = length in yards.

Maintopmast = mainmast × 607 and ÷ 1000 = length in yards.

Foretopmast = maintopmast × 91 and ÷ 100 = length in yards.

Mizzentopmast = maintopmast × 717 and ÷ 1000 = length in yards.

Maintopgallant mast = maintopmast × 508 and ÷ 1000 = length in yards.

Foretopgallant mast = foretopmast × 508 and ÷ 1000 = length in yards.

Spritsail topmast = bowsprit × 36 and ÷ 100 = length in yards.

For later ships we have what is called the old United States Navy Rule of 1840 and that rule gives us the following:—

Main top, breadth is ½ beam of ship (moulded) ⎤

Foretop, breadth is ⁹⁄₁₀ main top   ⎬ lengths = ⅔ breadths

Mizzen top, breadth is ⅘ fore top   ⎦

Lower trestle-trees, length = length of the tops; depth = ⅗ diameter of mast at deck; thickness = ½ depth.

Lower cross-trees, length = breadth of tops; breadth = breadth of trestle-trees; depth = ⅔ of breadth.

Topmast trestle-trees, length = ⅖ length of lower cross-trees; breadth = ½ depth of lower cross-trees; depth = ½ depth of lower cross-trees.

Topmast cross-trees; length of aftermost one = $\frac{3}{5}$ of after lower
cross-trees; length of middle one = $\frac{5}{6}$ of after one; length of
foremost one = $\frac{5}{6}$ of middle one; breadth = the breadth of their
respective trestle-trees; depth, or thickness, $\frac{4}{5}$ of their breadth.

Caps of bowsprit = length, 4 times the diameter of jib-boom;
breadth, $1\frac{1}{2}$ times the diameter of jib-boom; thickness, $\frac{1}{2}$
breadth.

All other caps = length, 4 times the diameter of respective topmasts
or topgallantmasts; breadth, $1\frac{1}{2}$ times the diameter of respective topmasts or topgallantmasts; thickness, $\frac{1}{2}$ breadth.

The length of all tops must be $\frac{2}{3}$ of their breadth,
and be made light, with the upper cross-trees upon the
top, over the lower ones, fayed down on the battens and
well keyed together.

The forward quarters of the top should be sufficiently
rounded to prevent chafing the sails.

In this rule the base for all measurements is the ship's
beam and therefore an easy rule to work to.

Ship's masts were made in sections, the lower part
being designated as the lower mast and further speci-
fied as to whether it was fore, main or mizzen lower
mast, this being the same with all the masts. The next
spar above the lower mast was called the topmast;
above that came the topgallantmast; then the royal
mast, the skysail mast and highest of all, the pole sur-
mounted by the ball or button-like truck through which
the flag halliards were rove.

Quite a number of ships had the topgallant and royal
mast in two separate spars, joined with trestle-trees,
cross-trees and cap, the same as the topmast head was
fitted. Ships generally had the royal and skysail mast
in one stick, and these were designated as standing skysail masts to distinguish them from those on ships that
had fidded royal masts where the topgallant and royal
masts were in two sticks. The skysail mast was gen-

erally referred to as the skysail pole, and was a separate stick that stepped into a shoe at the top of the top-gallantmast, extending up abaft the royal mast through a cap set aft on the royal masthead and sticking up above the royal far enough to hoist up the skysail yard on it.

Taking these various masts as first made in round, tapered sticks we may finish them ready for stepping into the model's hull.

The length of the lower masthead is measured down from the top of the spar and this part of the stick is cut square. Beginning at half the length of the masthead, below this, flatten two opposite sides of the mast for the hounds and glue on two flat pieces, their grain running up and down with the spar, so that the after edge is even with the after side of the spar and project-ing forward about half the mast's diameter.

As ship's tops and trestle-trees always set level, fore and aft, the top of the hounds must be the same so that if the mast rakes aft, the top of the hounds will accord-ingly tip down towards the front or forward edge of the mast.

After the trestle-trees are put on, the hounds can be whittled down to the same thickness and shaped as shown in the sketch of the masthead. The length, breadth and depth of the trestle-trees can be determined by the preceding rule, but no mention is there made of how much of the top is to be forward and how much aft of the mast. The tops and trestle-trees being the same length, they should extend forward of the mast $\frac{2}{9}$ and aft $\frac{3}{9}$ of their length.

This does not give us, as yet, the location of the cross-trees which are on either side of the lubber's hole and the third or after one, the same distance farther aft. But when we find that the lubber's hole, or the square hole, as sparmakers termed it, was in breadth ⅖ of the breadth of the top and in length 2/7 the breadth of the top, we have everything necessary to figure the sizes and spacing of everything required to build the tops on lower masts of ships built after the year 1800 and somewhat earlier.

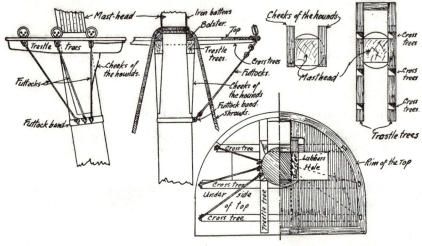

Fig. 52

To make these small trestle-trees and cross-trees you will need a hard, close-grained wood. Use either boxwood, maple or white ash; and to score down into the trestle-trees, use a small, square-edged file, cutting across both trestle-trees at one and the same time to insure their being exactly alike. Space the trestle-trees apart the thickness of the masthead and with a touch of glue in each score set the cross-trees in place across them and clamp in a vise until the glue is hard.

The top itself can be cut out of very thin maple or mahogany, preferably, though pine will do, about 1/16 of an inch thick. Round the edges and cut out the lubber's hole.

In a real ship there are battens, similar to the cross-trees below, that go across on top of the tops and are bolted or keyed fast to them giving double the strength, for the cross-trees must be tapered quite thin on their outer ends or they will appear clumsy.

Fit small chocks crossways between the trestle-trees, to fit snug about the masthead, and another one just forward of these to make a housing for the heel of the topmast. The forward cross-tree goes between the mainmast head and the heel of the topmast. Fit a bolster on each side of the masthead, on top of the trestle-trees. In shape this is like a quarter-round moulding and takes the crush of the shrouds.

The dimensions of the caps can be determined from the rules before given. Drill a round hole for the top-mast allowing for the rake of the mast, but square-up the hole that is to fit over the masthead and notch the masthead so that it will not slide down but stay level with the top of the masthead. Be sure that caps are parallel with the tops of trestle-trees and that the tops are parallel with the deck.

You will find it a great help to lay out a plan of where each block is to be attached and put in small eyes made of small bank pins before stepping the spars in place. Then there are the futtock-shrouds and band and the small cleats to hold the stays that can all be put on so much better and easier at this time than when the model is half rigged.

To permit bracing the yards sharp up, when the ship is "on the wind," that is, when close hauled, the forward topmast-shroud should be opposite the center of the masthead. This locates, therefore, where the forward futtock-shroud should be put through the rim of the top. Old-time ships, using rope futtock-shrouds, had

hooks on the futtock- or foothook-band, to which these
shrouds hooked and they also hooked into hooks in the
lower strappings of the lower topmast deadeyes. But
modern ships, that is, after about the year 1820, used
iron rods for futtock-shrouds. Therefore, in making a
small model (⅛ scale), the same wire that straps the

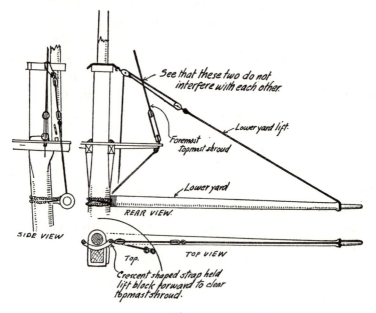

Fig. 53

deadeye can be used as the futtock-shroud after sticking
it through the hole drilled through the top. By drilling a hole through the mast and reeving this wire up to
form the futtock on the other side, a neat job can be
made; painting a black band around the mast where the
wires go through.

Another part that causes much trouble is the crescent-
shaped strap that goes over the masthead and cap and
hangs down on either side forming an eye into which

the lift-blocks for the lower yards hook. Fit this band close abaft the topmast so that the eyes extend forward to about the center of the topmast. This prevents the lift-tackles from chafing against the forward topmast-shrouds,—a very common error with ship model makers, yet one very carefully avoided by the men who rigged the real ships. This is another of the many "ear-marks" to look for in judging good models.

In the early navy ships and in merchant ships also, it was generally the custom to make the mainmast the heaviest spar in the ship; the foremast in all its proportions being $\frac{9}{10}$ the size of the mainmast and the mizzen, $\frac{5}{7}$ the size of the main. This meant all the various parts of the mainmast such as the main topmast, main topgallantmast, main royalmast and all the yards thereon as well. But after about the year 1840, for the sake of being able to make quicker repairs, the navy regulations made all spars on the fore and main the same size.

Topmasts had but little or no taper, being practically a parallel stick because the parrel or sliding band to which the topsail yard was swivelled, had to travel up and down this spar and much taper would give too much play to this parrel. This sliding band or collar was sheathed with rawhide to take the chafe of the well-greased or slushed topmasts and before it came into use the yards were held to the masts by parrel-straps made of hide with round, wooden beads threaded on them. These encircled the mast and could be slackened when the yard was to be hoisted or lowered and also tightened to hold the yard snug against the top-mast when sailing. This was done by means of yard tackles rove out along the yard with the hauling end rove in through a block at the mast and then led down to the deck. With this rig the topmasts could be tapered as was done on the older style of ships.

The topmasthead should be squared-up and the trestle-trees and cross-trees fitted, but with no cheeks, platform or top such as the lower masthead had. The foregoing rule gives the dimensions for all these parts and for the upper cap as well.

The topgallantmast, royalmast and pole were generally made in one stick with a shoulder or stop, as sparmakers called it, where the shrouds fitted. Some of the larger sized ships, where this would make too unwieldy a spar, had caps and cross-trees fitted to the head of the topgallantmast and also had fidded royalmasts. Those ships generally had the royalmast, skysailmast and pole in one stick and carried skysail yards in place the same as their royal and other yards.

Those ships that had only royalmasts, standing, that is, rigged as permanent spars, used to have skysail poles that could be extemporised in "flying-fish weather." They had a cap set *abaft* the mast through which the skysail pole was shoved up above the royalmast top, high enough to hoist the skysail, its lower end resting in a socket on top of the topgallantmasthead. The skysail pole ran up abaft of and parallel to the royal, far enough apart to let the royal parrel slide up and down.

To hold the topmast, topgallantmast, and, where it is a separate spar, the royalmast, from slipping down after being hoisted up through the tops and caps, a wooden or iron fid was slipped through a hole cut in the heel of the mast and extended out, each side, to rest on the trestle-trees. This fid was twice its width in depth, to give strength, as all the weight and strain on the mast came on this fid. Its width was half the diameter of the mast.

To summarize the foregoing into a few words for the benefit of the man who wants to build a ship model and who doesn't care whether it is a ship of 1776 or 1840,

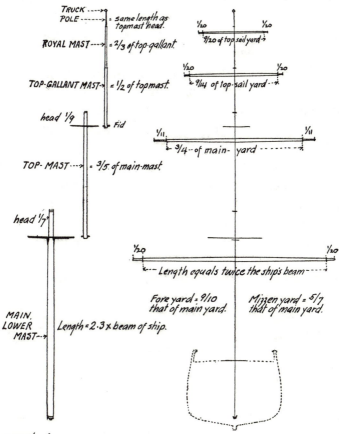

Length of :-
Bowsprit = 6/10 main-mast of which 2/3 is to be outboard.
Jib-boom = 1/2 main-topmast, outside the bowsprit cap.- Length additional
        inside the cap to be 2/3 of the length outside.
Flying jib-boom = 2/3 length of jib-boom, outside the cap.- Pole additional
        1/9 of whole length.
Spanker boom = 1/2 length of main-lower mast.
Spanker gaff = 4/5 length of spanker-boom.

Fig. 54

Swedish, French or American, the preceeding diagram (Fig. 54) will be sufficient to guide him in getting out a set of spars that will be shipshape.

Ship's yards are very much the same all the way up from the mainyard to the royal, in so far as their shape goes, but getting smaller and smaller as you go aloft. The taper has been given in a foregoing table, but when ironwork began to supersede the ropework, about the ship's rigging, and iron wythes or bands and iron-stropped blocks came into use, it made a decided change in the shape and character of the yards.

The older style was the more picturesque with its shoulders or stops to prevent the eye-splices in the lifts, brace-pendents and foot-ropes from sliding in along the spar. Just inside the yard-arms the yard was left square where the sheave for the sheet ropes was in-serted in it. Then it rounded and tapered, becoming larger as it went inboard, until it became octagonal. It was octagonal for the middle third of its length.

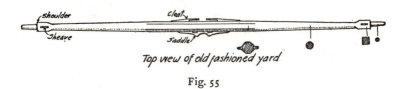

Top view of old fashioned yard

Fig. 55

On the forward face of this octagonal part, two cleats were fitted to prevent the strops, put around it here for the halliards, clew-garnets, etc., from slipping and on the after face, a yoke-like saddle was fitted to steady the yard against the mast. Such a shaped yard requires care in whittling it out but if neatly done the final ap-pearance of the model, so fitted, repays one for the trouble taken.

The later style of yards, from about the year 1812 on,

were round spars their entire length and simply tapered
in shape with a slight shoulder at the yard-arms where
the iron eye-bands or wythes were fitted. The saddles
were retained, but the cleats disappeared as iron bands
took the place of all the strops at the mast. An iron-rod
jackstay, rove through eyes in the top of the yard, succeeded the hemp-rope jackstay to which the sails were
lashed with rovings, in earlier days.

Top view of new style of yard.

Fig. 56

There is one thing about yards that it is necessary to
call particular attention to because nine out of ten
model makers, and artists as well, make this mistake,
and that is, to be sure to get the yard-arms on the main
yard and topsail yards, the only sails that generally
have reefs in them, long enough to equal the breadth of
the sail across the lowest, and therefore the widest, reef-

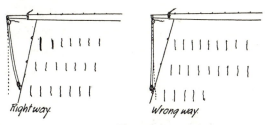

Fig. 57

band. The foresail doesn't widen out on the foot like
the mainsail, so that is usually workable. Some ships
had reefs in their topgallant sails, and when they did,
the yard-arms had to be long enough to let the reef
tackles, hooked into the outer ends of the yard-arms,
stretch them tight across the yard.

In the 1860's, when freight rates took a drop and a reduction in crews followed, as a matter of economy the big single topsails were divided into two sails with a lower topsail yard, as it was termed, swivelled to the lower cap and supported underneath by a stout iron rod down to the trestle-trees below.

This yard being stationary, tackles, called topsail downhauls, were rove from the lower yard-arm up to the topsail yard-arm to pull that yard down close to the lower topsail yard. This was necessary because the upper topsail sheets were made fast and the sail was never clewed up. Instead, the yard itself was hauled down, and as the wind in it prevented it coming down of its own weight, hence the need of a topsail downhaul.

Instead of a clewline, there was a topsail spilling line rove around under the foot of the sail by which it could be gathered up to spill the wind out of it. The standing lifts of this yard were just long enough to keep the yard at the slings from touching the cap.

Fast passages were made by keeping the ship moving at all times. Many a fine passage has been spoiled by rolling about a week or more in absolute calm down under the equator. It was to conquer this region of calms that studding sails were invented.

A ship comes driving past Cape Horn, homeward bound, under two-reefed topsails with two men at the wheel exerting all their strength to keep the big brute of a hull running a straight course as she logs twelve to fourteen knots an hour. She hauls up to the northward, through uncertain air belts, until she picks up the southeast trades and again she comes rushing homeward with every sail set and with white water piled up around her bows to the lee catheads. Sometimes the royals have to be doused in a hurry as extra heavy puffs lay the old ship down till she begins to scoop seas over the top of her lee bulwarks and the main deck becomes a swimming pool. But when the ship, after a week or so of this kind of sailing, begins to heel over less and less and finally a report like a cannon shot echoes down on deck as the big topsail comes back with a slap against the mast as the ship fetches up at the end of a weather roll, then you will see the old man's brow begin to wrinkle, and hear the men cuss. Days of downright hard work are to come.

They are in "flying fish" weather, and then begins the job of rigging out the studding-sail irons, swaying the yards aloft into place and pointing through the boom-irons, lashing on the blocks and reeving off the gear. Sails are overhauled in the sail locker, passed up on deck through the booby-hatch, and bent on to yards, with halliards sheets and tacks. Booms are run out far beyond the mainyards and one after another, the studding sails are swayed aloft and sheeted home. The light cloth of which they are made swells out to an air imperceptible in the heavy, hard canvas of the regular sails. The set of the studding sails and the trim of each tack and sheet are watched by the lynx-eyed mates, as a cat watches a mouse, and the ship, a glorious spectacle of sail on sail, a towering mass of white canvas, surges ahead through the calm water. Gulf weed slips past, Portuguese men-of-war glide astern, and the old man chuckles as he checks up the ship's position and finds a fair day's run to her credit.

It was this creeping ahead when others stood still, becalmed, that made passages. There was a little English tea clipper, the *Ellen Rodgers,* that newer, larger ships had outclassed in the matter of speed. The captain, to keep her in the trade, increased her sail area by putting her mainyards on the foremast and giving her a new and larger set of mainyards,—the mainyards being six feet longer than the foreyard. The *Kent, Falcon* and *Robin Hood,* three of the fastest of the new clippers, were in a calm, north of the line, one day in 1862, when the *Ellen Rodgers,* with her new sails, appeared over the horizon astern and rapidly overhauling the whole fleet, passed them and was soon out of sight ahead. The *Falcon* was 122 days from Shanghai to London, on that passage, and the *Ellen Rodgers* made it in 116 days. That is a good illustration of what carrying sail will do.

How the studding sails were rigged is what puzzles many model makers. The first thing to get clear in mind is the fact that there were two classes of spars used, booms and yards. The booms were those that were kept in place, rove through two iron bands attached to the regular yard, on its upper side, just aft of and clear of the jackstay. The outer iron was fitted into the end of the mainyard. The inner iron or band had a hinged clasp that could be opened and the inner end of the boom raised up out of it.

The yards were light spars lashed to the head of the sails and went up or down with the sail. The sizes of these spars are given in several tables in the appendix to this volume. The blocks through which the halyards rove were fastened to the outer end of the yard's arm on the under side, and the blocks for the sheet of the studding sail, above it, were lashed at the outer end on the top side of the studding sail boom.

The halliards were made fast to or "bent on," as sailors phrase it, in the middle of the yard so that the sail extended out beyond the yard's arm above it. The

sheet, being led down on deck, also acted as a brace and
the tack, the rope on the inner, lower corner of the sail,
led down on deck and it was by hauling down on this
and slacking away on the sheet and halliard, that the
sail was taken in, being pulled right down to the deck.

The lower studding sails, on the foremast, were so

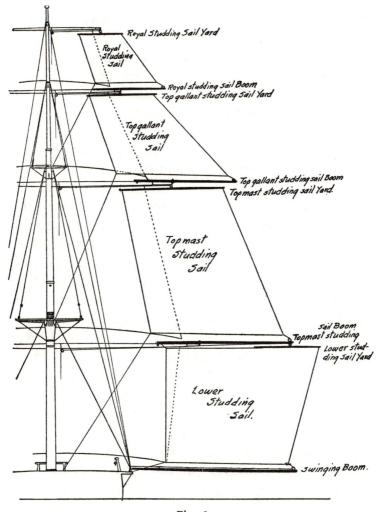

Fig. 58

broad across the head that the yard only extended about half way and the halliard was rove through a block on the end of the studding sail boom, the inner clew being hauled up to the yard by another rope led up into the foretop. The foot of this lower studding sail, only set on the foremast, was extended by a spar called the swinging boom it being that spar which served as a boat boom, to keep the ship's small boats away from the side when at anchor. These booms were swivelled to the rail or on the forward end of the fore channels.

Bowsprits have gone through a great evolution since the days when they were rigged like a mast with yards and square sails and stuck up in the air at an angle of about forty-five degrees.

Those bowsprits went down through the decks like a mast and were stepped against two big timbers in the 'tween decks, the rule in 1750 being that the line of the bowsprit should be from the upper part of the stem to the heel of the mainmast. This, the angle of rise above a horizontal line, was termed the stive; in later years spelled steeve. Canvas, with its edges nailed down in white lead and with a strip of lead over it, kept the water from leaking in around the bowsprit just as the mast-coat kept the water out around the masts, on the deck. They did not use iron so much in the old days but depended on rope gammon lashings to hold the bowsprit down in its bed on the stemhead. These lashings were passed through holes in the knee of the head, the stem, or part of it, and this explains why this part of the ship, which to many seemed a superfluous ornament, was made the shape it was. It gave the gammon lashing a better leverage to hold the bowsprit down against the heavy strain when all the masts pulled against the headstays. In later years, somewhere about

1820, the iron gammon strap was introduced, but years of development of the head-knee, with its figurehead and ornamental trailboards, could not abolish it in a day and it was not until the bald-headed clippers came out in the 1850's, that this fancy and cumbersome knee of the head disappeared.

Standing up above the stem, with the thickness of the bowsprit between them, were two timbers built solidly down into the bows of the ship, called knight-heads. These held the bowsprit firmly from moving sideways and the older the ship the more conspicuous were these knightheads. In the last of the clippers they were hardly noticeable as the forecastlehead all but hid them from view.

The clippers did not require such a heavy stepping for this spar as their head sails were comparatively smaller than those of a packet ship or frigate. Their bows were so much longer and they were so sharp forward that they did not have that ardency or inclination to run up into the wind, that the older, bluff-bowed ships had when driven hard against the water and inclined on one side. It was because of the need of much head sail that the bluff-bowed craft carried, besides their bowsprits, a jib-boom, a flying jib-boom and a jib-of-jib-boom.

On the 44-gun frigate *United States,* a sister ship to the *Constitution,* these spars were as follows:—bowsprit, 65 feet long, one-third of which was inside the knightheads; a jib-boom, 48 feet, 6 inches long, one-third of its inner end lapping on top of the bowsprit; a flying jib-boom, 58 feet long, that butted against the cap on the end of the bowsprit through which the jib-boom extended. This flying jib-boom set alongside of the jib-boom and extending through a cap on its end, set off horizontally to port, and on the end of this flying jib-boom was a cap, set off to starboard, through which the jib-of-jib-boom extended, its inner end extending in, parallel to the flying jib-boom and butting against the jib-boom cap. In actual feet the bowsprit extended 43 feet beyond the bows of the ship; the jib-boom, 32 feet, 4 inches beyond the bowsprit cap; the flying jib-boom, 25 feet, 8 inches; and the jib of jib-boom, 16 feet; giving a total length from the knightheads to the end of the jib of jib-boom, of 117 feet. Some length of spar to be sticking out ahead of a ship only 175 feet long on deck!

On the 74-gun ship-of-the-line *North Carolina,* these spars, all measured from the knightheads, were bowsprit, 53 feet; jib-boom, 91 feet; flying jib-boom, 109 feet; and jib of jib-boom, 128 feet. This ship was 209 feet long on the spar deck. These figures are given because many persons are skeptical as to whether ships ever carried such spars and these figures are taken from government data. They certainly did carry them and it was the net work of ropes required to rig out all these spars that made the old sailing ships so picturesque.

The packet ship *Patrick Henry,* 160 feet long, had a bowsprit 30 feet outside the knightheads, a jib-boom 25 feet outside the cap and a flying jib-boom 16 feet long, a total length of 71 feet. The clipper ship *Queen of the West,* built in 1843, a ship 180 feet long, had a bowsprit, outboard, of 29 feet 6 inches, a jib-boom 26 feet 6 inches, and a flying jib-boom 17 feet, a total length of 73 feet, or 44 feet shorter than the bowsprit on the *Constitution.*

Bowsprits in old ships, ships prior to about 1820, were generally round spars all their length, the same as masts and this was probably due to the fact that rope-gammon lashings were used. A row of small cleats was fastened to the spar to prevent the gammoning from sliding down the spar, but with the introduction of iron straps as gammonings, bowsprits were found to be more easily fitted by leaving them square as far as this point. Outside this they were chamfered eight-sided and then rounded.

The fitting of the bowsprit in its housing, on a model ship, is very important and should be done with the thought in mind that some day it may be broken and have to be repaired; for when the forecastle head is fastened down on top of it there is no way of getting at it again. Always fit a stop at its heel so that if a new bowsprit has to be shipped there is something to hold the heel or inboard end in its proper place.

The bowsprit cap in American ships always stood vertical and the dolphin striker under it the same, while many foreign ships carried their dolphin strikers so that the lower end stuck out forward. Italian ships had dolphin strikers with an S-shaped twist like a cow's horn. But the smaller caps on the jib-boom and flying jib-boom ends, were fitted square to the spar and set off to one side, *on the upper quarter of the spar*. The heel or inboard end of the jib-boom butted against a fixed piece shaped the same as the spar, as shown in the ac-companying sketch (Fig. 59), and in later-day ships had an iron hasp to hold it down. In the old timers,

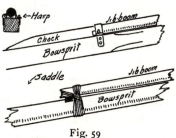

Fig. 59

they lapped back on the bowsprit, one-third of their length resting in a short hollowed saddle, under the inner end and were lashed fast to the bowsprit with rope. The other, outer jib-booms, were fastened in a similar manner,—butting the cap and fastened with an iron bale or hasp on ships after about the year 1812, or lashed with rope on ships of an earlier date.

On each side of the bowsprit, at its outer end, chocks

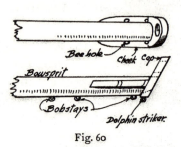

Fig. 60

were fitted to butt against the after side of the cap; and through bee-holes in those chocks were rove the fore-topmast stays leading aft to bull's-eyes set in the ship's bows (Fig. 60). Where the strain was not so great, as on parts of the running gear that rove through wooden parts, such as the cross-trees, sheaves were inserted to make the ropes run free and by going over a roller the wear and chafe was reduced to a minimum. But the foretopmast stays carried so heavy a strain that they would crush a sheave or shear off a pin on which it rolled and in such places a reamed-out hole was bored, its edges rounded off so as not to cut the rope. At sea, such holes were called bee-holes, and the stay, parcelled and served and then leathered, was rove through these bee-holes.

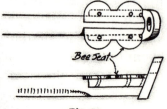

Fig. 61

On very old ships—ships along in the seventeen hundreds—besides this chock there was a small platform built on, called a bee-seat (Fig. 61). These ships had their foremasts set so far up in the bows that both the fore-stay and foretopmast stay were rove through the bee-seat, which was built double to receive them.

CHAPTER V

MASTHEADS

TO MAKE a neat looking top on a model ship's masthead is one of the hardest jobs in model making. The secret of having it look well is in carefully keeping to the relative sizes of all the various parts and these sizes may be easily determined by the old shipbuilder's rules, given elsewhere in this book. The old English rule was five inches of head for every three feet of mast's length. The United States Navy rule was .29 of topmast length, and the topmast head was .32 of topgallantmast length.

First square up the masthead as long as it should be and then flatten off on the two sides where the cheeks are to go. Below this, a little less than half the length of the masthead (⅖ to be exact), form a slight shoulder to make the hounds of the mast (Fig. 62). On these flattened hounds glue two thin pieces of white pine and when the glue has set shape the cheeks and bevel their top edge so that, as the masts rake aft, the top of the cheeks will be level.

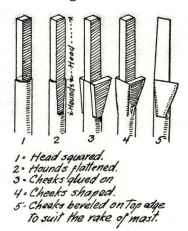

1 - Head squared.
2 - Hounds flattened.
3 - Cheeks glued on
4 - Cheeks shaped.
5 - Cheeks beveled on Top edge
To suit the rake of mast.

Fig. 62

The next step is to make, of maple or boxwood, the trestle-trees and cross-trees that are to fit over this masthead down on to the cheeks. Clamp together, in a small vise (Fig. 63), the two pieces of wood for the trestle-trees and with a small, square-edged file cut notches across, being careful to get them perfectly square, to receive the cross-trees, one on each side of the masthead; another, a little farther aft than the space between these two; and another, far enough ahead of

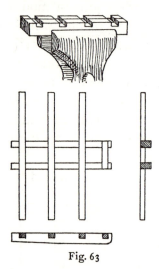

the front one to leave a hole large enough for the topmast to go through. These notches cut about one-third through the trestle-trees and the cross-trees should fit tight into them. Put glue under each cross-tree, where they touch the trestle-trees, keeping the latter just far enough apart so that they fit snug over the masthead and then clamp them in the jaws of a vise until they squeeze down flush and leave them until the glue

Fig. 63

sets. Then, with glue in all joints, place the cross-trees over the masthead down snug on the cheeks and let the glue harden.

The platform of the top should be of $\frac{1}{16}$ of an inch mahogany or maple, cut to size and shaped with the square hole in the center. Men-of-war had their tops almost square, the forward corners only slightly rounded, but merchant ships had smaller tops, more rounded in front into almost a half circle (Fig. 64). Cut

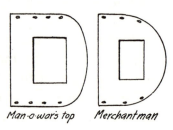

Man-o-war's top   Merchantman

Fig. 64

off the ends of the cross-trees so they are about a six-
teenth of an inch shorter than the top, on each edge.
Glue the tops of the cross-trees and clamp the tops in
place. That will hold
them until the deadeyes
can be fitted and the futtock shrouds which also
hold the top in place. A
few pins made into eye-
bolts also hold the tops to
the trestle-trees. Be careful to bevel or taper off
the size of the cross-trees
so that they are half as
thick on their outer ends
as they are at the trestle-
trees and round the edges of the top.

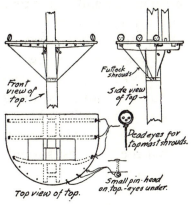

Fig. 65

The cap that goes on the top of the masthead, to hold
the topmast, is four times, in length, the thickness of
the topmast; in width, one and one-half times; and in

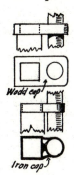

Fig. 66

thickness, three-quarters the thickness of
the topmast. Most builders get their tops
too clumsy looking. If these proportions
are followed, the caps will be as they were
on real ships.

Iron caps may be made by soldering a
thin strip of shim brass, bent the shape required, the two after edges lapped and
soldered, and a drop of solder spread over
where the two sides are pinched together
between the two masts (Fig. 66). Then
file off neat, to shape, with square and round rat-tailed
files, which are two of the handiest and most used files
in model work.

Don't try to solder eyes on this band but make eyes in the ends of small half-inch bank-pins and push them into the wood or drill clear through, if there is an eye on each side and run a piece of copper wire through, bending eyes in each end.

The topmast cross-trees are similarly built with fore and aft trestle-trees; two or three athwartship cross-trees, depending on the size of the ship; but with no platform or top as on the lower masthead. The most important point is to keep the forward deadeye in all rigging, so that it is opposite the center of the topmast, so that the foremost shroud does not stick out forward to interfere with the lifts of the yard.

CHAPTER VI

THE STANDING RIGGING

IN RIGGING your ship model don't be in too great a hurry to begin. Finish everything there is to do on the hull, the hatches and houses, even to the deck buckets, and be sure, above all, that you have holes enough drilled in the fiferail and pinrail to accommodate belaying pins for all the ropes, the "running gear," as it is called to distinguish it from the fixed stays and shrouds that are termed "standing gear."

If you are not up in ship's rigging sufficiently to visualize where each rope is to go, you had better do some planning. Lay out diagramatically the lead of each rope, to see where it is to stop and how it leads, to run clear of others, and be sure that every eye-bolt and cleat that will be needed to fasten ropes and hook blocks to, is on the masts and yards, as it is difficult to attach them later.

Another very important point is to get the proper kind of rigging, for some cords and threads shrink so much in damp weather that they will pull the masts out of their proper angle of rake and in dry weather they will be so slack that they will hang like drapery. Get a hard-laid, waxed, linen cord, such as harness makers use to sew leather. Winne & Co., Reade St., New York City, sell this cord in various thicknesses and in just the right sizes for model ship's standing rigging. It looks just like tarred hemp rigging, for each strand stands out distinctly and it is twisted up good and hard. Once put up it stands as put and does not come and go as will a cotton cord, painted black.

One of the prettiest features about a ship is the proper graduation in sizes of ropes. This sets a model off to advantage more than anything else. Just what sizes these should be may be found by using the rules given in the appendix. Even if you do not strictly adhere to proper sizes, these old tables are very useful in that they show you, for instance, that the mainstay is the heaviest stay on the ship. Take the mainmast, for instance. If it were a spar 22 inches in diameter, the shrouds should be $\frac{6}{22}$ of this diameter or six inches in circumference, about two inches in diameter. The mainstay, by this rule, is one-half the diameter of the mast or eleven inches in circumference, equal to $3\frac{2}{3}$ inches in diameter. Be guided by the proportions set forth in these rules, for they are the actual sizes used in the olden days by the builders of ships and they are not guesswork.

The process of rigging a model should be carried out just as if it were a real ship. Begin with the bowsprit and put on the bobstays and then the bowsprit shrouds. The fore, main and mizzen lower masts come next but be sure in putting up the shrouds to start with the forward starboard shrouds; then follow with the forward port shrouds; next with the second gang of starboard shrouds, and then the port. The shrouds are made in pairs. The one rope that makes the first shroud goes up and around the masthead and comes down forming the second shroud, the two being seized together forming a loop at and around the masthead. They form the first "gang" of rigging, as it is technically termed.

Old-time ships, rigged with burton-pendants, always put this pendant on first, before the shrouds. It hung part way down the mast and was used to hook tackles into to hoist heavy articles. The fore and aft stays were the last to be passed around the masthead.

When the lower rigging is all set up, put up the top-masts and their rigging, in the same way. Now is the time to do that tedious job of rattling down, that is, making the rope-ladders up the shrouds. Don't be so anxious to see the model all rigged that you neglect to rattle down until the last thing, or you will have cause to regret it. On a model like the clipper ship *Sea Witch,* there are over two thousand hitches made in putting up her ratlines, and this can be done far easier when only the shrouds are up and there are no braces or backstays to interfere.

THE BOWSPRIT

Ships generally had two bobstays made fast to the bowsprit close to where the headstays from the fore-mast made fast, so that one counteracted the pull of the other. Many carried a third stay called the cap bobstay, because it was made fast to the bowsprit away out at the end, close behind the cap (Fig. 67). On old timers, bobstays were cable-laid rope, and were rove through holes cut right through the stem,

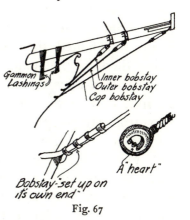

Fig. 67

being "set up on their own end," that is, the end was laid back along the rope and seized fast in three or four places. The outer ends were similarly seized fast into hearts, a heart-shaped, hardwood, sort of deadeye with an open center scored for ropes (Fig. 67), instead of the three individual holes of the deadeye. Another heart was strapped fast to the under side of the bowsprit and then the two hearts were laced together with a lanyard about one-third as heavy as the bobstay.

The bowsprit was held down in its bed at the stem of

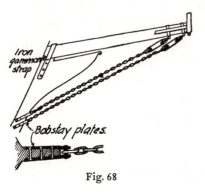

Iron
gammon
strap

Bobstay plates.

Fig. 68

the ship, by a couple of gammon lashings of rope rove through holes in the knee of the head, as that piece of the stem was termed.

It is difficult to determine the precise date when chain was first used for bobstays, but it was about 1820 or soon after. Iron bands took the place of the rope collars that held the hearts to the bowsprits and a heavy iron gammon strap, holding the bowsprit down on the top of the stemhead, supplanted the rope gammoning. Instead of going through the stem, the chain bobstays were held by an iron bolt in the ends of two iron straps projecting out beyond the stem (Fig. 68) to which these straps were rivetted, one on each side for each bobstay. On many of the older ships, where the knee of the head was very heavy, the bobstays

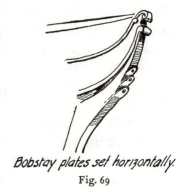

Bobstay plates set horizontally.

Fig. 69

could not go clear down to the stem, as this knee would interfere, and on those ships the bobstay plates were set horizontally, lapping one over the other where the bobstays came tangent to the knee (Fig. 69). Such old ships as the *New Hampshire, Minnesota, North Carolina, Ohio* and other 74-gun ships, as well as the *Constellation,* 36-gun, and *Constitution,* 44-gun classes of men-of-war, were all fitted this way and so were most of the old packet ships; but after about the year 1820, when chain bobstays came into vogue, the side plates on the stem were generally used to fasten the bobstays, well down on the cut-water.

Bowsprit shrouds went through the same evolution as bobstays. When of rope they went around the outer end of the bowsprit, just behind the cap, and led aft, just under the bee-seat or chock, to eyebolts in the ship's bows that gave them a good spread to help resist the side strain the headsails put upon the bowsprit. They were kept low enough down on the hull so as to exert a slight down-pull against the jib's up-pulling influence.

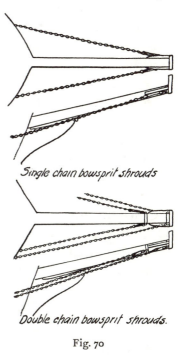

Single chain bowsprit shrouds

Double chain bowsprit shrouds.

Fig. 70

One very common error made by model builders is to attach this shroud so far aft on the hull that it will interfere with the anchor cables. Another is in attaching the shrouds to the ends of the catheads. This is not where the shrouds should go. The jib-boom backropes go there. The bowsprit shrouds should set up to hearts

or bull's-eyes at the bowsprit and be shackled to eye-
bolts down in the bows of the ship, above and a little
abaft of the hawser-holes.   Chain bowsprit shrouds
were shackled at their inboard end into eyebolts in the
bows and set up to bull's-eyes just aft of the bowsprit
cap (Fig. 70).   Large ships, of 2000 tons, carried two
chain bowsprit shrouds on each side.

Running so nearly in line with the bowsprit, this stay
does not show very clearly in pictures and many that
are shown are incorrectly portrayed.   Only recently I
was shown a set of paintings, very highly colored and
showing much rigging, but the artist had made the
same mistake in every picture.   The bowsprit shrouds
were shown going clear way aft, abaft the catheads and
very low down on the hull.   Where the artist expected
the anchor and cable to go is a mystery.   And yet, future
model makers will point to those pictures as their authority for rigging a model.   Let them but try to cat
the anchor or let the anchor go from the cathead and
they would carry away that bowsprit shroud every time.
Don't rig a model so it is impractical.   Men didn't
build ships that couldn't be worked, even if some artists
did draw pictures of them so rigged.

THE LOWER SHROUDS

To set up the mast shrouds, seize a deadeye into the
bight of the cord you are using for lower rigging and
with a touch of glue applied wind tightly about seven
turns of fine black thread, around both parts, close up
to the deadeye, and tie it fast or by bringing the end
back under the last two turns and pulling it tight a
neater job is done as it does not make the unsightly
knob the knot does.   The glue helps the thread to hold
and keeps it tight and snug.   Leave end enough to put

three or at least two such lashings on the shroud (Fig.
71). Be sure to have the odd eye in the deadeye so that
it will be uppermost when the shrouds are in place.
Reeve the other end of the shroud up through the
lubber's hole, forward around the masthead, down
through the lubber's hole,
aft of the mast, and then
seize in the other deadeye
so that the distance between
the lower and upper dead-
eyes is equal to about four
or five times the diameter of
the deadeyes, that being

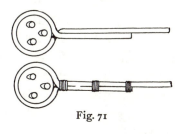

Fig. 71

about the proper drift or length of lanyards to use.

The size of the lanyards should be about one-third
the diameter of the shrouds. There is a heavy, black,
linen thread that comes on large spools, and is called
shoe button thread, that makes good lanyard stuff. Put
a knot in one end. A figure-eight knot makes a bigger
lump than an ordinary square knot and will not pull
through the hole in the
deadeye.

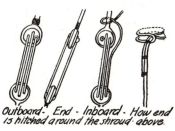

Outboard · End · Inboard · How end
is hitched around the shroud· above.

Fig. 72

Reeve the lanyard from
inboard out, so the knot is
on the inside of the forward
deadeye. The lanyards
should show straight up
and down on the outside,
the crossing over from the
front holes to the middle holes and from middle holes
to the after holes being on the inboard side of the deadeyes. Remember, that we are setting up the forward
starboard shrouds, and when you cross the deck on a
real ship and begin reeving the port lanyards, they are

rove off in the same way, left to right, so that the knot
comes on the inside of the after upper hole and the lanyard goes forward as you reeve it instead of aft as it is
on the other (starboard) side (Fig. 72). The end of
the lanyard goes inboard, through the last lower hole,
and is then taken up and clove-hitched around the
shroud just above the deadeye, the loose end being
stopped fast to the standing end on real ships, but on
small models a touch of glue will hold it jammed in
between the other parts.

Be careful to get all the upper deadeyes exactly the
same distance above the ship's rail so that when all are
in and you lash on the sheer-pole, just above the deadeyes, it will line up parallel with the ship's rail. On
real ships this sheer pole is a bar of inch iron wound
or served, as sailor's term it, with marlin. When all are
lined up true pass several turns of thread around both
shrouds, close up to the mast, in the lubber's hole of the
tops, and draw them close together and tie. In a real
ship they are seized together here, forming a loop
which is passed up over the masthead before the cap is
put on. Be sure you press the shrouds down good and
snug, where they go around the masthead, for there are
a number of them to go on.

On some of the old men-of-war, the forward shroud
was set up with a tackle so that it could be slacked to
allow the lower yard to be braced up sharp. I remember seeing in New York, a big clipper ship having
an extra shroud that went up to the cap of her masthead. She was one of the last of the big fellows of two
thousand or more tons burden.

Sometimes there is an odd shroud when a ship has
five, seven or nine shrouds to a side. In that case the
last shroud is a single one on each side, and the ends

lap by each other far enough to make an eye large enough to go over the masthead and are spliced into each other, forming a cut splice.

If the scale of your model is large enough to permit it and you want her to be exactly like a real ship, you should "serve" the shrouds with fine black thread where they go around the masthead and around the deadeyes. To serve a rope is to wind a small tarred cord (marlin on real ships) edge to edge, tightly around it so that it is completely covered. To worm, parcel and serve a rope, the old sea term of "worm and parcel with the lay, turn and serve the other way," should always be borne in mind.

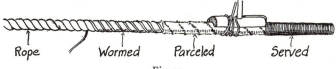

Rope   Wormed   Parceled   Served

Fig. 73

The three or four strands of a rope so stand out that sailors "worm" it to make a neat, smooth surface. Following the twist of the rope, they wind a piece of small rope to fill up the V-shaped score between the strands. Thin cloth, torn into strips about two inches wide, is then wrapped over it and tied down at intervals with twine. Then, with what is known as a "serving mallet," tarred marlin is hove on tight and so close together that it makes a smooth surface on the rope. Two or three turns around the mallet and another around the mallet handle enables the man to pull this serving on very tightly (Fig. 73).

This "serving" protects the rope where it would chafe around the masthead or deadeye and it should be carried a foot or two beyond (Fig. 74). The rope to

Fig. 74

be "served" must be stretched tight while being "served." It is a tedious job, at best, and all kinds of mechanical devices have been invented to try to spin this serving on in a lathe, but I get the best results in doing it just as we used to do it at sea, only in miniature, and instead of having to pass the spool of thread with every turn, I pivot the spool onto the handle of the serving mallet so it turns just hard enough to keep the thread tight. A small wedge, back of the spool, will adjust the tension on the thread (Fig. 76).

There is no royal road to learning and there are no short cuts by which the tedious process of rigging a ship's model may be overcome and still have a shippy-looking job. Men have told me how wonderfully they have rigged models by using short cuts in making all the lower rigging separate, all rattled down, before they put it on the model; but if they were satisfied with the bungling-looking job, when done, I was not. The only way is to set up the rigging just as we set it up in the old days on the ships and then it looks like ship's rigging. But "where ignorance is bliss 'tis folly to be wise"

Fig. 75

is an old saying as true now as the day the phrase was coined.

I have seen lower rigging where the ratlines were sewed on, strung around, across and back and up and across (Fig. 77), like stringing popcorn, but it shows up badly. The

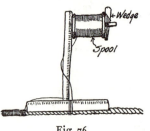

Fig. 76

only way is to hitch each ratline to the shrouds. Clove hitch each one and be careful not to pull the shrouds together in the middle, as so many do (Fig. 78). The space or step between the ratlines should be 14 or 15 inches.

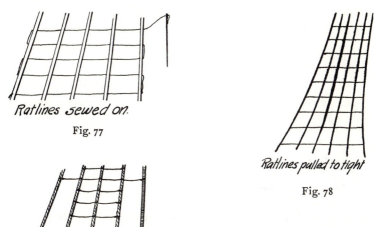

Ratlines sewed on.

Fig. 77

Ratlines pulled to tight

Fig. 78

How ratlines should look.

Fig. 79

On old-time ships it was customary to carry the ratlines clear across all of the shrouds (Fig. 80). On men-of-war, with nine shrouds, the ratlines would only cross seven of them, the forward, and after ones being left free. On line-of-battle ships and frigates, with their great spread of rig-

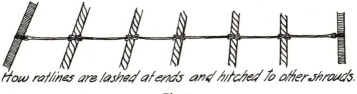

How ratlines are lashed at ends and hitched to other shrouds.

Fig. 80

ging, this made a veritable network, but they carried so many men and sent so many aloft to reef or furl sail, more ladder space was required than on merchant ships, especially those of a later period.

About 1880, ships began using iron rods served with marline or oak battens lashed on the outside of their shrouds, in place of tarred rope ratlines; and these, instead of going clear across the whole spread of the shrouds, only crossed three shrouds. About every sixth ratline, ratline stuff was carried clear across to the outer shrouds or "swifters," as they were called (Fig. 81).

Wood Ratlines

Fig. 81

On old-time capstans, the big, wooden capstan bars were always tied together from the end of one to the end of another, all around the circle, to prevent their being catapulted out if the capstan ever got away from the men heaving on it and spun around. Those bars would then be as deadly as cannon balls and as a precaution they were all "swiftered" together. That is how shrouds and backstays were "swiftered" together to keep them their proper distance apart.

If the masts on your model are properly stepped so that they fit snug and fetch up solid at the bottom of the hole they are stepped in and not simply tapered and jammed into a hole, which, as the wood dries out, allows the tapered spar to go in deeper; and the cheeks and trestle-trees are pinned as well as glued to the mast-head, you will not be troubled by the lower rigging becoming slack, except to the small extent that change in temperature and humidity will cause and that nothing can prevent. If the model be kept in a tight glass case in which a cup of salt is placed, it will be well protected against the weather.

THE STAYS

The fore-stay comes next in the process of rigging and just where it sets up to depends on the type of ship. On small ships, around the year 1700, this stay was a single rope, and the loop around the masthead was made by having a small eye spliced in the end. After this was passed from forward aft, around the masthead, the other end was rove through this eye and all pulled through until it came to a big, knot-like knob formed by working a turk's head in the stay at a point where it would stop the eye and so form a large loop around the mast.

Forestay of a ship of 1700.

Fig. 82

If you cannot splice this small cord then take a knife-blade and scrape ¼ inch of the end of the cord so that it tapers down thin. Touch it with glue and then bend it around a nail or piece of wire of the size you want the eye to be (a trifle larger than the cord itself) and then lap it back on itself in glue. Then take very fine black thread and wrap it neat and close up to the eye so as to cover the scraped thin end and you will have made a neat eye.

I would not advise you to try to make a turk's head or wall and crown knot on

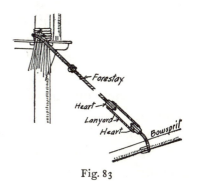

Fig. 83

very small models.   Just tie a plain knot.   Where one rope pulled on another like this, the under rope was always covered with leather to take the chafe (Fig. 82).

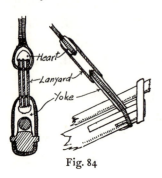

The lower end should be seized fast in a heart which is set up taut by a lanyard (Fig. 83) to another heart lashed to the bowsprit.

Later ships, and larger ones like those built for the early American navy, had this fore-stay doubled, the two parts, each with an eye in their end, going up around the masthead where they were seized together at the back or after side of the mast.   These two stays were fitted with hearts in their lower ends,

Fig. 84

but as jib-booms were added to these ships a yoke was used to set up the lower ends to and this yoke straddled the jib-boom and had a lashing around under the bow-sprit (Fig. 84).   This left the jib-boom free to be housed, or run in, in very bad weather.   One stay lashed ahead of the other about three or four feet farther out on the bowsprit.

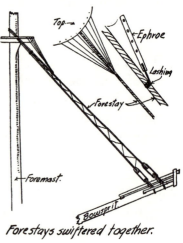

Forestays swiftered together.

Fig. 85

On many of the old-time men-of-war models you will see these two stays and others, laced or "snaked" to-gether in the same way, with a light line that zigzags back and forth, hitched to first one and then the other. This is another use of the "swifter." The stays are said to have been so snaked, or "swiftered" together that in case a cannon-ball should cut one they would not all go adrift but be held in place by the "swifter" until connected up, or "stoppered," as the sailors termed it (Fig. 85).

On the forward edge of each top, extending down to the stay, fore-stay, main-stay and mizzen-stay, on old sailing men-of-war, there was a net-like affair called a "crow-foot," the use of which many men do not understand. This was to prevent the heavy bolt rope on the foot of the topsail from hooking under the top or injuring the sail by slapping back against the rim of the top and cutting the canvas. It acted as a buffer and consisted of a light line rove continuously through holes along the front rim of the top, and thence down through holes in a hardwood batten, called an "ephroe," whose lower end was lashed to the stay. This line went up to the top again on the other side, and down again, and so on (Fig. 85).

Instead of carrying the two parts of the fore-stay, one ahead of the other, set up with hearts and yokes, along about 1820 these fittings, picturesque but clumsy, began to disappear and the fore-stays were both carried down to the same place, one on each side of the bowsprit, under which they passed, being seized fast, the end of one stay to the standing part of the other on the opposite side. Sometimes, however, they were passed through the eyes of a short strop under the bowsprit and set up on their own end or standing part.

Along in the 1860's, when ship's bows were made longer on clippers, this fore-stay, still doubled, came down to the knightheads, the two extreme timber heads away up in the bows, one on each side of the bowsprit, and there passed through lignum-vitae bull's-eyes, iron strapped to the knightheads, where they were doubled back on themselves and seized fast,—"Set up on their own ends," as the saying was (Fig. 86).

The main-stay was similar to the fore-stay in the manner in which it was fastened around the masthead. In the later day clippers, instead of being made in two pieces, lashed back of the masthead, it was in one continuous length passed around the masthead and seized

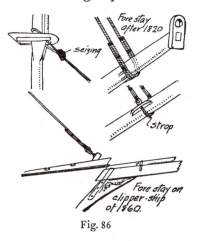

Fig. 86

together down in front of the foremast, about four feet away from it. The main-stay was the largest rope on a ship. It was set up at the lower end to the knightheads. Small ships had only one stay, but large craft were fitted with two, the main-stay and another, called a preventer - stay or spring - stay. The relative sizes of these stays are shown in the case of the frigate *Macedonian*. Her fore-stay was 13 inches in circumference and the fore-springstay, 9½ inches. Her main-stay was a rope 13 inches in circumference and her springstay, 10 inches. The mizzen-stay, 8 inches in circumference, had no spring-stay.

Ships, along in the 1820's, had their main-stays set up to the windlass bitts and later ships, such as the craft I went to sea on, the ships of the 1880's, set their main-stays up to bull's-eyes strapped to iron bands around the cross-piece, the "bolster," as it is called, in the fore-topsail sheet bitts, just forward of the foremast, and about three feet above the deck.

Where the main-stay crossed the foremast it was covered with a piece of leather sewed on and to prevent its sawing up and down, an oak batten was fastened vertically on each side of the mast with a score or hole for the stay to pass through. On later ships, those after 1850, where the maintop-mast stay also came down and set up to the fore-topsail bitts, this batten was long enough to take it also.

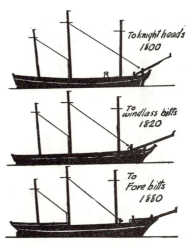

Fig. 87

The mizzen-stay should run on an angle nearly parallel to the main-stay. Sailors were a hard-headed, hard-fisted, practical set of men and they had leisure to do a lot of thinking and much of this was devoted to their ship's appearance. Every spar and stay was carefully studied. It had to stand or run just so,— until hard and fast rules were developed and in rigging or sparring ships these rules were strictly adhered to. If this mizzen-stay does not parallel the main-stay, the ship somehow will look odd. Put it parallel and note the difference. That is

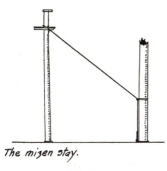

The mizen stay.

Fig. 88

what years of sailors' observance of such things has developed.   Where this stay comes to the mainmast, a heavy bull's-eye was lashed to the mast.   In ships after

Right way   Wrong way
to lead the main-stay, at the top.

Fig. 89

1850 it was iron-strapped with an iron band around the mast.   The stay was rove through this bull's-eye and led down aft of the mast to another bull's-eye, in an eye-bolt in the deck, through which it rove and was turned back and seized to itself.

One common error made in rigging models is in leading the fore, main, and mizzen-stays *over* the forward end of the top instead of down through the square-hole or lubber's hole, as it is called, *under* the forward end of the top.   The strain on that stay would crush the top, which is only a light platform. What leads many novices to do this is the thought that the stay should lay against the mast above the shrouds.   In actual practice the stay is passed around and over the shrouds on the masthead, being wormed, parcelled, served and then covered with leather.

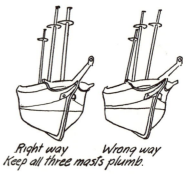

Right way   Wrong way
Keep all three masts plumb.

Fig. 90

There are many things to keep in mind when setting up rigging.   Be sure that the masts are all in line, looking end on at your model; that the masts stand plumb and are not pulled over to one side or the other by setting up the shrouds too hard on one side (Fig. 90).

Another thing to watch out for is to get just the right rake or slant aft to each mast to conform to the particular ship or to the date to which the ship belongs. This amount of rake is given in a previous table. You will often see a ship model on which the masts come closer together at the top than they do at the deck and you can put down that model as being faulty (Fig. 91). No ship was ever so rigged. The fault lies with the man who rigged the model in pulling the delicate upper masts too tightly together. The stays are sometimes correct but in reeving the yard braces they are pulled so tight as to slack up the stays.

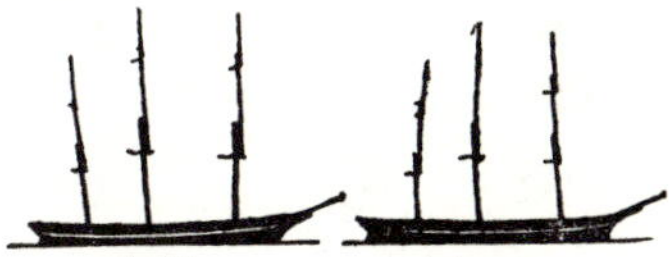

Right   Wrong
Slant or "rake" to the masts.

Fig. 91

It is always a good practice to step the masts so that they slant aft a little more than is actually called for and then, when the stays are set up, the tension on the mast keeps them snug and taut. They will, in time, lose this tension, as the continual alternation of damp and dry days serve to tighten and slacken the cords. On a real ship this has to be constantly attended to and you cannot hope to completely overcome it. Springs or rubber, under the foot of the mast, have been tried, but in time will give out and you are in a worse fix than ever. The secret lies in using a linen cord, well stretched and waxed. I have a model of a bark rigged with linen and for six years her shrouds and stays have stood as taut as when first rigged. I also have another little model of a ship rigged with various sizes of cotton cords, painted black, which are taut and trim as ever on a damp day, but when it comes out dry and hot, the stays slacken and hang in bights so you can almost tie a sheep's shank in them. Many men, by the way, after using linen rigging, make the mistake of using cotton lanyards which stretch far more than one will believe.

If you want to tighten your lower rigging without

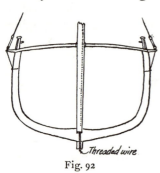

setting up on all the lanyards in the deadeyes, with a small bit bore your mast holes clear down through the bottom of the ship, and then screw up from the bottom, in this hole, a small machine bolt with the head cut off (or a threaded wire), so that it just touches the heel of your mast

Fig. 92

which has a small metal disc or flat nail head on the bottom to meet the wire (Fig. 92). By screwing up on this bolt, the masts can be lifted up, thereby tightening the rigging; but this, on an accurate model, distorts the scale by lengthening the masts.

Fig. 93

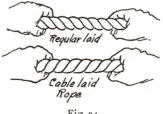

Regular laid

Cable laid Rope

Fig. 94

Ordinary ropes are so twisted that when you hold a short length between your hands, the strands come over the top and slant down towards your right hand. Cable-laid rope is just the reverse; the strands come over the top of the rope near your right hand and slant downward towards your left (Fig. 94). All these shrouds and stays should be made of cable-laid, four-stranded rope.

Before setting up the topmasts, if the model is of a vessel built after 1812, she may have fore and main spencer gaffs rigged on her masts. Not all vessels were so fitted. Some captains would not be without them and some would not have them on their ship. They were fitted just like the brailing foresail on a schooner, with a standing fore-gaff, except that instead of the hoops and jaws of the gaff being large enough to go around the bulky lower masts, a smaller diameter spar, called a spencer-mast, named after the man who invented the rig, was fitted from a step on the deck, up abaft the mast, its top being housed in chocks between the trestle-trees (Fig. 95). The jaws of the gaff were

held to the spencer mast by the usual parrel strap,—a piece of tarred ratline stuff with eight or ten lignumvitae beads or parrels to keep it from sticking as the gaff was hoisted or lowered, by means of a single becket block, hooked into an eye in the top of the gaff, at the jaws, and a double-block, hooked into an eye-bolt in the under side of the cross

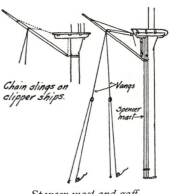

Spencer mast and gaff.

Fig. 95

trees, for the throat halliard to reeve through. The peak halliard had the same purchase only there was no becket on the block on the gaff, the standing end of the halliard making fast to the gaff out beyond the block and the throat halliards coming down on the port side and the peak halliards to starboard.

On clippers and later-day craft, the gaff was permanently set up with a chain bridle from the after end of the top to the gaff, instead of using a rope peak halliard (Fig. 95). When rope was used, they were generally belayed to a wooden cleat, one on each side, on the after quarter of the mast. This gaff was kept from swinging about by vangs, one off to each side to the ship's waterways. The after sail of this kind was of a much older origin and was not known as a spencer at all. It was called the "spanker" or, by some, the "driver." As it is better to leave this sail till later, we will not detail it here. It is sure to get broken if the spars are put on now, but the spencers can be rigged easier now than later. Some ships carried only a fore spencer and some a spencer only on the main mast. A few carried them on both masts.

The futtock shrouds and lower topmast deadeyes come next, the former doing for the topmast shrouds what the chain-plates, below them on the hull, do for the main rigging. They hold the deadeyes against the pull on the topmast shrouds and have to be fastened to the top of the lower shrouds or to a futtock-band around the mast. Sometimes they were set up with a bentinck shroud carried down to the deck and set up taut with a tackle.

The oldest method is where the rope futtocks hooked into the straps of the deadeyes that projected through the underside of the rim of the top and were carried down, not quite vertically, but in farther, so that the top overhung it a little and were hitched around the shroud, the end laid along it and lashed fast to the shrouds.

Later, an oak batten, termed the futtock-staff, was seized fast to the inner edge of the shrouds and the futtocks were hitched around this staff (Fig. 96). This answered the purpose very well on merchant ships but on the heavily rigged men-of-war, with nine and eleven lower shrouds and four futtock shrouds, the rigging became pretty well jumbled up at this point. As there was an advantage to be gained

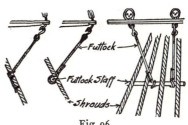

Fig. 96

by hoisting the yards as close up under the top as was practical, to give them room to swing, braced sharp up under the stay, the mast, therefore, could not be used to attach the futtocks to except the angle was made so great that it lost its power to hold the topmast rigging strain. To overcome this, the bentinck shroud was evolved. All four futtock shrouds on the fore and mainmast and three futtocks on the mizzen, were brought down to a point at an iron ring. On the underside of this ring a heavy shroud was spliced in and this shroud kept the topmast shrouds taut by being led across and down to a heavy tackle hooked in the waterways on the opposite side of the ship (Fig. 97). Large ships, including line-of-battle ships and frigates, such as the *Constitution* and *Constellation,* generally carried double bentinck

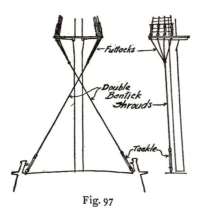

Fig. 97

shrouds, one for each side; but smaller sized craft, sloops-of-war, brigs, etc., only carried a single bentinck shroud where all the futtocks (generally only three on a side) were brought to one common center abaft of the mast and a single shroud was hooked in that extended down abaft of the mast to a tackle hooked into an eyebolt in the deck (Fig. 98).

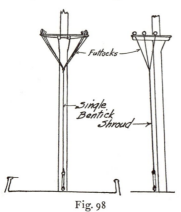

Fig. 98

To hold the futtock in place, for the lee one will swing out against the main yard as they slacken, short pieces of rope with an eye in each end, called cat-harpins, were made to lash across from side to side and hold the futtock snug. Some crossed them from the forward end of one futtock staff to the after end of the other, and some lashed both ends to the same futtock staff but carried the cat-harpin around the mast (Fig. 99).

The topmast rigging is put over the mastheads in the same sequence as the lower shrouds. The burton pendants come first of all, then the forward starboard pair of shrouds and forward port pair, etc. The breast backstays follow; then the standing backstays, the spring-stay and the stay. The breast backstay, to take the side strain on the topmast, was carried down abreast the topmast head as near as was practical, which brought its chainplate

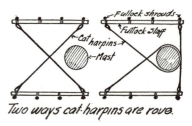

Two ways cat-harpins are rove.

Fig. 99

between the fourth and fifth chainplates of the shrouds in the channels. Instead of a deadeye, this chainplate set inboard a little from the shroud's chainplates and had an eye in the upper end into which the blocks of a heavy tackle could be hooked, for this breast backstay stood out so far that it prevented the lee yard-arm from swinging around unless it were fitted with tackles that could be slackened instead of being set up permanently with deadeyes. The standing backstays led aft of the last lower shroud, setting up with deadeyes and chainplates.

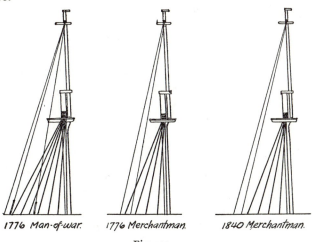

1776 Man-of-war.   1776 Merchantman.   1840 Merchantman.

Fig. 100

Men-of-war carried a second backstay,—a shifting backstay that set up with a heavy tackle to an eye chainplate in the channels between the deadeyes of the two after lower shrouds. It set inboard about six inches so that the blocks would clear the deadeyes and lanyards of the lower shrouds. This way of rigging was the style in 1776 and as late as 1800 or a little later. Merchantmen, not having so many lower shrouds to spread so far on the channels, carried two fixed backstays to the topmast but no breast backstay. The forward of these two set up between the two after shrouds, but ships of about 1840 set up their two backstays aft of the lower rigging (Fig. 100).

The leads of the fore, main and mizzentopmast stays

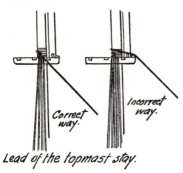

Lead of the topmast stay.

Fig. 101

were so different that it will be necessary to consider each one separately. All of them passed around back of the masthead and down across the trestle-trees in a fair line to their point of attachment below. They did not, as so many amateurs assume, lead over the forward end of the topmast cross-tree and then down (Fig. 101).

Topmast stays in the days of the caravels were picturesque. They were looped over the mast and had a fiddle-block strapped into their lower ends. Two single blocks were seized around the bowsprit; one near the outer end and the other in about six feet or so. A smaller rope was made fast around the spar just outside of the inner block. It was carried up to the lower sheave in the fiddle-block, then down through the block on the bowsprit end, and up through the upper, larger sheave in the fiddle-block, down through the inner,

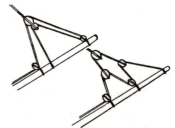

Two ways of rigging caravals fore top-mast stay at bowsprit end

Fig. 102

single blocks and in along the bowsprit and was belayed

at the bow of the ship (Fig. 102). This crow-foot purchase distributed the strain on the bowsprit and the stay could always be set up taut.

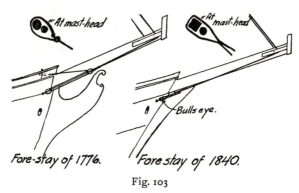

Fig. 103

Ships of 1776 carried two stays one of which was a little smaller in size than the other. A frigate of that period carried a 3½ inch in circumference topmast-stay and a 2½ inch spring-stay. The former reeved through the port bee-hole and the latter through the starboard bee-hole in the bee-seat just behind the bowsprit cap, the porthole being a foot or more aft of the starboard one. They rove around the topmast-head with an eye splice and a stopper knot in the same way as the fore-stay, and were set up taut, after reeving through the bee-hole, by a tackle hooked to an eyebolt outside on the ship's bows, the hauling part coming in to a belaying pin (Fig. 103).

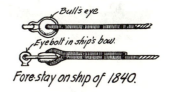

Fig. 104

Some time after 1800, this topmast-stay and spring-stay became one. The same rope was carried up around the masthead and the two parts were seized together forward of the mast and far enough away to leave a loop big enough to permit the topgallantmast being lowered down through it. At the bowsprit end both ropes were rove the same distance aft of the cap, one to port and one to starboard, through bee-holes in the bee-chock that butted against the after side of the cap. From here they were carried aft to the bow of the ship through a bull's-eye hooked on there and set up on their own ends (Fig. 104).

The maintopmast-stay took a decided change in the way it was led, beginning about the year 1828. Previous to that date the universal practice was to make the forward end of this stay fast at the after side of the foremast-head. But by 1850, the vessel so rigged was the exception. They then all carried their maintopmast-stays down to where the main-stay belayed, to the windlass-bitts or foretopsail-sheet bitts just forward of the foremast at the deck, and were set up on their own end through a bull's-eye strapped around the bolster of the fore bitts (Fig. 105). Where it made fast at the

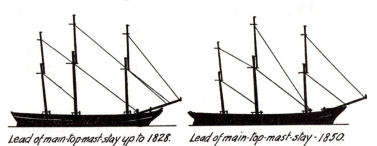

Lead of main-top-mast-stay up to 1828.   Lead of main-top-mast-stay - 1850.

Fig. 105

the foremast-head, a strap or collar was fastened around the masthead, under the shrouds, with a bull's-eye through which the maintopmast-stay was rove and turned back on itself and seized fast.

This was the usage on very small craft such as brigs

and small barks or ships. But the ships of three hundred tons and over carried two maintopmast-stays having a preventer or spring-stay under the main-stay. Both came from the maintopmast head, the preventer underneath, and rove through large, single blocks hooked into straps or collars around the mast and led down abaft the foremast. The maintopmast-stay was set up with a heavy tackle made up of a fiddle-block on the end of the stay and a single block hooked into an eyebolt in the deck at the starboard after side and just clear of the mast wedges and coat (Fig. 106). The hauling end hooked under a cavil or rove over a sheave in the after vertical post of the pin rail around the head of which it was hitched. The preventer stay rove in the same manner—only it was on the port side.

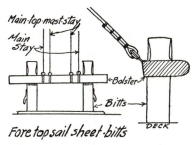

Fore topsail sheet-bitts

Fig. 106

Ships were only small craft before the year 1800 and with all hemp standing rigging, the topmast-stays were so set up with tackles that the stretch could be readily taken up. Many a ship, however, rigged in the freezing northern climate, has been totally dismasted when suddenly caught in a gale or hurricane upon reaching the hot southern latitudes that softened the tar in the ropes and stretched the rigging so that the masts were left unsupported to carry all the strain. Heroic seamanship on several occasions saved a ship's masts. Tail blocks were seized fast to the shrouds, up near the tops, and a rope was rove zig-zag, back and forth from port to starboard, and back through a block on every shroud.

This rope was then led down through a snatch-block or leader-block on deck and hove taut on the capstan. This process was what is called "swiftering the rigging" by which the slack shrouds were pulled tight by pulling them inboard.

On one or two old British Admiralty models I have seen this process demonstrated. It was done to illustrate the process of "swiftering" the shrouds, but must not be confounded with regular ship's rigging. It is merely an expedient to be resorted to in case of emergency.

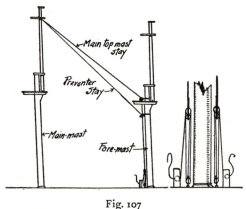

Fig. 107

Some idea of the way the old hemp rigging stretched can be formed when we read that a line-of-battle ship's main-stay stretched out twelve feet, and that after a cruise of only two months, two feet had to be cut off the fore-stay.

By having their topmast-stays so set up it was possible to keep the topmast heads where they belonged in taking up the stretch in the stays by setting up on these tackles. The maintopmast-stay made a true continuous line with the fore-stay, but the preventer-stay led under the after edge of the fore-top with the hanks to which the foretopmast-staysail was seized sliding up and down on it (Fig. 107).

About the year 1828, ships began to appear with the maintopmast-stay carried down to the windlass bitts. Some captains, evidently a little skeptical of this new-fangled rig, carried the stay this way but also hung on to a stay to the foremast head as well. The latter was a shorter stay and so less liable to stretch, but on the other hand, if the foremast carried away, the maintopmast was sure to go with it. The appearance of wire rigging, however, settled the question in favor of the stay coming down to the bitts and that is how the clipper ships were rigged.

Some people, for argument's sake, say they have seen the old square staysail style of rig in the 1880's. So have I. Some of the old packet ships turned into whalers have carried their antiquated style of rig a century beyond their time, but we are speaking of the general trend in ship's rigging and not isolated examples in shipping. The old *Constitution* and *Constellation,* for example, built in 1797, are still afloat, long after all of their kind have disappeared from the sea. They are still rigged with square staysails.

The mizzentopmast-stays set up at the mainmast head just the same as the maintopmast-stays set up at the foremast head, except that in later-day ships they were made fast there and not led down to the deck as was the maintopmast-stay on clippers.

Most merchant ships carried only two topmast cross-trees, but men-of-war, from frigates up, had three on the fore- and mainmasts and two on the mizzen. The futtock shrouds were rigged in the same manner as the lower futtocks, according to the time the ship was built, but instead of the topgallant shrouds being set up with deadeyes and lanyards, bull's-eyes with a single hole were used, the shrouds leading down through this, doubled back up along the standing part of the shroud and seized fast to it.

The topgallant shrouds were rattled down; that is, cords were put across from shroud to shroud, to form a ladder, so the royal yard, when lowered, could be reached from the top of the topgallant rigging. But

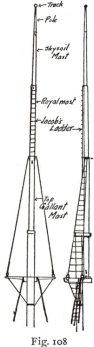

men-of-war, clippers and a few big ships carrying standing skysail-yards, had a single rope ladder, called a Jacob's ladder (Fig. 108), up the after side of the royalmast to the top or within reach of the skysail yard when lowered.

Ordinarily the topgallantmast, the royalmast and the long naked pole, with its truck, a round ball on American ships and a flat, round button-shape on foreigners, sticking up above all the rigging, were all in one spar with shoulders where the topgallant and royal rigging went around it to prevent their slipping down; but, as said before, a few ships carried a top-gallantmast that was headed; that is, fitted with trestle-trees, a single cross-tree and a cap into which the royal-mast fitted. Such a ship was distinguished as having fidded royalmasts and generally carried a mast that included both the royal and skysailmast with its pole in one and the same stick. The long tapered pole above all the rigging, was a feature that distinguished American ships from foreigners whose short, stubby poles

Fig. 108

and flat trucks gave them a heavy, squatty appearance
(Fig. 109).

Put up the topgallant rigging on your model next,
remembering that there was a difference in the size between the lower rigging and the top-
most rigging. The topgallant rigging
is decidedly lighter than either, and as
a No. 40 black linen thread is about
the size to use on the topmast rigging
of an ⅛ inch scale model, No. 80 or
No. 100 should be used for the royal
and skysail rigging.

American truck-Foreign truck

Fig. 109

In fitting topgallantmasts and topmasts also, the mistake is too often
made of not fitting them snug through the cap and
trestle-trees and in leaving too great a space in the
doublings (where the two spars lap each other at the
masthead) between the
lower masthead and the
heel of the topmast (Fig.
110). There should only
be room enough to get the
thickness of the rigging
between them.

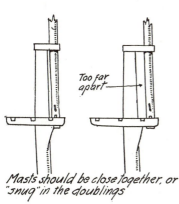

*Too far
apart*

*Masts should be close together, or
"snug" in the doublings*

Fig. 110

Faults like this are the
cause of rigging becoming
so slack on some models.
The greatest fault, how-
ever, is in not fitting the
fid and heel properly. Be-
cause it is a mere model the fid is just stuck through any
old way. Great care should be taken that the appar-
ently insignificant, but really most important little fid,
is heavy enough to support the strain and *that it lies*

snug down on the trestle-trees. If it does not, when the rigging tightens, on a wet day, the strain will push the topmast down (Fig. 111) and when a dry day comes the rigging will hang loose. This error is made so frequently that I want to impress upon future model builders the importance of this point, trivial as it may seem.

So many men have asked me how to keep the rigging tight on their models. The best way is to fit the fid correctly and use linen cord.

Masts too far apart push the trestle-trees out of alignment

Fig. 111

Another point is to cut a small notch in the after side of the topmast at the heel or lower end, that will lodge over a hardwood chock, between the trestle-trees, that is glued and pin-fastened besides lodging on the shoulder of the mast below it where the masthead is squared up. A topmast so put up, with a small wedge inserted in front of the topmast at the trestle-trees, will not work down and cause slack rigging (Fig. 112).

The trouble is most people look upon model building as a mere pastime and make indifferent models. To make a good model you have got to do good, careful work. As you go aloft and the spars and trestle-trees become tiny, only the best of material can be used and also the greatest of care in fitting the spars and rigging.

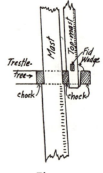

Fig. 112

Another point that is the cause of much slack rigging in model ships is the neglect, just as in the case of the fid, to shape the topgallant and royalmasts with proper "stops" or shoulders to support the shrouds. There should be a decided yet not too clumsy ridge where each set of rigging lays over a mast. The older the ship is supposed to be the more pronounced was this "stop" for the reason that rope was not so strong and was therefore made larger to stand the strain and accordingly it required a larger "stop" to prevent its pulling over (Fig. 113). On very early ships, in the 1700's and in the days of the caravels, this stop was a very noticeable swelling or enlargement of the spar.

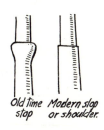

Old Time   Modern stop
stop   or shoulder.

Fig. 113

In putting up the shrouds so many men tie a square knot which is so bulky and has so many turns to slacken up in time, that it is no wonder the shrouds gradually loosen up. Pass the cord only once back of the spar and then with very fine thread and just a touch of glue binds the two shrouds snug close up to the spar (Fig. 114). Put the starboard topgallant shrouds over first, the port second, then, after the shrouds, the starboard backstay and port backstay and then the stay.

A seizing in glue will not stretch-but a big bulky knot has several turns to stretch and slacken.

Fig. 114

But by this time we must rig out the jib-boom. On the old-time ships this always lapped back on the bowsprit one-third its length; two-thirds sticking out beyond the bowsprit cap. The inner end of the jib-boom rested in a saddle fastened on top of the bowsprit to receive it and at this point it was lashed to the bowsprit which, as noted, was a round spar in old ships, which was left square, for a couple of feet in from the cap, where the bee-block and bee-seat were fastened to it (Fig. 115).

A jib-boom was all that was carried by ships from about 1700 to 1780 when the two square sails, the sprit-sail and sprit-topsail, were in the height of their glory. Jibs had come into use about the year 1708, but the sailors of those days, with their bluff-ended, beamy ships, had more faith in the square sails under the bowsprit. Their ships were so clumsy aft that they steered none too well, and when we remember that they had a huge beam for a tiller that extended from the rudder-head almost to the mizzenmast, its forward end sup-

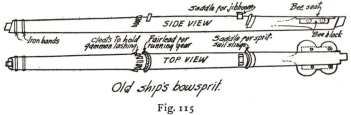

Old ship's bowsprit.

Fig. 115

ported on a greased beam up just under the deck, and with tackles rove off to each side, their ends wound around the barrel of a hand steering-wheel that some-times took several men to turn, and that the tiller would only swing to an angle of about ten to twelve degrees each way, it is not to be wondered that their ships were somewhat unwieldy on their helm. When it came to quick manœuvring in an engagement, where life was at stake, the sailors of that time depended more upon these kite-like sprit-sails, to spin their ships about, than they did upon the helm.

With the finer-shaped, less burdensome ships, jibs, being far handier to manipulate, won out in the long run and the sprit-sails gradually disappeared from the sea. The sprit-sail was carried as late as 1862, more as an auxiliary sail, however, than a regular one, for my father-in-law, the late Capt. T. R. Webber, sailed on the ship *Contest,* 1150 tons, to China, in that year, and she carried this sail which the sailors then nicknamed the "bull-driver." In the China Sea they were over-hauled by the *Alabama,* Capt. Semmes, due to the wind dying out, and the *Contest* was burned and sank. Cap-tain Webber, then one of her crew, was afterwards landed in France.

The spritsail-yard, one-sixth shorter than the foretop-sail-yard, was held around the bowsprit by a rope strop (Fig. 116). In ships of about

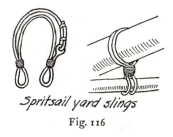

Spritsail yard slings

Fig. 116

1745, this strop had beads or parrels and was rigged to slide up on the bowsprit, having a tackle rove to an eye-bolt in the underside of the cap. But ships of about 1800 had this yard fixed in one place a pendant being hooked into the eye-bolt at the cap (Fig. 117). By 1820, the majority of ships had given up the use of sails on the spritsail-yard but retained the yard as a spreader for the jib-boom stays.

1745

1800

Spritsail yard rigging.

Fig. 117

In 1860, merchant ships had given up the use of the spritsail-yard, except in a few cases, and many carried it in two separate pieces known there as "whisker booms." They were fitted with hooks on the inboard end that fastened into a stout eyebolt, on each side, just aft of the bee-block. On men-of-war this was retained to the last days of sailing ships as it spread a tarred rope net, triangular in shape, to keep the jib, as it was hauled down, from getting under the jib-boom, and they even carried another net, spread between the flying jib-boom backropes, to catch the flying jibs (Fig. 118). It was a life-saver for the men who had to go out on the footropes and stow the jibs.

The jib-boom must be rigged before the topgallant or even the foretopmast-stay can be completed. This brings us to a consideration of the dolphin striker. Ships of 1750 and thereabouts that carried a sprit-topsail under the jib-boom, had no dolphin strikers at all, and all the

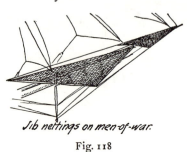

Jib nettings on men-of-war.

Fig. 118

very old ships, the caravels and galleons, had no rigging under their bowsprits. The sprit-topsail yard and the jib traveler, an iron ring encircling the spar, to which the jib-stay was attached, hoisted out and were hauled in along the naked jib-boom. But where jibs superseded square staysails, the dolphin striker began to appear, in a very small, modest way at first, until it grew to be a real spar with a mass of stays attached to it. The sprit-topsail was reluctantly given up for jibs and dolphin strikers and during the transition, the foot of the sprit-topsail was cut arching enough to clear the dolphin striker, in an effort to retain

The first primitave dolphin striker.

Fig. 119

this sail, but by 1797 it was fairly done away with. The spritsail, however, existed for many years after.

The short dolphin striker was bolted to the forward face of the bowsprit cap and its rigging was brought abruptly up to the bowsprit, outside of the spritsail-yard (Fig. 119). The handsome American frigates built in 1797, were rigged in this manner, but the use of flying jib-booms increased the number of ropes so that in order to accommodate them all it was necessary to make the dolphin striker double, in two pieces that forked, one on each side, from the cap (Fig. 120).

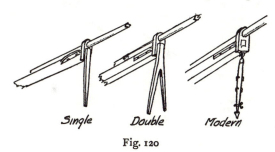

Single   Double   Modern

Fig. 120

In the 1820's, the swinging dolphin striker became popular. As in all changes made in ship's rigging, one or two vessels may have had it a few years previous, just as many retained the older style after this date. With the new dolphin striker the martingales or ropes that steadied it were led back to the ship's bow.

With the old, rigid dolphin striker, the head-rigging (a general term used to designate all the rigging forward of the bows) was led through holes bored through it; but with the round spar of the modern dolphin striker, these ropes were hooked under iron hooks that stuck out on each side.

At first the jib-boom martingales were of rope; then wire rope, when this patent rigging was invented; and finally, chain was used. Small craft had only a single martingale from the end of the jib-boom to the dolphin striker; but the clippers and large cargo carriers of 1860, rigged with inner and outer jibs, had a doubled martingale as shown in the accompanying sketch (Fig.

121). One ran from the end of the jib-boom and one
from just outside the inner jib-stay where the spar was
cut down in diameter to form a slight shoulder to
prevent the eye band, into which it shackled, from

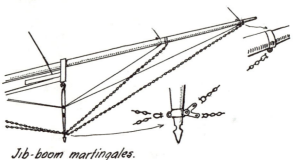

Jib-boom martingales.

Fig. 121

sliding in. Both of these were made fast at the lower
end of the dolphin striker which was usually finished
off with a spear-head ornament.

In the days of rope, eye-splices were fitted over the
lower end of the dolphin striker, but the chain martingales were shackled into a crescent-shaped iron, one to
each horn, the iron being bolted at its after edge to two
eyes or lugs on the iron band around the dolphin striker.

A cow-horn dolphin striker.

Fig. 122

Many of the French, Spanish
and Italian ships carried a
crooked, "cow horn"-shaped dolphin striker (Fig. 122). It seemed
to be a characteristic of Mediter-
ranean-built ships as I never saw it
on any other vessel. American
vessels were distinguished by their dolphin strikers
standing vertically, while foreign craft had them raked
directly in line with the foretopmast-stay.

In the 1860's, when ships began to have longer, easier

bows, their bowsprits were correspondingly shorter and
the jib-booms were brought clear down to the rail, at
first, with a dummy-shaped block that the heel of the
jib-boom butted against, which carried the line of the
spar back to the bows. In time, however, the jib-boom
itself came almost to the
ship's bows and the
heel-block was merely a
cleat for it to butt on,
being cut so that the jib-
boom went under it and
it was further held
down with an iron bale,
bolted to the bowsprit
(Fig. 123).

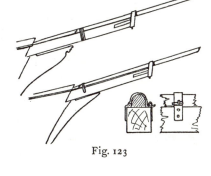

Fig. 123

With the jib-boom in
we can put up the head-stays that go to it. Until about
the year 1800, jibs were hoisted out to the bowsprit end
as well as up and down on the stay, so that in furling
the jib, the stay was slacked back or rather hauled in to
the bowsprit cap and the jib was furled on the end of
the bowsprit and not on
the end of the jib-boom,
as was done in later years.

There was a large iron
ring around the jib-boom
and in a clevis on this
ring, an eye-splice in the
lower end of the jib-stay
was put and secured with

Right way - Right way - Wrong way.
The jib-slay lead.

Fig. 124

a bolt through both clevis and eye. The stay led up to
the head of the foretopmast where it was rove through
a large single block (an eleven-inch block on the frigate
Macedonian) that was stropped around the foretop-

mast masthead just above the foretopmast-stay. From here this stay led down almost to the deck where it was hove taut with a tackle that hooked into an eyebolt in the deck on the after, starboard quarter of the mast.

There are two things to be careful about, and one is to so strap the block that it is close in to the mast so that the stay does not interfere with the swinging of the topsail yard (Fig. 124). Ships of a later period put a

Merchant ship · 1850.

Fig. 125

cheek-block against the topmast, on each side, close up under the trestle-trees, to insure the stays leading down aft of the front of the mast. The other thing is to lead this stay fair, clear of the shrouds, by reeving it through a bull's-eye or a bee-hole in the top if it cannot be rove clear by going through the lubber's hole. When the jib is hauled out on the jib-boom, the stay is set taut by the tackle on deck.

After the year 1800, hoisting jib-stays were changed to fixed-stays. A long loop or eye-splice went around the masthead and the stay went through a sheave in the bowsprit, down through a hole (the upper one) in the dolphin striker and set up to the bowsprit just forward

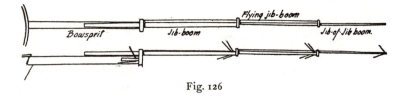

Fig. 126

of the spritsail-yard. On later ships it set up to bull's-eyes hooked into eyebolts in the ship's bows at the waterways of the main deck.

The packet ships of 1850 carried another stay, leading to the maintopmast head, making three stays to the same place,—the flying jib-stay. Each of these was a little smaller than the one below. The jib-stay was

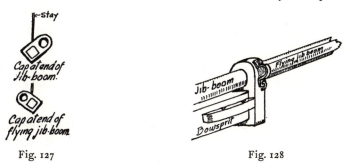

Fig. 127   Fig. 128

hooked on the starboard side of the dolphin striker and the flying jib, opposite it, on port (Fig. 125).

Men-of-war and packet ships built frigate-fashion,

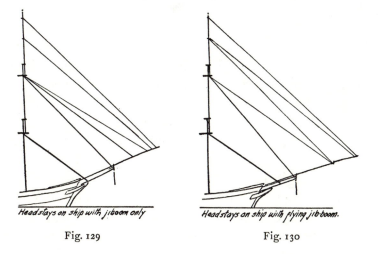

Fig. 129   Fig. 130

that operated just after the War of 1812, reached the height of perfection in sailing ships so far as carrying spars and sails were concerned. They had bowsprit, jib-boom, flying jib-boom and jib-of-jib-boom, though but few ships carried the latter spar (Fig. 126). The jib-boom lay directly on top of the bowsprit, but the flying jib-boom was off center so as to clear the jib-stay and was shipped on the upper port quarter of the jib-boom. The jib-of-jib-boom was shipped through a cap (Fig. 127) set just the other side of the flying jib-boom on the upper starboard quarter of the spar, and as these spars were pointed a little in towards the central line of the ship, all the headstays were kept in line,

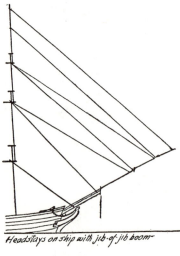

Headstays on ship with jib-of-jib boom

Fig. 131

though the heels of the various spars were off-center (Fig. 126).

The fore-topgallant and royal-stays had an eye-splice in their upper ends fitted snug over the mast. The lower ends did not both go to the ships' bows. After hooking under the hook on the dolphin striker, the topgallant-stay went to the bow. The royal-stay was seized fast to the topgallant-stay under the jib-boom's outer end.

What might be called the jib-boom shrouds and the flying jib-boom shrouds, were termed "back-ropes" by seamen and the manner of rigging them was more varied than the bobstays and martingales. When the spritsail yard was in its prime, the jib-boom shrouds were led through bull's-eyes seized to its upper edge. From there they came in to the head or bows of the ship and were set up with tackles. After the spritsail was done away with and it was no longer necessary to slacken and tighten these shrouds, the tackles were omitted and the ends of the stays were set up to bull's-eyes.

About the year 1800, merchant ships were rigged with the jib-boom shrouds or back ropes, set up with deadeyes (or bull's-eyes on small vessels) fastened on the forward side of the catheads out near the ends with no spritsail yard on which to spread them (Fig. 132). The men-of-war of that time,

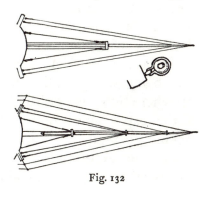

Fig. 132

with all their jib-booms to spread the shrouds of the flying jib-boom and jib-of-jib-booms, had iron outriggers from the cat-heads, with bull's-eyes on their outer ends (Fig. 132), through which the flying jib-boom and jib-of-jib-boom shrouds were led going back to tackles on the fore channels where they were set taut. They had to be spread well out to keep clear of the gear when handling the anchors.

Fig. 133

On modern ships with low-steeved bowsprits, it was not so difficult to climb out to the end when it became necessary to stow the jibs, but even they had a pair of hand-ropes, leading from the top of each knight-head (Fig. 133), or from an iron stanchion set

up on top of them, to the two parts of the fore-topmast
stay, where these stays were spread apart to go, one each
side, through the bee-blocks on the outer end of the
bowsprit.   Where the knight-heads did not stick up
above the forecastle-head rail, as on the clipper and
later ships, these hand-ropes rove through stanchions,
were carried aft at about an angle of forty-five degrees
from the eye in the top of the stanchion and were lashed
to eye-bolts in the deck (Fig. 133).   The outer ends,
after being seized to the stays, ended at the bowsprit
cap where they were lashed to an eye-bolt, one each side
in the cap.   Old-time ships, with round bowsprits
sticking up high in the air, had "footings" or wooden
steps, nailed across it at intervals, so that the men could
readily climb out with the aid of the hand-ropes.

Lead of top-gallant and royal stays up to 1828   Lead of top-gallant and royal stays 1850.

Fig. 134

The main-topgallant-stay, on old-time ships, led
across to the fore-topmast cross-trees, but the ships of
1850 carried it down to the cap of the foremast where
it led through a bull's-eye and was seized to the collar
of the lower shrouds.   The mizzen-topgallant-stay,
owing to the fact that the mizzenmast was much shorter
than the mainmast on nearly all ships, was led to the
cap of the mainmast head in the same way (Fig. 134).

Main-royal-stays led to the cap of the fore-topmast, through a bull's-eye and were seized to the collar of the topmast rigging, the collars being the loops around the masthead. Mizzen-royal-stays led to the collars of the main-topmast shrouds where they were seized fast. Topgallant-back-stays were one rope to a side and so were the royals and on small ships these often had no chain plates, but were set up to eye-bolts in the channels or on the main rails. Large ships used deadeyes and lanyards as on the rest of the shrouds, but very small ones that were in keeping with the size of the rigging.

Ships carrying standing skysail masts had stays and back-stays as a regular part of their rigging. Ships fitted with skysail-poles that went up abaft the royal-mast through a cap set aft, had these stays rigged only temporarily, when in mild weather, temporary braces being rove off to brace the yard around.

Small merchant ships, when down in the calm latitudes, set skysails by lashing the skysail yard fast to the royal-stay. The poles of the masts were greased or slushed the same as the topmasts, so that the loop or collar of the royal-stay could be hoisted clear up to the truck, taking the yard up with it, by slacking the lower end of the stay at the foretopmast.

No braces were rove, but about half-way out on the skysail yard, two ropes were made fast that led down to blocks under it, on the royal yard, and then down to the deck. These, by being kept taut, made the skysail yard and royal yard swing together and served as down-hauls to pull the skysail yard snug down on top of the royal. The skysail was furled by being rolled up with the royal.

CHAPTER VII

THE RUNNING RIGGING

THE various sizes of cords or threads, to represent the different pieces of running rigging, should be very carefully graduated into four sizes; the lower, top, topgallant and royal rigging, as with the standing rigging. Try to get a cord with the yarns twisted hard so that each strand shows distinctly the "lay" of the rope, as it is termed. Three-strand ropes are generally used for running rigging, but do not use the snow-white cotton thread or any cord, until you have dyed it a light brown color. Draw it through a shallow tin in which there is a thin mixture of raw umber and turpentine and before it dries, rub it off with a cloth. A regular light-brown dye can also be used. It may be possible to buy thread of the right color but don't use colored silks. Cotton or linen thread is the best and the gear should not be too tight as allowance must be made for the "come and go," due to atmospheric changes, which might pull the spars out of shape. It is not necessary to show all the running gear on a small model, but if it is built to a scale of $\frac{3}{16}$ or $\frac{1}{4}$ inch every detail can be carried out.

When a ship reaches a harbor, the sails are unbent, if she is to stay any length of time. This would be the case if she had to unload or load a cargo, except in a foreign port where the anchorage was dangerous and sail might have to be set in a hurry to claw off shore. When the sails were taken off, the gear, such as buntlines and leechlines, would be unrove and put away. So it is perfectly proper and shipshape to show a model without this gear (ropes and blocks are all classed as part of the ship's gear).

To better understand what all these queer-sounding ropes are named, let us rig up the foresail on a ship. The foreyard, on a modern ship of about 1880, is hoisted up and the pin in the cranse-iron is put into its place which holds the yard away from the mast a short distance and yet makes a hinged joint that will let the yard swing around so that the yard-arms go forward or aft (Fig. 135). It also permits the ends of the yard to teeter up and down. A chain is shackled into an eye-band on top and at the center of the yard to hold the weight of the yard. This chain is connected to iron rods that go up over the masthead or are bolted fast on each side of the cap. In the language of the sea the yard is them said to be "slung."

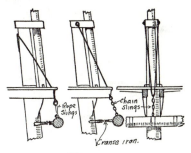

Fig. 135

Cranse-irons came into use about 1820 and before that time yards were held to the mast by parrel-straps which were controlled by yard-tackles. It makes a most interesting addition to the rigging of a model when all this gear is properly rove off.

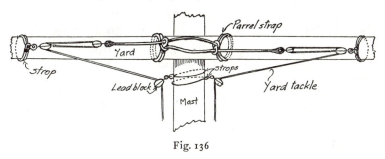

Fig. 136

In place of the iron bands about the yard, the parrel-straps were passed around the yard, doubled on each side of the mast, for there are two separate straps, and the ends are passed through their own bight forming a loop about the yard. One end was very short, with an eye spliced in it, and the other was long enough to go around the mast and reeve through the eye spliced into the short end of the opposite parrel-strap (Fig. 136). This long end was hooked to the block of a tackle rove out along the yard for the purpose of hauling it tight. The outer block of this tackle hooked into a strop around the yard. The eye in the short end should be up on one side and down on the other, thereby keeping the two parts of the parrel-strap clear of each other.

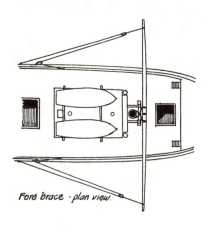

Fore brace - plan view.

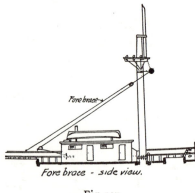

Fore brace →

Fore brace - side view.

Fig. 137

The hauling end of the yard-tackle was carried in through a single block hooked into a strop around the mast, just under the yard, and down to a belaying pin in the fife-rail at the foot of the mast. To control and swing this yard to any desired angle, tackles, called "braces" were rove, leading from the ends of the yard, aft, to pulleys or blocks on the ship's rail (Fig. 137). The kind of tackle and amount of purchase gained by it depended somewhat on the size of the ship.

To steady the yard, so that the ends would not teeter up and down, tackles termed "lifts," were rove from the end of the yard to a "block" at the masthead cap (Fig. 138), and the hauling end came down along the mast and was "belayed" or wrapped around and so made fast to a "belaying pin" in the fife-rail built at the foot of the mast on the deck.

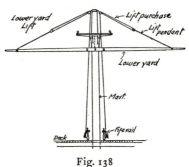

Fig. 138

These are the four parts common to all yards and they are all that are required to really handle the yard, viz.:—the *slings* and cranse-iron, the *halliard* and parrel, the *braces* and the *lifts*. The rest of the rigging on the fore-yard, except the foot ropes, all pertains to the handling of the canvas, that is, the sail. This sail is

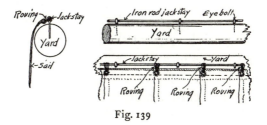

Fig. 139

stretched tight across the top or "head" as it is called, and lashed securely at each end to the yard with short pieces of rope called "earrings." Small seizings of rope yarn, termed rovings, hold the top of the sail, at frequent intervals, to an iron rod called the "jack-stay," rove or threaded through eye-bolts put in the top of the yard, about every two feet (Fig. 139).

The sail now hangs down like a curtain and several ropes are needed to hoist it up so that the men can go out on the yard and roll it up snug and tight and lash it with ropes so that the wind will not blow it away.

The first and most important of these ropes are the clewlines, because they hoist up the clews or corners of the sail. If you study the names of the various parts of the sails, many of the nautical phrases will have a meaning instead of being a mere jumble of unintelligible words.

The top of the sail is called the head; the bottom or lower edge is called the foot; and the two edges are the leeches (Fig. 140). But when the yard is swung so that one edge of the sail points up towards the wind, that edge is called the weather-leech or the luff of the sail, the other edge being the lee-leech.

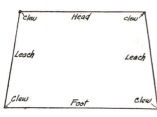

Fig. 140

Everything on the side of the ship against which the wind is blowing is termed the "windward" or weather side, as, for instance, the weather-yardarm, the weather-leechline, the weather-clewline, etc., to distinguish them from those on the opposite sheltered side, which is termed the lee side, and there they are called lee-leechlines, lee-clewlines, etc. If there is no such distinction, owing to the wind's blowing from directly aft or forward, then sailors use the distinction of starboard and port, which are always the same. The starboard side is the right-hand side and the port, the left-hand side, as one stands facing forward looking towards the bows of the ship. While the starboard-clewline is always known by that name, it may be a weather, or it may be a lee-clewline, depending on which side of the ship the wind is blowing at the time.

The four corners of the sail are called "clews." The edges around all four sides are bound with rope and in old-time sails this rope was made into loops at each corner to give a place to which the blocks and ropes could be attached. Later-day sails however, use iron rings, as iron hooks have been fitted to the blocks instead of rope loops held by wooden toggle pins (Fig. 141).

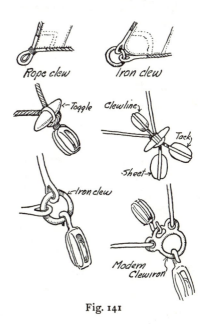

Fig. 141

When a sail is to be raised and furled, the first order given is to "man the clew-garnets." For some reason the clewline on the fore, main and crossjack, as the mizzen course is called, are designated as clew-*garnets,* but on every other sail the same rope is called a clewline. A single becket-block is hooked into an eye on the aft, underside of the yard, and the clew-garnet made fast to the becket on the underside of this block, goes down through the single block at the clew of the sail, up through the becket-block and down to a belaying pin in the fife-rail (Fig. 142).

When the sail was to be clewed up on old ships, the fore or main sheet or tack was slacked out, permitting the clew of the sail to be hoisted up close under the yard. On more modern ships there was a single, heavy rope, called the tail-rope, which was spliced into the

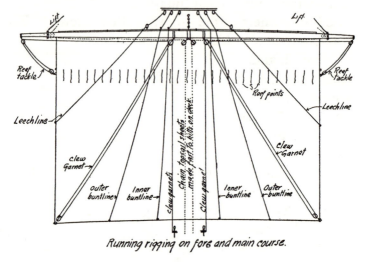

Running rigging on fore and main course.

Fig. 142

clew-iron and either the sheet or the tack-tackle was hooked on, according to how the ship was sailing, one being used at a time. Both were unhooked preparatory to clewing up the sail and the sail was kept from slatting by the tail-rope which was slacked out as that corner of the sail was clewed up on the after side of the rest of the sail.

About midway down the outer edges or leeches of the sail was a loop in the bolt rope or a cringle spliced in, viz.: a small iron ring. Very large ships had two. In fair weather, a rope, called a leechline, was made fast at this cringle and led up in front of the sail, through a block lashed to the jack-stay on the yard, to make it always pull from that place, and then up through a single block hooked into an eye-bolt under the forward rim of the top, the outer one of three blocks. The leechline was then led down along the shrouds, through an oak batten lashed under the shrouds, the same as a futtock-staff, where the futtock and lower shrouds crossed each other, through a fairleader, with three holes, lashed to the forward shroud directly over the belaying pin rail on the inside of the ship's bulwarks, and down to a belaying pin where it was made fast. In bad weather in the winter, or when south of Rio or north of Hatteras, this rope was untied at the cringle on the leech, and passed up aft of the sail and tied to the jack-stay on the yard where its lead block was. This gave greater purchase to pull the sail up and all bunt-lines and leechlines were so treated. It was called "doubling up the leechline or buntline."

Buntlines were rove in the same manner as leech-lines, small ships having only one buntline and large ships two, on each side of the center of the sail, called outer and an inner buntline. They came down to be-laying pins at the bulwark just forward of the leech-line.

Except for the lower sails or courses, whose clew-lines led in to the bitts, the same rule for belaying gear was strictly observed on all ships. From forward to aft, in the pin-rail along the bulwarks, came clewline, buntline and leechline, then clewline, buntline, and leechline, and each one always following in rotation. The courses were belayed forward in the pin-rail, the topsail gear aft of it, the topgallant next aft of that, then royal and then the skysail gear.

The clewline was the only rope that pulled the sail up abaft of itself. All the others gathered the sail up

in festoons on the forward side (Fig. 143). In furling
sail, after all these ropes were pulled as far as they
would go, the order was given to "Lay aloft and furl!"
The crew then had to roll this canvas up in a snug roll

and lash it fast with long
ropes called gaskets.

The gaskets were hitched
fast at one end of the jack-
stay, about three on each
side of the yard, at equal

Fig. 143

intervals. These were kept made up into a snug coil
hanging to the yard but were let fall preparatory to
clewing up the sail (Fig. 144). At that time they were
passed around and around, both the sail and the yard,
going down aft of the yard,
under it, and up on the
front, for the secret of making a neat furl was to get
the sail well up on top of
the yard (Fig. 145).

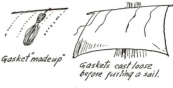

Gasket "made up"

Gaskets cast loose
before furling a sail.

Fig. 144

The bulk of the sail
comes naturally in towards the middle and makes quite
a big bundle. This is termed the "bunt" and is so heavy
that it often takes nearly all the men on the yard to roll
it up on top of the yard. That is why men-of-war and
large craft had what were
called "bunt-jiggers." A
"jig," in the language of the
sea, refers to a handy tackle
and is to a ship what the jack
is to an auto. These bunt-
jigs or jiggers, were hooked up under the tops and there
was a mat-like net made fast to the jack-stay, aft of the
sail, called the bunt gasket (Fig. 146). The end of this

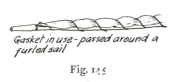

Gasket in use - passed around a
furled sail

Fig. 145

was passed around under the bunt and up forward until the jigs could be hooked into it when it was comparatively easy to parbuckle or roll the big bulk of sail up onto the top of the yard when the bunt gasket was lashed fast and the jigs unhooked (Fig. 146).

Fig. 146

This was the old-style way and in later years it was the style of furling sails adhered to by all American ships. They "stowed," which meant the same as furled, their sails "at the bunt," and it was a means of distinguishing an American ship from a foreigner, most of whom adopted the method of clewing their sails straight up to the yard-arms so that the canvas was evenly distributed. This made a more even distribution of cloth to be sure, but it did not give to a ship the smart symmetrical appearance of the bunt-stowed sails on the American ships (Fig. 147). It also brought a heavier strain on the outer ends of the yards which was soon apparent in the clumsy, stubby-looking spars of an English ship when compared with the tapered and more delicate looking spars of a Yankee.

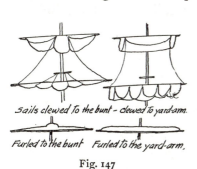

Fig. 147

A few sails were fitted with one to four rows of strings called reef points or reefing nettles, fastened to reef bands, horizontally across the sails, at intervals under the yard, the last reef reducing the area of the sail to one-half its full size.

Topgallant-sails (those that reefed) had only one row of reef points. The courses had two and the top-sails three or four. Mizzen courses or crossjacks, gen-erally had none and the mizzen topsail always had one less than the fore and main.

Cringles were fitted so that each end of the reef could be well lashed with a rope called the "reef earring," a new, strong piece of about five-eighths diameter manila, with an eye-splice in one end and the other pointed or neatly whipped. The mate generally kept these in his own room and gave one to each of two of the best seamen when they started aloft to reef. Among the sailors this was considered an honor, an acknowledgment of their superiority as a seaman, to be given the dangerous position astride the weather or lee yard-arm ("riding the Flemish horse") to pass the earring. The weather earring was always the pre-ferred position. A verse of sailor's poetry alludes to this weather earring:—

> "A sailor on the topsail yard
> While reefin' softly sings,
> I'd rather pick some cherries here
> Than be pullin' these 'ere strings.
>
> I'd rather of a kicking mule
> Be the undisputed boss,
> Than pull this weather earring out
> On this 'ere Flemish hoss."

The "Flemish horse" is a short foot-rope under the yard-arm, for the man who has to sit straddling the yard-arm, and is independent of the regular foot-rope.

The reef tackles consisted of a single block hooked into an eye at the outer end of the yard-arm, with another hooked to the leech of the sail in an extra cringle put below the lower reef band. The fall or rope led inboard, under the yard, through a second sheave in the same double block the clew-garnet rove through or, on some ships, it had a separate, single block from which it led straight down to the bitts just aft of the clew-garnet's belaying pin. On some ships the reef tackle rove through a sheave in the yard-arm up to a block on the masthead and down to the deck.

In general this is all the rigging for a square sail and a knowledge of the purpose for which each rope is rove should enable one to rig any of the other yards. The same operations have to be gone through with each. Many sails, however, are far simpler as they have no reefs to bother with, and the lifts are a fixture with no adjustment, up or down.

It is a difficult matter to describe ship's running rigging in the great number of variations that have occurred going back to ships of earlier periods. There was no sudden and complete change or abandoning one style of rigging and adoption of a new style by all ships. It was a gradual change that spread over many years. All the changes were made to accomplish the same end, but as the decks, hatchways, houses, cannon, etc., were arranged differently on the different types of ship it became necessary to lead the various ropes differently. Fighting ships, whose bulwarks were really breastworks behind which the men fought the cannon, had much of the running rigging led down to the fife-rails on decks, at the foot of each mast, instead of encumbering the bulwarks with the ropes.

On more modern ships, the lower yards were stationary, but in the days of oak and hemp, they were hung at the middle of the yard by a rope sling from the masthead, and also were equipped on small ships, with one, and on large ships with two, heavy tackles with treble-sheaved blocks above and double blocks below, called "truss-tackles," one hooked to the forward end of each trestle-tree. The fall, or hauling end, led to sheaves in the deck-bitts from which they could be led to the capstan.

Topsails were fitted to hoist up and down in a variety of ways, according to how heavy they were. Later-day ships had chain for the topsail tye, or single part, that was shackled to a band around the middle of the yard and led up through a score, cut in the topmast, just under the trestle-trees, over a large iron sheave in this score. This chain came out on the after side of the mast, with a large, flat, iron tye-block on its end, with its sheave scored to take a chain "runner," long enough to travel through the tye-block as the yard was hoisted and lowered. On the starboard end of this chain runner on the foremast and *vice versa* for the main-mast, a wire pendant was shackled that went down to an eye-bolt in the channels, just inside of the topmast backstays. In the port end, a tackle, with double block aloft and a single becket-block below, hooked into an eye-bolt in the port channel opposite. The hauling end came down to a large single block hooked into an eye-bolt in the waterways (a leader block) so that this hal-liard could be passed along the deck and all hands and the cook could lay hold of it and pull, for it took every-one on the short-handed merchantmen to masthead a topsail.

The hauling end on the fore-topsail-halliards was always to port, the main-topsail-halliards to starboard, and the mizzen to port. They alternated from side to side so that all the heavy strains would not come on one side of the ship. On each mast, in the same manner, the halliards alternated so that the fore-topsail-halliards being to port, the fore-topgallant halliards should be to starboard; the royal to port and the skysail to starboard. The halliards on the mainmast were just the reverse as its topsail-halliard was to starboard and so on. This is another feature by which the inexperienced model maker's ships may be recognized.

Before the days of chain the topsail tyes were made of hide rope with cable-laid rope runners and to prevent the twist of these ropes unwinding and twisting the falls of the tackle so it could not be worked, a timenoguy or "gill-guy," as sailors term it,

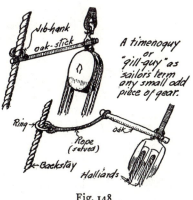

Fig. 148

was lashed to the tye-block and seized to a ring or iron jib hank that travelled up and down on the nearest backstay (Fig. 148).

Just previous to 1800, and for many years before, instead of cutting a score in the mast it was the custom to fasten the end of the tye around the masthead so that it led down outside the trestle-tree, on one side. From there it rove down through a single block seized to the top of the yard, in the middle, then up through a cheek block fastened to the mast, close up under the trestle-trees, or to a single block strapped around the mast-head, so that it hung down on the opposite side from the standing part (Fig. 149). From there it lead down, leaving length enough to permit the lowering of the yard to where a tackle was hooked on that led down to the deck as before described.

A few small vessels used this rig until even a much later date.

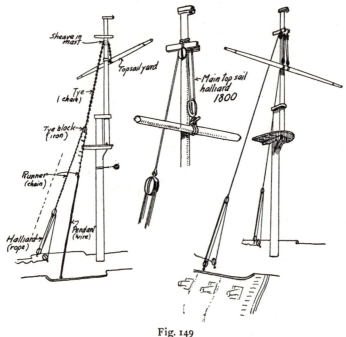

Fig. 149

Large frigates and the still larger line-of-battle ships and also East Indiamen, with their immense topsails and heavy 60 to 70 foot yards, carried double topsail halliards. There were two single blocks on the yard and three at the topmast cross-tree (Fig. 149). One hung in the center, on the forward side of the mast, and one on each side, through which the topsail tye was rove and instead of a runner, each end of the tye had a tackle rove from it to the channels on each side so that both ends could be manned at the same time. Vessels of an earlier date had these tackles led aft in near the center of the deck, where they were rove to a pair of bitts built in the deck.

A very ingenious but rather clumsy way of reeving topsail tyes, so as not to weaken the masthead, was used by seamen in the 1660's (Fig. 150). They made the upper cap on the masthead like a pillow or bolster, wide across and rounded on top, so that the tye rope went over it, on each side of the topmast, in a shallow groove, just as if it were a sheave, only the sheave did not roll. It was a double tye, both ends being fastened to the yard, and the halliard block rove on the bight, or in the loop of the rope that hung down on the after side of the mast. The falls or tackle were rove through the fourfold block above and sheaves below, in a bitt head just aft of the mast.

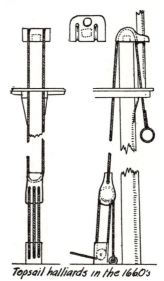

Topsail halliards in the 1660's

Fig. 150

The topsail-yard lifts and, for that matter, all the lifts, top, topgallant and royal, were fixed, wire rope pendants lashed at yard-arm and masthead to let them down to just the proper distance so they would not hit on the cap of the mast below. On ships in the early 1700's, and on small ships, tarred rope was used, except for the topsails.

The lifts on the big clippers and semi-clippers of the 1880's, vessels of 1500 to 2000 tons burden, were a span of wire rope with one end made fast at the yard-arm and then rove through a bull's-eye at the masthead. The other end was brought down and seized to the same side of the yard, half way out from the mast. This gave a double support needed by the large yards. Each side of the yard was fitted in this way with doubled lifts, as they were termed.

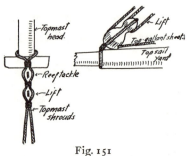

Fig. 151

Before the introduction of wire rope, ships were rigged with hemp and had their topsail-yard lifts rove from the masthead down and out through the upper sheave in a fiddle-block at the yard-arm (the lower sheave of which was for the topgallant sheet), thence back (Fig. 151),

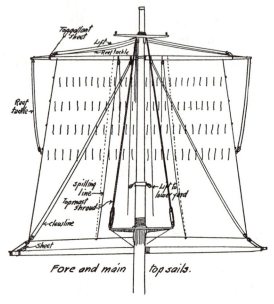

Fore and main   top sails.

Fig. 152

up and through a sheave (the lower one of two seized in between the first two shrouds of the topmast rigging) and so down to the deck at the bulwark. The reef-tackle was reeved through the upper sheave that was seized in the topmast rigging (Fig. 151).

Instead of having buntlines and leechlines, on account of their having to be reefed and the yard lowered to do so, topsails had only one set of "brails," called "spilling-lines" (Fig. 152). These kept the sails from bellying out by being hauled tight after the yard was lowered so that the men could haul it out snug across the yard and reef it. They rove from the forward side of the yard, seized to the jack-stay, down under the foot of the topsail, through a cringle, up to the yard, through a single block opposite the standing part, and down to the deck through a bee-hole in the top.

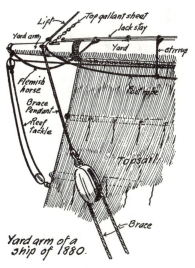

Fig. 153

Topsail sheets, with the rest of the gear, have gone through various stages of evolution. Hemp, hide and chain have been used alternately. With chain only one part was used and that rove over a sheave set in a score just inside of the shoulder at the yardarm (Fig. 153). It was led inboard under the yard through an iron eye fairleader half way in and then rove into an iron block, one for each side, hooked into lugs on the underside of the central band on the yard and thence down until there was length enough of chain to have some remaining under the yard even when the topsail was clewed up and furled. A tail-rope was then spliced in and carried down to the bolster piece of the bitts. When sheeted home there should be length enough of chain to allow a couple of round turns being taken around the bitts.

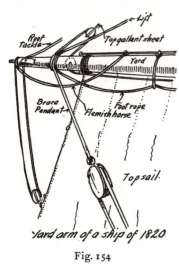

Fig. 154

With hemp or hide, the sheets were usually rove the same way, hide being used where the constant chafe occurred in the blocks at the yard-arm, and hemp used the rest of the way. The big single topsails were so powerful that the sheet had to be rove through a single block in the clew of the sail and the end hitched to the yard-arm, doubling up on the purchase in order to get power enough to sheet home the sail (Fig. 154).

Going still farther back we come to the days when sheaves were not cut in spars but fiddle-blocks were stropped to yard-arms the upper sheave taking the lift-fall and the lower sheave the topsail sheet.

Instead of a fiddle-

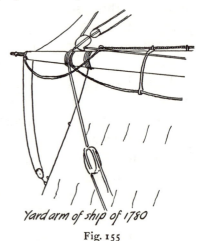

Fig. 155

block, sometimes two blocks, one large and one small, were stropped, one behind the other (Fig. 155), the sheet block generally being a shoulder-block, the shoulder preventing it from being pulled down so flat on the yard as to jam the topsail sheet.

The topgallant and the royal sheets were a single part from the clew of the sail reeving through a sheave in the yard-arm (or through a single block) in through a single leader-block at the middle of the yard and so down to the rail.

Topgallants and royals on large ships were usually fitted with clewlines, bunt-lines and leechlines in the same way as the courses. On small craft, where the sails were small, and on men-of-war, with many men to do the work, these upper-sails had only one line which had a span on its end, one leg of which was made fast on the leech and the other on the foot of the sail so that this one line, when clewed up, acted on both buntline and leechline.

Skysails, where carried as standing sky-sails, were fitted in the same way as royals.

Fig. 156

Topgallants and royal halliards consisted of a single tye from the yard up through a sheave in the mast, just under the cross-trees, coming out on the after side of the mast and going down nearly to the rail where there was a purchase long enough to permit hoisting the yard (Fig. 156). As in the case of the purchase or tackle on the topsail halliard, each of these purchases had a gill-guy, travelling up and down on a backstay, to keep them from twisting.

Skysail, royals and topgallant yards were held to the

mast by tarred-rope or hide-rope parrel-straps, which were passed around, abaft of the mast, with eye-splices in each end that were seized to the yard (Fig. 157). Where tarred-rope parrel-straps were used they had leather sewed over them and the mast was kept well

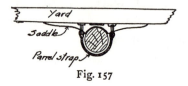

Fig. 157

slushed with grease to facilitate its sliding up and down the spar.

Topsail parrel-straps had wooden rollers or "beads" threaded on them, that rolled and prevented the parrels from sticking to the mast. On the very large ships there were several rows of beads, with spacers between them, forming a wide band that would not jam or stick (Fig. 158). About 1840, an iron collar or band, pivoted to the yard, was substituted for the old-style parrel-straps and these were covered with raw-hide laced on, the lacing being on the outside; the smooth leather surface on the inside sliding on the well-greased topmast.

If some model builders were obliged to "tail on" to the halliard of one of those topsails they would know better than to paint a ship's topmast.

Sheets and tacks on the fore and main sail, and also on the mizzen, on such ships as carried this sail, which was called the "cro'jack," are seldom shown on ship models and it is hardly

Fig. 158

appropriate to do so unless the model is to have sails on it. When the sails are unbent and sent below into the sail locker, on a real ship, such gear as sheets and tacks are unrove and stowed away.

The sheet is the rope that pulls the foot of a course aft and the tack pulls it forward. For each sheet there should be an eye-bolt in the outside planking of the ship, at the deck level, and a sheave set in the bulwarks at such an angle that it will be in line with the sheet as it pulls from the clew of the sail (Fig. 159).

The sheet is a large rope, as big around as a man's wrist, which is rove through a large single block hooked into the cringle of the sail. One end leads to and is hooked into the eye-bolt with a pair of sister hooks or split-hooks (Fig. 159), as some people call them, that are

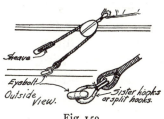

Fig. 159

spliced into a thimble in the end of the rope; the other end leads in through the sheave in the bulwarks and is belayed around a cavil or pair of bitts (Fig. 160).

This rope is too heavy to belay around a belaying-pin and either a cavil or bitts is provided, about six feet from it, as it requires several men to hold the strain on a sheet after it has been hauled in and the last man of all has to take the turns that hold it. There must be room for these men, as they hang on until the last man says "All fast," which is their signal to let go.

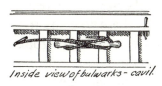

Fig. 160

The tacks are a heavy tackle consisting of a single becket-block which is hooked into the cringle of the sail, and a double block hooked into a ring-bolt in the waterways put there for that purpose. This is for a mainsail. With a foresail, on modern ships, the double block is hooked to a ring-bolt on the cat-head.

Old-time ships with foremasts so far forward that there was not spread enough for the foot of the sail, had this block on the end of a stout, short wooden spar called a bumpkin so fixed to pull the sail to the right place, being held down by several guys to the stem, etc.

The fall of this tackle was hove tight by taking it around the capstan. "Boarding the fore tack," as this was called (Fig. 161), was generally hard pulling even with the leverage of the capstan to assist.

When sailing on a wind, close hauled, the sheet, on the side that swings forward, is unhooked and laid in on the rail and on the other side the tack is unhooked

Boarding the fore-tack.

Fig. 161

and that tackle laid on the forecastle head. In order to have control over the sail while these various manœuvres are being executed, there is a stout tail-rope, kept spliced into the cringle, long enough to permit the sails being clewed up and yet with end enough to get hold of on deck.

The location of the sheaves and eye-bolts for the sheets and the ring-bolts for the tacks may be determined readily by swinging the fore and main yards as far around as the rigging will let them go. The tacks should be a little farther forward than the weather yard-arms and the sheets well aft of the lee yard-arms.

The fore sheets generally go through the bulwarks in the waist, as the mid-length of the ship is termed, a little nearer the main than the fore rigging, while the main sheets lead through just ahead of the mizzen-shrouds (Fig. 162).

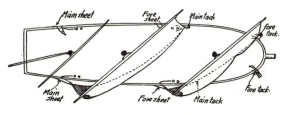

Fig. 162

Instead of ring-bolts and tackles the old-time ships, of the 1700's, had sheaves set in vertical timbers bolted on the ship's side, which were called the "chess-trees" and through which the sheets and tacks were rove (Fig. 163); then through horizontal sheaves in the bulwarks, inboard, to where they were belayed. The chess-tree permitted the sheave to stand vertically in line with the lead of the main tack.

Fig. 163

Braces are the tackles that swing the yards so that the sails may be properly set to catch the wind on their after surfaces. They show up so prominently on a model that care should be taken to have them rove properly. The heavy lower sails require purchases or tackles while the light, upper yards and sails can be braced about with a single rope. So often, however, we see models where the same kind of a single whip purchase is rove on every brace from the main yard clear up to the skysail yard and horizontally back and forth with no resemblance to a real ship at all.

The main-braces have been rove aft to the quarters
of the ship for generations, but the fore-lower-braces,
instead of leading to the main-masthead, beginning
about 1830, were carried down to the rail, similar to

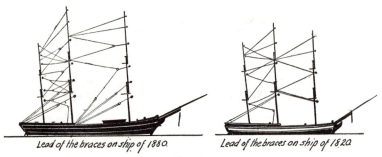

Lead of the braces on ship of 1880.   Lead of the braces on ship of 1820.

Fig. 164

the main-brace (Fig. 164). Previous to the year 1800
there were many variations in the lead of braces. Many
were fastened to the stays of the mainmast and returned
down along these stays to the foot of the foremast. This
separated the many braces so that in tacking ship the
various gangs of men hauling the braces did not get in
each other's way.

Another feature that distinguishes the older craft is
the absence of pendants on the brace-blocks, the blocks
being stropped close up to the yard-arm.

Beginning with the later ships and going backward,
we find that the big cargo craft of 1880 (which were
worked short-handed to save expenses, as freights were
very low) had a three-part purchase on both fore and
main yard (Fig. 164). There was a single becket-block
on the end of a pendant from the yard-arm, and a single
block on the forward end of the main channels for the
fore-brace; but on the main, this block was hooked into
another pendant from the brace bumpkin, away aft,

sticking out from each quarter of the ship that held the block abreast of the after mizzen-shrouds. This was kept from dragging down in the water, when swinging the yard, by a gill-guy made of tarred ratline stuff, which was fastened to the mizzen-topmast-backstay (Fig. 165).

Do not make the pendants so long that the brace-blocks will come "block and block" or "two blocks," which means so that they touch each other when the yard is "braced sharp up"; or swung around as far as it will go.

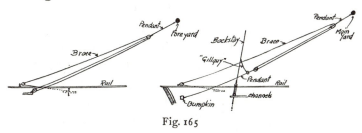

Fig. 165

Hooked into eye-bolts on the top of the ship's rail, are large, flat, single blocks through which the hauling end of the brace is rove, leading from there down inside of the bulwarks to belaying pins in the pin-rail on the bulwarks, about eight feet forward of the leader-block, to give the men room to hold it until the end is belayed.

Previous to about 1820, ships that were fitted with cannon along their bulwarks had their fore-braces rove with one end fast to the main-stay just clear of the foot of the main topsail. After reeving through the single block on the fore-yardarm, it came back through a single block strapped to the stay, to keep it down clear of the foot of the fore-topsail. It was then led up under the main top through a single block hooked into an eye-bolt in the main trestle-trees and on merchant ships came down to the main-fife-rail (Fig. 166); but on men-of-war and merchant ships in the early 1770's, when all ships had more or less armament on their decks, this brace, instead of going up under the main-top, was led down forward along the main-stay to a leader-block lashed to the stay, from which it was led straight down to a belaying pin in the after part of the foremast fife-rail.

Crossjack (mizzen-yard) braces, on later-day ships, led forward, almost horizontally, to the mainmast, the standing end being fastened to eye-bolts in the cheeks of the mainmast and, after leading through the block at the mizzen yard-arm, are rove through a single block hooked to the futtock band. In ships of an earlier period, where the mainmast had to be kept clear to permit the parrels of the main yard sliding up and down, this block was seized to the after lower-main-shroud. It was then belayed at the bulwark instead of to a pin in the fife-rail to which it led in the other way of rigging.

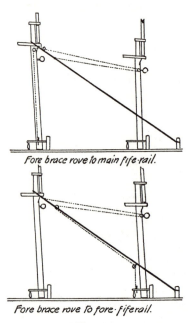

Fore brace rove to main fife-rail.

Fore brace rove to fore-fiferail.

Fig. 166

The one vital point to watch out for is to see that the crossjack-yard, when swung around, does not bring the braces out so far as to rub foul of the main back-stays (Fig. 167). When this occurs, due to the length of yard, the wide spread to the main shrouds, or the short distance between the masts, the brace-block should be made fast far enough in from the end of the yard to keep the braces clear.

Topsail yard braces went through the same stages of evolution that characterized the lower braces. The ships of 1880 had the brace-block on the yard at the end of a pendant. The standing end of a runner was made fast around the main-topmast,

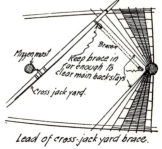

Lead of cross-jack yard brace.

Fig. 167

close up under the trestle-trees and was rove through the block at the yard-arm and down to the ship's rail, where a whip, or two-part purchase, was hooked onto it with draft enough to permit the yard to swing. The

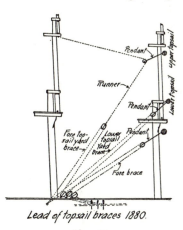

Lead of topsail braces 1880.

Fig. 168

standing end of this whip-purchase was hooked into an eye-bolt in the main-channels, the hauling end coming down through a leader-block on the rail where it was led inboard to a belaying pin just aft of where the fore brace was belayed (Fig. 168).

On ships that carried double-topsails, with the lower topsail-yard swiveled at the fore-cap, the brace-block was at the end of a wire rope pendant, as on the upper-topsail, but it had no runner, a two-part or whip purchase being rove as on the upper-topsail brace. The leader-block on the rail was between the fore brace and the fore-upper-topsail brace-leader block and it belayed the same way to a belaying pin between the two. The main upper and lower topsail braces rove off in the same way as the fore-topsail braces.

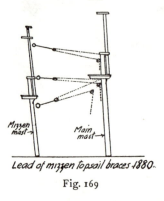

Lead of mizzen topsail braces 1880.

Fig. 169

The mizzen topsail braces were rove forward to the mainmast head and the mizzen-upper-topsail led to the cap. On large ships, the end of the brace was made fast at the maintopmast head, going aft through the brace-block and then across again to the block on the mainmast cap and down to the deck. The mizzen lower topsail brace was rove forward to just under the main-top above the crossjack braces (Fig. 169).

Single topsail-yard braces, of about 1820, in the case of the fore-topsail were made fast at the main topmast-

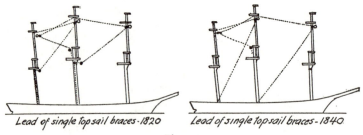

Lead of single topsail braces - 1820   Lead of single topsail braces - 1840.

Fig. 170

stay, a few feet down from the mast (Fig. 170). They rove forward, to and through the single block on the yard-arm, and back to a lead-block on the main-stay; then aft to a block on the cheek of the mainmast and down to the deck. By 1840, however, about every other ship had the hauling end of the topsail braces rove down from the yard-arm to the rail (Fig. 170). The maintopsail brace was made fast in a similar way on the mizzen topmast-stay, through the brace-block on the yard and aft to the mizzenmast just as the fore was rove to the mainmast.

On ships of the 1660's the topsail braces followed down along the main-top-mast-stay and down to the fore bitts. Topgallant braces were rove with a whip purchase, except on small ships of four or five hundred tons where the sail was so small that it could be braced around with a single rope. Most royals were braced in this manner. When rove single, they came from the

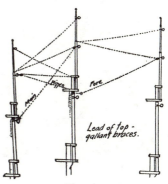

Fig. 171

topgallant-yard-arm, aft to a lead-block on the main-topmast-stay, then aft to another lead-block under the cross-trees and so down to the rail. When rove double, the standing end was made fast around the head of the topgallantmast, across to the yard and then aft the same as with the single brace (Fig. 171).

In the case of the mizzen topgallant brace, when single it rove to a sheave in the after end of the main-topmast trestle-trees; and when double, it led the same but the end was carried back to the maintopmast cap.

Fore and main-royal braces were a single rope from the yard-arm to leader-blocks at the topgallant-mast-head. Mizzen-royal-braces led forward to the cap of the main-topmast.

Tying or setting up the standing rigging is easy work compared to belaying the running rigging, particularly in places where the foretopsail-halliards come; alongside the forward deckhouse, where the long boats on top prevent reaching down to the belaying pins. By the time the model is nearly rigged, the strings and threads are so thick there is but little room to move in.

To belay the threads you should use a long-pointed pair of tweezers and a piece of wire or crochet needle

To reach in and belay the threads you need a pair of tweezers and a fork ended wire.

Fig. 172

with the hook broken off and the end filed to a fork or crotch-end. By holding the thread with the tweezers you can manipulate it so as to twist it around the belaying pins (Fig. 172). It is sometimes most exasperating when, after great patience you have succeeded in twisting the thread around the belaying pin, to have the thread slip from the tweezers and all the turns untwist. To prevent this, touch a tiny drop of glue on to the pin and then each turn, as you put it on, is held fast. Hitch the thread on the last turn and pull all snug before snipping it off with the scissors.

If you want to have the coils of rope hanging on the pins, as on a real ship, leave the thread long enough and make the coil by winding around something round, like around a pencil, and touch this with glue or the stiffness of the thread will cause it to uncoil like a spring. Don't leave the coils in a perfect, mechanical-looking roll. Pull and flatten out of shape so they will look as though they lay over the pin on the deck of some ship; as if human hands had laid the "fakes" of the coil and they had not been turned up in a lathe (Fig. 173). In making threads fast to the belaying pins do not wind them around and around in the same direction all the time but cross the turns over so as to make a figure-eight twist (Fig. 174).

Braces have a most aggravating way of twisting so that the falls, or tackle part, are all wound up and they could not possibly be pulled through the blocks. This

Too perfect a coil does
not look natural.
Coils are never 100%
perfect.

Fig. 173

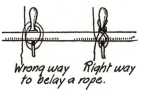

Wrong way   Right way
to belay a rope.

Fig. 174

is generally due to the untwisting of the brace pendants. A good way to prevent this is to use wire for the pendants, which holds the brace-block free and clear of twists. Painted black it looks like tarred rope or the wire rope used on ships of a later date. But if the model is to a large scale this cannot be done for it will look badly.

One thing that causes twisted purchases on running gear and is also responsible for ruining the appearance of many models, is pulling the gear too tight. We all know how story-writers love to describe the rigging on men-of-war as being hove taut as fiddle-strings. The rigging did have a neat, taut appearance when the yards were braced up square and true by both braces and lifts, but in reality it was not actually taut but only relatively so. It was neater looking than the undermanned and more slovenly appearing merchantmen, as the ships lay in port, where most writers, who have described them, saw them; but at sea, Yankee seamanship on these merchantmen kept their ships as trim as a vessel could be kept and the old packet ships and clippers rivalled any man-of-war in this respect.

Jib and staysail running gear, if properly rove off, help wonderfully the appearance of a model. A ship has a barren look without them and I like to see downhauls and sheets rove, even if the latter are generally stowed away when the sails are unbent.

Jib halliards consist of a single becket-block aloft and a single block on the jib. As shown on a model without sails they would be hooked into the eye-bolts on the jib-boom or the pendant that permits the foot of the jib going a few feet up the stay. Like the halliards on the yards, they alternate, one each side; the fore-top-mast-staysail to port, the jib to starboard, the jib-top-sail to port, and the flying-jib to starboard. They belay in the pin-rail on the bulwarks ahead of all the other gear, the farthest jib out being the farthest pin forward.

Seized to the stay, just above the jib-boom, is a single block for the jib downhaul, each sail being so fitted, and these downhauls, a single rope, are led back to cleats inside the forecastle-head bulwarks or rail or to belaying pins in a rack across the forward end of the forecastle-head. The staysail downhaul being the inner port pin, the jib, the inner starboard pin, the jib-topsail, the outer port pin, and the flying-jib, the outer starboard pin.

Jib sheets and the way they lead have been more incorrectly portrayed by marine artists than any other part of ship's gear. They will show the proper rig and lead them to the right place, but common sense should teach them that the angle they make to the sail is quite

impractical. Sailors sheet their sails to get out the maximum pull, yet we frequently see handsome portraits of ships where the jib-sheets are a straight pull in line with the foot of the sail (Fig. 175). Such a jib might look picturesque with its flowing, flapping after leech, but it would not propel a ship. The sheet should pull nearly equal on both foot and leech, just a trifle more on the foot to get the most out of it.

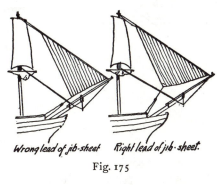

Wrong lead of jib-sheet   Right lead of jib-sheet.

Fig. 175

Hooked into the clew (the after lower corner of the jib) was a tarred rope pendant with two long ends and round oval-shaped blocks stropped into their ends. One of these led to starboard, and the other to port of the stays aft and had a whip purchase rove through the blocks leading in to the forecastle-head (Fig. 177).

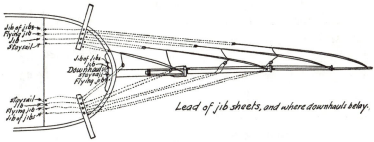

Jib of jibs
Flying jib
Jib
Staysail

Jib of jibs
Downhauls
Staysail
Flying jib

Staysail
Jib
Flying jib
Jib of jibs

Lead of jib sheets, and where downhauls belay.

Fig. 176

One end of this whip purchase was made fast to an eye-bolt in the deck, and a few feet aft of it the other end rove through a bull's-eye stapled fast to the deck or to the top of the inboard end of the cat-head (where these extended in on ships with forecastle-heads) and from there aft to cleats or belaying pins through the after end

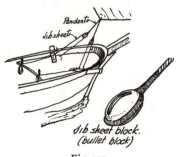

Fig. 177

of the forecastle-head decking. The leads for the jibs were usually put in a row, close together, the innermost jibs being rove through the innermost fairleaders, etc. (Fig. 176).

The reason for having jib sheet-blocks so round and oval-shaped was to prevent any corners from catching as the blocks were dragged back and forth over the various head stays (Fig. 177).

Staysail halliards, on the main and mizzenmasts, were rove in the same manner as the jibs on the foremast. Ships prior to 1840, instead of jib-shaped staysails, carried what were designated as square-tack staysails. Their stays ran across from mast to mast, at a much less acute angle. They also carried a hoisting staysail, that fell into disuse after the wars when crews became smaller.

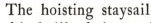

Fig. 178

The hoisting staysail had its halliards fastened at the main-topmast-head, but instead of its tack being made fast it was secured to a block that the hoisting stay was rove through and had a tackle to hoist it up almost to the fore-topmast-head (Fig. 178). The block had a ring traveller around a rope jackstay that extended from the foremast cap up just abaft the foretopmast to the foretopmast cross-trees. The luff of the staysail was held by toggles to this jackstay.

Jibs and staysails on more modern ships slid up and down the stays seized to iron jib-hanks. Wooden hanks were also used made of hardwood bent in a circle, the two ends being notched so they hooked together and then locked, the lashing holding them securely. Previous to this, these sails were fastened on stays with short pieces of rope having a loop or becket in one end and a wooden toggle, fitted snug in an eyesplice, in the other, as signal flags are still fastened together (Fig. 178).

CHAPTER VIII

FOOT-ROPES

FOOT-ROPES are not exactly standing rigging, yet more like it than anything else, as they are made of tarred rope and permanently fixed to yards, jib-boom, etc. They are the ropes the men stand on when they go out on the yards to reef or furl the sails, and, until the sailor learns to keep his knees constantly kicked back, so that the foot-rope throws his breast against the yard in front of him, he finds it a rather precarious foot-hold. Here, again, we find a good reason why sailors sing their weird songs or chants. In rolling up a heavy sail, the men, lined up along the after-side of the yard, at the signal, "Yo! ho! Heave 'em!" the word *heave* being emphasized, all hands give a hearty heave or pull to raise the canvas. In doing so they naturally kick their legs out backwards to counteract the weight in front. Without this unity of effort, the sudden swinging backward of the foot-rope would take the rope out from under a man and throw him off the yard.

English laws compelled English ships to carry back-ropes, to prevent men from being thrown backwards off the yard. With a topsail ballooning up like a wall in front of the sailor, so hard with wind he can't make a dent in it or get a wrinkle to grab hold of with his fingers, there is little on which to hold onto; but Yankee ships had no safety appliance such as a back-rope. Stick there like a fly or go overboard, was the result.

The foot-ropes had an eye spliced into the outer ends that went over the yard-arm and a rope grommet that fitted up against the shoulder of the yard. The inner end had a small eyesplice in it and was seized to the eye of the jack-stay on the opposite side of the yard nearest the mast, so that the two crossed each other, and this made the foot-rope, in close to the mast, a long easy sweep to stand on. On the smaller upper yards that was all there was to the foot-ropes, one on each side; but as this span became too long, on the longer, lower yards, it was held up in loops by short pieces of tarred and served rope, called stirrups. The foot-rope rove through an eyesplice in the lower end of this stirrup and the upper end of the stirrup had an eye that was seized to the jack-stay eye-bolts, hanging down, as all foot-ropes did, on the after side of the yard.

Under the jib-boom, the foot-ropes were made fast; on the inboard end, to eye-bolts in the bowsprit cap and the outer ends were seized to the jib-boom back-ropes. On old-time ships, where the bowsprit steeved up high in the air, turks heads, like knots, were worked at intervals of about three feet to prevent a man's feet from sliding down along the foot-rope.

All yards carried foot-ropes and on the lower and topsail yards, and on upper topgallant sails, when fitted to reef, there was an extra, short foot-rope, on the ends, that went by the name of "Flemish horse." This was for the man who straddled the yard-arm, facing inboard, whose duty it was to pass the reef-earring, when a sail was being reefed. This "Flemish horse" was made fast on the extreme outer end of the yard-arm, the inner end lapping in past the other foot-rope, and was seized to a jack-stay eye-bolt about three feet in from where the main foot-rope was made fast at the shoulder on the yard. This had no stirrup as it was only a short loop.

In putting foot-ropes on a model, the greatest diffi-culty is to make them keep their shape for, when hang-ing down in loops, the stirrups are inclined to kink and the foot-rope will draw up close to the yard. One way to prevent this is to stiffen the stirrup with shellac; another, is to work a piece of fine wire into the center of the cord forming the stirrup, to hold it down.

If made to an $\frac{1}{8}$ inch scale, the foot-ropes will look better if made of wire, the stirrups to be soldered to the foot-rope and then all painted black.

The foot-ropes should not be brought in to the center of the yard and made fast there. They should lap by each other, so as to make the slope easier for a man to stand on.

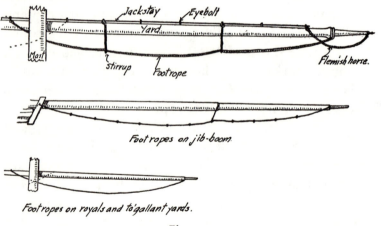

Foot ropes on jib-boom.

Foot ropes on royals and to'gallant yards.

Fig. 179

CHAPTER IX

THE BLOCKS

LANDSMEN call them pulleys, but sailors always speak of them as "blocks,"—single blocks, double blocks and treble blocks, according to the number of sheaves they have (Fig. 180). It requires about eight hundred blocks, ranging in size from 30-inch down to 8-inch, to fit out a full-rigged line-of-battle ship. Such a ship had an endless assortment of jigs or jiggers as they were called. Standing jigs fitted to every-

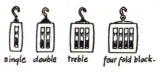

single   double   treble   four fold block.

Fig. 180

thing while on the poorer, thrifty merchant ships, one or two jigs, called "handy-billies," had to answer, being shifted from rope to rope and attached by strops as required. The "watch-tackle" was another name for this much-used set of blocks (Fig. 181). Excluding all such little-understood blocks and many buntline and

A watch-tackle.

Fig. 181

leeching blocks besides, to rig a model of a full-rigged ship, one has to make close to two hundred blocks and about sixty deadeyes, be-sides about two dozen bull's-eyes. The latter are all of one size; the deadeyes about four different sizes; and the blocks are a variegated lot according to where they are fitted. The older the style of ship, the more blocks and deadeyes are required.

The old saying that "pigs is pigs," doesn't hold good when you come to ship work, for while all blocks are

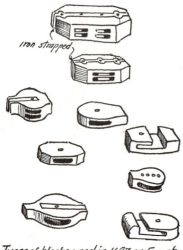

Iron strapped

Types of blocks used in 1697 on French galleys.

Fig. 182

blocks, if you don't get the right size and shaped block in its proper place, the appearance of the model is ruined. "Brace-blocks" have a large diameter sheave and are a thin, flat-shaped block as is the "tye-block" on the topsail halliards which is much thinner in appearance than jig blocks or other halliard blocks. On latter - day ships, where chain was used for topsail halliards, the tye-block was an iron one, with iron sheave, iron strap and iron shell, shackled to chain tyes. Before the days of iron, tye-blocks were double-scored and stropped with

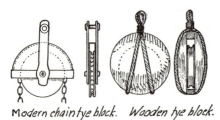

Modern chain tye block.   Wooden tye block.

Fig. 183

Topsail halliard block on the caravals. a sole block

Fig. 184

rope to withstand the heavy strain put upon them (Fig. 183). Going back to the days of the caravels, we find this important block a sole-block, with a large score in its head, big enough for the heavy rope that served as a topsail tye, to be rove through it, bent back and toggled to the standing part and not even seized or clinched (Fig. 184).

Jib-sheet blocks were known as "bullet-blocks," and were round as an egg but longer and of oval shape (Fig. 185). They were rope-stropped so there was no corner or shackle or anything to catch as they were dragged back and forth across the head-stays when tacking ship.

A bullet block used on jib sheets.

Fig. 185

Before sheaves were inserted in the ends of the yards, for topsail sheets, topgallant sheets and royal sheets, these ropes were rove through blocks

Yard arm

A shoulder block

Fig. 186

stropped fast to the ends of the yards, at inner end of the yard-arms. An ordinary, single block would lay down so close to the yard as to jam the sheet, due to the angle at which the strain came, and to prevent this a small toe or projection was left on the under side of the block, holding it up so the sheet could not jam. These were known as "shouldered-blocks" (Fig. 186).

"Fiddle-blocks" were blocks having two sheaves and instead of the sheaves being set side by side, on one pin, the shell of the block was long enough to let one sheave set below the other, the lower one being a little smaller so that the ropes did not interfere with each other, and the shape of the shell resembled in outline a fiddle, from which it took its name (Fig. 187).

A fiddle block

Fig. 187

Modern ships seldom used this kind of block and we have to look back to about 1700 to find them much in use.

Where rope-stropped blocks were used it was a simple matter to make the blocks lie so that the score lay in any desired direction; but when iron-stropped blocks came into use care had to be exercised to see that the hook or shackle lay with the score or across it, as the occasion required. Where the hook or shackle pointed in the same direction as the score, it was termed a "front-hook" or shackle and where these pointed across the block it was a "side-hook" or shackle. And where the shackle was strapped fast in the block, with the pin uppermost, it was termed an "upset shackle-block." If the straps extended through, below the lower end of the block, with a bolt and thimble to attach the end of the rope to a becket, as it was called, it was termed a "becket-block" (Fig. 188).

1 Block with front hook
2 Block with side hook
3 Block with the front shackle
4 Block with side shackle
5 Block with upset front shackle
6 Block with upset side shackle
7 Block with becket.

Fig. 188

Boxwood makes the best blocks for models. Buy a carpenter's two-foot rule and you will have enough wood to make all the blocks you will need for one ship, at least. Cut this wood into strips of various sizes to make the different sized blocks required, using a fine, flat file to shape the wood. To bore the holes, representing the sheaves, where the rope goes through, use a number 65 or for very small blocks, a number 70 drill. The most important tool of all in block making is a knife-edged file to make the scores in the edges of the blocks. This kind of file is not obtainable in all sections of the country, but it is an indispensable tool. A very small saw may be used but it is apt to spoil a block unless great care is exercised. The file is by far the better tool for the purpose.

Shape one end of the block to be, on the end of a strip of boxwood. Bore the hole or holes and file the scores and then file a score to take the strapping of the block. Then with file or saw, cut off the block and finish the end.

Showing the several processes of making a boxwood block.

Fig. 189

This sounds easy, but when you try to hold so small a piece of wood your fingers are all thumbs in their clumsiness. So take a crochet needle and file the hook off the end. By inserting this into the hole bored in the block, you can hold it while finishing with a file. Some of the smaller blocks are no larger than a mustard seed and the wood left on their sides or cheeks is so delicate when the scores are filed in them, that they cannot be held in any other way than by something inserted through the hole, for the shell will break if you try to hold them between the points of a pair of tweezers. A small pair of round nosed pliers, one jaw of which is filed to a size that will fit in the hole bored for the score, makes a very good tool to hold blocks while being filed.

Real blocks are not made of one solid piece. The two sides, called the cheeks, are each made separately, out of white ash, which is light, strong and durable. Two narrow end pieces hold them apart and through these the two rivets, at each end, hold the cheeks together.

The wooden or iron sheave is scored to fit the shape of the rope, and an iron pin, which goes through both cheeks and through a hole in the center of the sheave, serves as an axle for the sheave to revolve upon. Over each end of this pin a small diamond or circle of thin sheet copper is bradded on to keep the pin from falling out (Fig. 190).

Some block makers upset one end of this pin so as to form a square head which, when let into one cheek, prevents the pin from turning and wearing down through the wood, which sometimes happens when a ship has been laid up for a long time and the sheave and pin become rusted together.

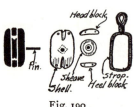

Fig. 190

About 1880, patent roller bushings were invented and manufactured. These prevented blocks from "freezing," as it was termed, when they rusted fast. The hole in the sheave was made larger and small steel rollers were inserted around the pin, held in place by two brass rings into which their ends were fitted to keep them spaced apart and clear of each other. The friction of the rolling sheaves was thereby reduced to a minimum (Fig. 191).

Another improvement was iron strapping that was scored out of the inside faces of the cheeks and, being close up to the sheave, strengthened the block by giving iron to hold against the strain on the iron pin, in

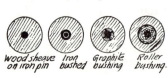

Fig. 191

place of wood (Fig. 192). The upper ends of these iron bands or straps, extended up over the end blocks, in the form of a loop into which an iron hook or shackle was fitted, thereby doing away with the rope strapping on the outside of the block, and where a becket was required, for a rope to be attached under the block, these straps were simply extended down below the block, far enough to put a small bolt through them.

There was no set rule as to the size of blocks to be used on a ship and block lists were varied in olden times as much as they are still fought over today. Captains and mates had their own ideas as to blocks and we find evidence of this in books where it is recorded that the British captains explained that the slowness of their ships, when compared with the speed of their American competitors, was due to the cheap grass rope and small blocks used on the British ships, whereas the American packets used hemp ropes and large diameter sheaves in their blocks.

Fig. 192

A sheave six times the diameter of the rope, is about as small as it is safe to use, but many a Yankee ship has had ten or even twelve-inch sheaves in her brace blocks, using one and a quarter inch diameter rope, where foreign ships had eight-inch sheaves. The free running of the large sheaves makes a wonderful difference in the ease in hauling braces. The sailor looking for a ship to sign on, can tell which are "work-houses," to use the slang of the sea, by the stingy little blocks they are fitted with. A farmer can tell a horse by looking at his teeth and a sailor can judge a ship by certain earmarks, just as readily, and the blocks were always one of the first items sized up.

CHAPTER X

Steering Wheels

STEERING wheels are by far the hardest part of a model ship to make, they are so delicate and so complex that it is difficult even to make a good casting of Babbitt metal, if you had a mould, for the metal is apt to chill before it penetrates all the little grooves in the plaster mould.

Wheels vary in size with the type and tonnage of the vessel and large craft, over 1000 tons, often carried a double-wheel so that more men could lay hold of it and hold the strain on the rudder. Big clippers, frigates and line-of-battle ships all carried double-wheels. Small wheels were made of iron but all the large ones were built up, hub, spokes, rim and handles of wood, the rim inlaid with white holly and embellished with inlaid designs in brass. A scale as small as $\frac{1}{8}$ of an inch to the foot brings the spokes of a wheel down as small as an ordinary pin. It is easy enough to bend a brass rim and drill holes for the spokes to pass through it, but the hardest part of all is to make the small hub and fasten all these spokes so that they are spaced true.

If you lay the rim on a board and plan wires for the spokes, with a flat-headed nail in the center of the wheel, set down into a hole bored in the wood, you can, if careful about it, get a drop of solder so as to unite all the parts and make a steering wheel. But the difficulty is to get all these points hot enough to take the drop of solder and have it flow evenly around all the ends of the spokes and yet hold on to the nail head.

Patience and careful work alone will succeed. I find the only way I can do this is to use an alcohol flame and a blow pipe, blowing a small tongue of flame on to the points on which a tiny drop of solder is laid after applying a good big drop of soldering fluid to make it stick (Fig. 193).

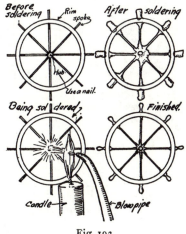

Once the center, with all its spokes, is soldered fast it is an easy matter to heat each end and with a drop of solder fasten the rim to each spoke end and puddle enough solder on each spoke so it can be filed to imitate a wooden handle.

Fig. 193

Once you succeed in making such a metal wheel it is a good plan to make several castings from it by using dental plaster and Babbit metal, the same way as in making anchors.

Aside from soldering the spokes at the center of the wheel, the next greatest difficulty is in keeping the rim thin and flat enough so that it does not look clumsy (Fig. 194). On a round-rimmed wheel the rim should be only about three times the diameter of the spokes and it is a tedious job to try to bore the spoke holes and not break out through the side of the rim.

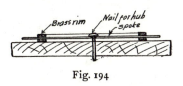

Fig. 194

Wooden steering wheels had heavier rims in proportion to the size of the spokes but there we run up against the difficulty of trying to imitate the turned baluster-

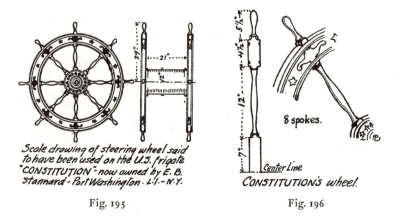

Scale drawing of steering wheel said to have been used on the U.S. frigate "CONSTITUTION" now owned by E. B. Stannard · Port Washington · L·I· · N·Y·

Fig. 195

8 spokes.

CONSTITUTION'S wheel.

Fig. 196

like spokes (Fig. 195). If one has a jeweller's lathe and is building to a scale of ¼ inch to the foot it will be

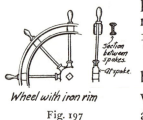

Wheel with iron rim

Fig. 197

possible to show all these little niceties of construction, but on a ⅛ inch scale it is hardly practical.

Eight spokes was the usual number in a wheel but on the large wheels, five and six feet in diameter, eight spokes would make too long a reach between them. Six feet in diameter is 18 feet in circumference which, with eight spokes, would space them over two feet apart, but twelve spokes bring this spacing down to fifteen inches. which is about what the interval of reach should be.

King spoke

Fig. 198

An iron shaft, with a wooden spindle for winding the tiller ropes around, extended aft from the wheel supported on stanchions just high enough

off the deck so that the lower spokes did not hit
(Fig. 199). Where there were two steering wheels
with a spindle between them the
stanchions were forward and aft
of the wheels; but with a single
steering wheel, one stanchion
was aft of the wheel, then came
the spindle, or barrel as some

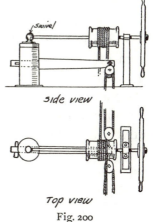

Side view

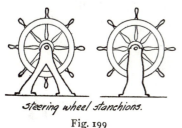

Steering wheel stanchions.

Fig. 199

Top view

Fig. 200

termed it, with another support aft of it. The forward
stanchion was usually a single wide board cut to a more

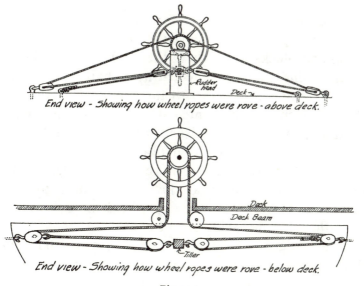

End view - Showing how wheel ropes were rove - above deck.

End view - Showing how wheel ropes were rove - below deck.

Fig. 201

or less fanciful design, but the after one was a double
or A-shaped support to give steadiness (Fig. 199). The
double wheel always had two A frames.

The tiller ropes were wound several turns around
the spindle then leading down through holes in the
decks (Fig. 200) they went around sheaves that led
them off one to each side of the ship and from there
in to the end of the long wooden tiller where there
was another block and this rope was rove off with one
or more turns to give sufficient purchase to handle
the strain on the rudder and tiller (Fig. 201).

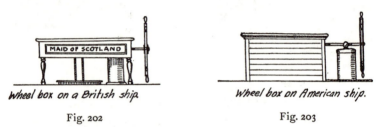

Wheel box on a British ship.

Fig. 202

Wheel box on American ship.

Fig. 203

Many merchant ships, after 1800, had their tillers
aft of the rudder-head, above the deck, so all the wheel
ropes and blocks were where they could be readily got
at, the spindle being protected by a shallow box built
over it set up on legs clear of the deck. This cover on
American ships was painted white, but on the Clyde-
built ships it was of varnished teak and generally had
the ship's name lettered on it (Fig. 202).

Those ships whose tillers were under the deck had a
box cover that went clear down to the deck to keep
water out of the small opening where the tiller ropes
went through the deck (Fig. 203).

The rudder head extended up high enough above the
deck to serve as a support for the steering wheel shaft,
through a swivelled bearing on top of it.

Previous to 1800 or, maybe, a few years later, it was the custom, centuries before, to have a long wooden tiller that mortised through the rudder head and extended away forward close up under the deck beams. On big three-deckers this tiller was a huge balk of a timber that extended clear up almost to the mizzenmast, its forward end resting and sliding on a greased beam built across the ship just under it.

One can realize, after knowing what huge tillers the old ships carried, why three and sometimes four men could hardly hold the steering wheel in stormy weather, and it explains why there were no hatchways or companionways leading down from the deck aft of the mizzenmast and why the steering wheel was placed just aft of the mizzenmast.

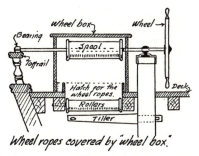

Fig. 204

The *Weazel,* a little 10-gun brig, of 1776, that was only 80.5 feet long on deck and 25 feet beam, had a tiller 12 feet long. The 28-gun ship *Thisbe,* 124 feet by 33.6 feet, had a tiller 18½ feet long and the 36-gun ship *Flora,* 140.8 feet by 38 feet, had a tiller 21 feet long. Iron tillers came into use about 1840. The sloops-of-war in the American navy at that time were fitted with iron tillers that mortised through the rudder head, above the deck, stuck out forward, and had an S-shaped bend that went down between the transom and the aftermost deck beam and then extended forward under the beams a short distance to where the side tackles were hooked on (Fig. 205).

The rudder head and space for the tiller to swing

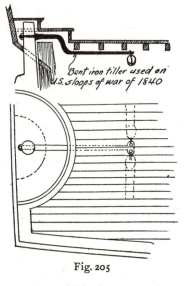

Fig. 205

was built up in two half-circular platforms against the ship's stern. Iron tillers on small craft were nothing new as the brig *L'Atlante,* of 1796, carried a long tiller sweeping close above her after deck and controlled with hand tackles rove off to each side from the end of it (Fig. 206).

This method of steering with hand tackles was an universal practice on small craft for years,—it was not until in the 1880's that small iron quadrant steering gears began to appear and this, several years later, was succeeded by a worm-screw steering gear that eliminated all lost motion.

I can distinctly remember seeing the hand tiller tackles used on the end of wooden tillers, twelve to fifteen feet long, on the big Hudson River sloops and schooners, in 1884; and the big Scotch-built cutter yacht *Thistle,* that raced against the *Volunteer* for the America's cup, in 1887, steered with a long tiller. On some of the small coasters a peculiar steering gear was used. The wheel with its spindle was mounted right on top of the tiller and the tackles, rove off

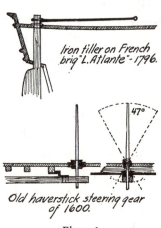

Fig. 206

to each side, were taken around this spindle, so the wheel travelled back and forth across the deck on the tiller end as it swung (Fig. 207).

Such expedients often were the result of crowded

Odd steering gear of small coaster.

Fig. 207

Iron tiller on ship of 1880

Fig. 208

decks, the after cuddy or cabin coming so close aft to the wheel (Fig. 209).

Sailors are whimsical creatures I know from years of associationship with them, and in a measure I share their feelings. I'd always try to find out if the captain of a ship took his wife along, and though many did and stories of kindness of the wife in helping alleviate the hard lot of the forecastle crowd were reported about, I never would ship on a ship with a woman aboard. And many a time have I refused to ship on a craft because she had one of those, to me, ungainly looking big wheel-houses built over her steering gear aft. No doubt this house was a comfort. I have been half frozen

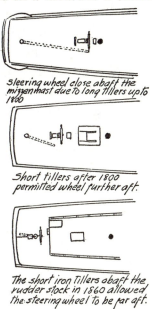

Steering wheel close abaft the mizzenmast due to long tillers up to 1800

Short tillers after 1800 permitted wheel further aft.

The short iron tillers abaft the rudder stock in 1860 allowed the steering wheel to be far aft.

Fig. 209

at the wheel, when it was so cold that the tricks at the wheel were cut from two to one hour, for no human being could stand at a wheel two hours at one stretch, and I've melted under a tropical sun when the pitch in the deck seams was running like water, but I always felt as if I were safer and the lives of all on board were safer, if the man at the wheel was out on a clear deck where he could see and be ready to meet all emergencies, instead of being cooped up in a "chicken-house" and relying on some one out on deck to pass the word what to do. It didn't seem ship-shape to me. Many of the old packet ships carried such deck or wheel-houses and also the big Cape Horners, but I never was shipmates with one of them and never want to be.

The seventeenth and eighteenth century three-deckers had their big double steering wheel down under the poop deck where the men at the wheel could see nothing but the compass, being conned by an officer above how to steer. Suppose this man was shot down in action, as many, no doubt, were; it was a clumsy and, to my way of thinking, a dangerous way to steer a ship.

Fig. 210

On the old-time little caravels the helmsman stood on one deck with his head and shoulders sticking up in a half dome-shaped hood handling the vertical heaver or haverstick which controlled the tiller and rudder (Fig. 210).

CHAPTER XI

The Ship's Galley

INSTEAD of calling them kitchens, seafaring folks always spoke of the place where they did the cooking of their victuals, as the galley. Just where this galley was located depended upon the size of the ship and the trade in which she was employed.

There was a little fishing smack, laid up over winter in the muddy reed-grown banks of the Harlem River, New York, that I came across in my wanderings years ago. She was only about sixty tons burden and carried deck loads of oysters. In the little square cuddy aft, so near the stern that the tiller came right up to within an inch or so of the companionway, was the galley. The skipper, sitting on a stool, could steer, holding the tiller in one hand, his other arm resting on the after edge of the house, and his legs he could stick down the stairs if he wanted to warm his shins. On each side, under the deck, a box bunk was built in and the forward end of this small living room was taken up by a small cook stove and a couple of boxes made into cupboards. The smoke-stack went up through an iron ring in the cabin roof, the pipe turned off to the lee side by an elbow. One, or, at most, two men, constituted the crew on such a craft.

But many a larger coaster had the same galley arrangement, for craft that carried deck loads and where all hands and the cook bunked together aft, as on river schooners and some of the little Down Easters where captain, cook and crew were all one family, were of the same kin.

Fishermen and Grand Bankers had four to six bunks aft, with a pot stove lashed fast in the center of the cabin floor to keep them warm. The stack of this stove went up through the middle of the cabin roof with an athwartship, dome-shaped sheet iron hood to carry the sparks off to leeward so as not to burn the mainsail. But the cooking was done on a range, down below, just aft of the foremast, in a room opening forward into the long forecastle, where ten or twelve bunks lined the walls so that food could be easily passed to the crew. The cabin mess was carried aft. The smoke pipe, with a bonnet top, came up through a water iron set in the deck alongside of the cuddy that gave access to the galley below.

Everything was strong, for these craft got washed fore and aft with green water, when carrying on sail to get their fish to market or when hove to, riding out a gale that piled the Atlantic seas up over these shallow banks, in waves that were fierce things to ride over in a craft that jumped and pitched like a bucking broncho.

How different in the West Indies, the Spanish Main of olden times! There, stubby little schooners, beach-combers among shipping, with occasionally a Chesa-peake schooner, as trim and neat as a pilot-boat to give a contrast and whose long tapering masts put to shame the slender, crooked sticks in the native-built craft, there, in a waist-high box filled with sand, just abaft the foremast, negroes cooked their fish on a wood fire and warmed up their case oil-can full of native drink.

Before deck houses came into vogue, when ships themselves were relatively small craft, the galley was always down in the ship under the deck. A stone fire-place below, with a brick chimney, was built on the upper deck in days long gone by, and after that came square sheet iron and later on round sheet iron chimneys built up from the cooking fireplace below just abaft the foremast. This is the way in which such ships as the old man-of-war *Constitution* and the frigates of 1776 were equipped.

As early as 1757, records show that one Gabriel Snodgrass, a surveyor for the British East India Company, in an audience before the Lords of the Admiralty, explained that the "east-indiamen" had removed their galley from the center of the lower hold to the bows of the ship; and Sir Walter Raleigh, as far back as 1587, objected to the cook room in the center of the hold of the ship.

No doubt there was less motion of the ship's tossing about felt down at the axis of the ship, as it were, but the smoke and smell permeated throughout the ship, and in bad weather, when hatches had to be battened down to keep out the sea, between the smell of rotten bilge-water shaken up and the confined smoke and fumes of cooking, it must have made the cook room anything but a desirable place to work in.

With the galley just abaft the foremast and with a smoke pipe through the deck above and a wide grating overhead to let the heat escape, cooking on an "India-man" was heavenly compared with the old men-of-war who, for years later, clung to the galley in the lower hold.

Ships began to grow in size after the year 1800. Of course there were a few large ones before then, but we are speaking of the rank and file of merchant ships; and poop decks and forecastle heads appeared where formerly ships were flush-decked. When the forward deck-house emancipated the sailors from their rat-like nests up in the wet fore-peak, it also gave the ship's "doctor," as sea cooks were nicknamed, a light, ventilated room in the after end of this deck-house in which to boil salt-horse and salt-pork, burn cracker-hash and brew pea-soup and make bootleg coffee, for sailors delight to claim that the cook ground up old rubber sea-boots for that purpose.

The three-masted schooner, *J. Percy Bartram,* had a little square house, just abaft the foremast, in which the galley occupied the starboard side and the forecastle, the port side aft. A narrow carpenter's shop extended across the forward end with a door on either side. The galley and forecastle both had a door opening aft with a sliding panel in the partition so that food could be passed from the galley to the forecastle without going out on deck. The smoke pipe from the "shipmate range," went up through the roof, with an elbow on top into which fitted a length of pipe that the cook had to swing every time we tacked ship. An iron, bracket-like leg, off to leeward under the fore-boom, supported this pipe near the outer end and kept it about a foot above the top of the house.

Small coasting vessels, such as schooners, brigs and brigantines, had a little square box of a galley in which the cooking was done. When ready for sea, this little galley was lifted up on top of the main hatch and lashed down to ring-bolts in the deck and when in port, unloading cargoes, the galley was set forward, off to one side, on the deck.

CHAPTER XII

PUMPS

THERE are many varieties of pumps used on ships, from the hollowed-out log pump to the diaphragm pump. Little, homely ships had any kind they could get. By the year 1880, modern pumps were in use, but the old timers, of those days, used to tell about the box pumps with leather valves and to discuss the methods that were approved before iron supplanted wood.

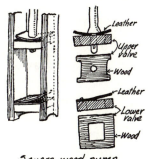

Square wood pump.

Fig. 211

It was as easy to gouge a groove out of two halves of a split log, and then to dowel and lash the two halves together, as it was to take four boards and make up a box (Fig. 211). The latter had four seams to make watertight whereas the logs had but two.

Round wood pump.

Fig. 212

The ploughing out of narrow slots for feathers, or pine stopwaters, and getting them so that they matched up true, was the most difficult part of pump making (Fig. 213).

The use of iron pipe wonderfully simplified pump making. Iron valves could be made stronger and smaller and with the larger opening for water the pump became more efficient.

The greatest depth in a ship is just aft of the main

mast and here is where the pump well was always built. It consisted of a boarded-up hatchway extending from the deck to the bottom of the ship, similar to the elevator shaft in a modern building or a dumb-waiter shaft in an old-style apartment house. Down one side of this well there was a built-in ladder, so that, if necessary, a man could go down and clear the pump. Previous to about 1850, there was a hatchway on top of this well, giving access to it. The modern iron pump did away with this deck hatch but the well

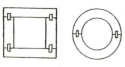

Fig. 213

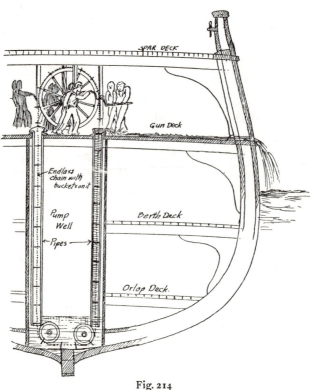

Fig. 214

was retained, and access to it being had from under the poop deck, everything on deck was made watertight.

On the big two- or three-decked men-of-war, the pumps were below the upper or spar deck, on the deck that was just above the water-level.

After 1650, the so-called chain pumps were in general use. They consisted of two pipes with an endless chain, going over sprocket wheels, carrying a series of valves that returned down one pipe and came up bringing water in the other. Long crank arms were extended fore and aft, from the upper sprocket wheel, so that a gang of men could lay hold and heave (Fig. 214). The amount of water one of these pumps could discharge was prodigious. There was no lost stroke, as on the down stroke of a plunger pump, but a continuous stream of water poured from them, flowing across the deck and out through the scuppers into the sea.

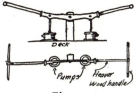

Fig. 215

A later style of pump was the plunger pump or pumps, for by working them in pairs the down-stroke of one was the up-stroke of the other, the plungers being attached to a rocket-arm, pivoted between the two pumps, and with heaving arms, similar to the windlass heavers, each stroke brought up water (Fig. 215).

A later and more efficient style of pump, was known as the diaphragm pump. It had an enlarged basin at the top and instead of the plunger being only the size of the pump and making a long stroke, this basin was double or more the size of the pipe and had a large, round iron diaphragm, with a rubber lining, that lifted only a few inches but which sucked a great volume of water. The lift being much heavier, the power was

obtained by the greater leverage made possible by the
shortness of the stroke (Fig. 216).

On small vessels, a single, long, iron lever handle was
used, which shipped when needed and unshipped and

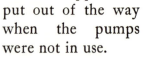

put out of the way
when the pumps
were not in use.

On large vessels these pumps
were worked in pairs and the
plungers were connected to
crank-arms, on a horizontal iron
shaft, fitted into bearings on

Diaphragm lever pump.

Fig. 216

each side of the main fife-rails, just aft of the mainmast.
Just outside the fife-rails, two large, round or channel-
shaped rimmed flywheels, with peculiar S-shaped
spokes were fitted. The crank-arms were long enough,

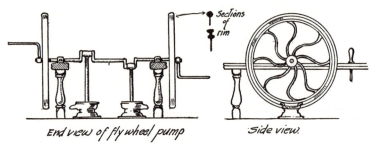

End view of fly wheel pump.   *Side view.*

Fig. 217

extending out beyond the wheels, for two men on a
side (Fig. 217). These crank-arms were removable
and fitted over the squared end of the crank shaft.

Such pumps make a most picturesque addition to a
model's deck and, like steering wheels, they are delicate
things to make and require much time to cut and file
them out of a sheet of metal, the rim being reënforced
with solder to the shape required. If neatly done,

however, they repay in appearance for the trouble taken.

American ships, when racked and strained by many hard passages around the Horn, were usually sold to the Norwegians, who invariably dismantled them aloft, leaving only the topgallant-sail yards crossed, with all under them, of course. They then rigged up a windmill, like a pin wheel, just forward of the mizzen-mast, that disfigured what was formerly a beautiful ship. "She's a stock-fisherman" was invariably a sailor's expression of disgust, when one of these ships hove into view.

Manning the pumps, sounds interesting in reading stories of the sea and the pumps look picturesque on a model; but manning the pump is the hardest work seamen have to do, for it is back-breaking labor, fit only for convicts in a chain-gang. Yet, when ships began to appear on the seas, with donkey-boilers and engines to heave the anchors, to pump, and to hoist topsails, so great was the real deepwaterman's disgust for anything mechanical, due to the inroads of steamships in the commercial field, that many sailors refused to ship on vessels so equipped, considering them thereby degraded by becoming "monkey-wrench sailors."

CHAPTER XIII

SHIP IRONWORK

ONE of the most important functions in an old-time wooden shipyard was the shipsmith, for such parts of the hull and rigging as had to be made of iron must be of the very best, both in material and workmanship. Men's lives depended upon it and the life of the ship itself was often in jeopardy when a faulty weld or a burnt iron might mean a total loss of ship, cargo and men. Those men required no plans; all they needed to know was the diameter of the spars and they could hammer out withes, straps, link-eyes, chain-plates, bobstay-irons and rudder-irons so complete in form and detail that not a key or cotter-pin was omitted. They knew where to put the strength of material, not from any theoretical formulæ, but from the experience of years.

To duplicate all these metal fittings on a model made smaller than a scale of $\frac{1}{8}$ of an inch to the foot, is almost an impossibility, unless one wants to work under a microscope. At $\frac{3}{16}$ of an inch to the foot good work can be done, however. At an automobile accessory or hardware store buy a box of assorted brass shims. They sell them in strips of about one inch in width and with three different thicknesses in each box. The thinnest is the thickness most used on ship models and can easily be cut with a pair of scissors. Cut strips of this about $\frac{1}{16}$ of an inch wide and with a pair of long-nosed tweezers to bend in eye bands for yard-arms or sling-bands, it can be bent and soldered and made into the ironwork for your model.

To make an eye band or withe, crimp the brass up and down so that the metal is doubled where each eye is to be. It will be a great help to have a long, tapered, metal point, like a crochet needle, of the diameter to match the yard where the band is to fit. Bend it around this, crimping up the lugs or eyes, as many as are wanted, one, two, three or four, and cut the strip long enough to let the two ends lap $\frac{1}{16}$ or $\frac{1}{8}$ of an inch. Hold this a second in the flame of an alcohol lamp, to heat it, and then dip into soldering fluid, and with the tweezers holding the lapped ends so that the size is just right, heat it again and touch a drop of solder to it; the solder generally flows over quickly and binds all

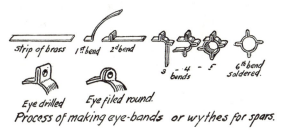

Process of making eye-bands or wythes for spars.

Fig. 218

the crimped up lugs and solders the lapped ends as well. If the solder flows too freely and floods the band, a quick, sharp tap on something hard will knock off all superfluous solder. If not, it is better to have too much than too little solder, for with a rat-tail file the band can soon be shaped inside, to fit the spar. Then with a No. 65 or No. 70 drill, held in a pin-vise, drill holes in each of the lugs and finish by filing off the square corners of the lugs so that they form round eyes (Fig. 218). Don't try to make these out of lead for they will not hold their shape and will corrode when painted. I made that mistake and in time found that just the

weight of the lead hanging on a thread would cut
through the eyes. If filed out of ivory or celluloid, one
cannot get them thin enough and they make unsightly
knobs that are anything but ship-shape in appearance;
but very good ones can, with patience, be drilled and
filed into shape out of copper.

For making eye bolts use small half-inch long bank
pins, "lils," as they are called, made of very small wire.
Cut the head off and anneal, or soften the metal so it
will bend into the shape of a small loop or eye without
breaking. Do not bend it in a long loop but make a
round eye the shape of the real eye-bolts on ships (Fig.

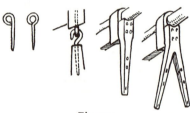

Fig. 219

219). A touch of solder
adds to their appear-
ance. Two of these eyes
hooked together, one
stuck into the under side
of the bowsprit or
through the bowsprit
cap and the other into
the dolphin striker, is a good way of attaching the
latter, unless the model is to represent an old ship of
1810 or earlier, when the dolphin strikers were bolted
to the forward face of the bowsprit cap (Fig. 219),—
single on small craft and double on large ships, when
there was a flying jib-boom and maybe a jib-of-jib-
boom beyond that with all its mess of gear to hold it
steady.

On the lower yards of $\frac{3}{16}$ inch scaled models, these
bank pin eyes will answer for the eyes spaced at intervals along the top of the yards to reeve the jackstays
through the iron rod to which the sails are seized with
spun yarn at each grommet along in the head of the
sail. But on the yards of smaller models and the royals

of the larger models finer wire is required to make these eyes so that they will be in proper proportion. Old-time ships with hide-rope parrels and yard tackles to hold the lower yards to the mast, had practically no ironwork, as do modern ships rigged with cranse-irons. An iron ring shaped like a letter D, called the "D" iron, was seized to the top of the yards of the older ships, the loop of the D standing up and lashed to

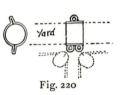

Fig. 220

the slings which held up the yards. On more modern ships there was a band, with an eye on top, to which the chain slings were shackled with a double eye below, into which, one on each side, were hooked the lead-blocks for the topsail sheets (Fig. 220).

The cranse-iron was a complicated affair. It had two bands, about two feet on each side of the center of the yard, connected on the after side with a yoke-iron. Around the mast was a split band, made in two sections, with lugs standing athwartship. Another yoke-iron ran from the mast, its ends going through the lugs and being threaded, the yoke, bands and all, were held rigid on the mast by screwing up a nut on each end. This yoke and the yoke on the yard were connected by a double-swivelled link, so that the yard could swing around in a horizontal plane or be tipped up or down in a vertical plane (Fig. 221).

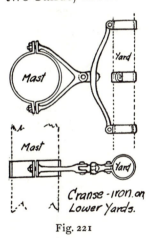

Fig. 221

There are two vital points to be considered in making this cranse-iron. One is to have the vertical pin, on which the yard pivots, far enough away from the mast so that the yard will swing around allowing it to be braced sharp up on a wind without its pressing on the lee shrouds or backstays before it is braced around enough. It will lie against the backstays when fully swung. That order so often shouted by the mate to "Heave! and backstay him," or "Lay him on the backstays," as we were hauling lee braces, still lingers vividly in my memory.

The other point is not to get the yard so close to the stay (the mainstay in the case of the main yard, and the forestay in the case of the fore yard) as to interfere

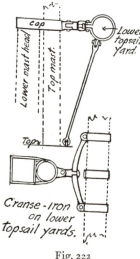

Fig. 222

with rolling up the bunt when stowing sail. It comes close. I well remember once stowing the foresail, off Cape Horn, on the bark *James A. Wright,* when our fore yard was braced sharp up on the starboard tack and all hands were trying to stow a frozen foresail. The mate himself was on the yard, for it was an effort to try to save the sail, already heavily coated with ice, and he told me to "Get under and boot it, Davis!" and being young and active, I crouched on the foot-rope and booted the sail up from the under side to try to get the canvas up on the yard between it and the forestay. But the sail was so big and stiff with ice it was an hour or more before we succeeded in stowing the bunt.

Some model makers go to the other extreme and put the yards too low down on the masts. The band for the cranse-iron should be fitted around the mast just above the futtock-band. Vessels so fitted did not send down their lower yards as was often done on the little, old-fashioned, rope-rigged craft using the parrel straps and yard tackles. Once a modern ship's lower yard was hoisted and the swivel pin put into the cranse-iron, the jeer tackle by which it was hoisted was unrove and sent down; but on the older craft, the jeer tackles, for they had two, one hooked into an eye-bolt in the forward, under edge of the trestle-trees, were kept in readiness to be used at any time.

Chain-plates are tedious things to make either for a real ship or a model. There are so many of them and each one, as you go aft, has to be just a little longer than the other, due to the increasing angle, for chain-plates should stand in line with the shroud or stay, except in a few cases on men-of-war where they have to straddle a gun port. And they must be kept in line where they are bolted to the hull. On merchant ships they were generally all even, but old-time men-of-war often used to have an extra backing-link extending down on every other chain-plate. The main and fore lower rigging chain-plates were heavier than those for the mizzenmast, and the topmost backstay chain-plates were shorter and of lighter metal, the topgallant being still smaller, each in proportion to the strength of the rigging it supported.

In olden times the deadeyes in the lower ends of the shrouds were spread out away from the ship's side by wide boards, called channels, to keep the shrouds from touching the rail above, and the connections from these deadeyes to the bolts in the ship's side below, through extra thick strakes of planking called the "chain wales," were pieces of chain; hence the expression, "in the fore chains," or "in the main chains"; and the plates bolted to the ship's side, into which their lower ends were hooked, were the chain-plates (Fig. 223). But

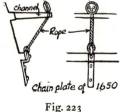

Fig. 223

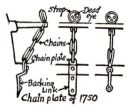

Fig. 224

nowadays no distinction is made and the whole chain-plate, of one stray or rod of iron, is termed the chain-plate. Some chains had three links and some only two long ones, the lower link terminating in an eye, not

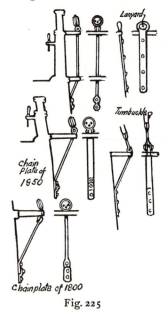

Fig. 225

being hooked into the plate but held by the same bolt that went through the top eye of the backing link and this link was made of round iron instead of flat iron (Fig. 224).

Different shipbuilders had their own individual styles in ironwork by which the ship-yard in which a vessel was built could be determined by one conversant with such matters. Many a time I have heard an argument abruptly ended when some ship captain said: "Blue-nose, nothing! That's a Bath-built ship. Look at her chain-plates!" And in discussing a ship's age, the expression "Why! That ship's as old as your great-grandfather. Look at those old link chain-plates," shows how the various styles in ironwork went out of date the same as the old-fashioned hoop-skirt.

Many model makers go astray in applying the same style of fitting to all types of ships, regardless of size or tonnage, because it looks picturesque.

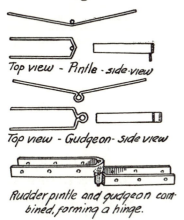

Fig. 226

They will put the heavy, cumbersome gear that belongs on a four hundred ton ship on a little eighty ton schooner. Shipbuilders of the year 1770 knew as much, if not more, about shipbuilding, as the men of 1880, and in building a small coasting sloop or schooner, they adapted the ironwork to the use it was to be put to, just as the later-day men did.

Top view - Pintle - side-view

Top view - Gudgeon - side view

Rudder pintle and gudgeon combined, forming a hinge.

Fig. 227

Rudder irons consisted of what men called gudgeons on the stern-post and pintles on the rudder, the former being the eye and the latter the hook or pin that fitted into it forming a hinge joint for the rudder to swing on (Fig. 226). If your model is on ⅛ of an inch scale, use the pins bent into eyes and hooks and paint strips to represent the metal straps. But if on a 3/16 of an inch scale, use the shim brass cut into strips about 1/16 of an inch wide. Bend the brass so it forms a slight angle and solder a pin to it for the pintle and crimp

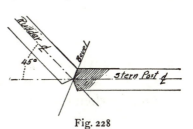

Fig. 228

the brass to form a socket or eye for the gudgeon. Bend them to fit over the rudder and stern-post and fit them so the pintles all fit even in the gudgeons (Fig. 227). Three pairs of irons will do for small craft and five or six for large craft.

To permit the rudder to swing 45 degrees each side,

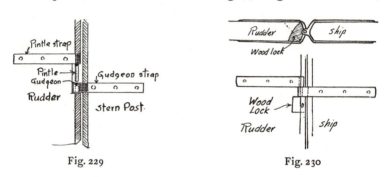

Fig. 229   Fig. 230

the edges of both rudder and stern-post should be chamfered. To find out how much, lay out a diagram representing the thickness of the stern-post, and then intersect this, at an angle of 45 degrees, with lines representing the thickness of the rudder, which is usually the same as the stern-post. A line connecting the point where the outer edges meet and the point where the center lines meet will give the bevels for

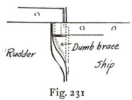

Fig. 231

both rudder and stern-post (Fig. 228). To hook the pintles on to the gudgeons you will have to cut out clearances under the pintles far enough to let the gudgeons go under the pintles before the rudder can drop down and form a hinge joint (Fig. 229).

The rudder being of wood and liable to float up off its pintles when the ship was deeply loaded, some means had to be employed to prevent this. Under the second pintle a bevelled block was cut out so that when the rudder was swung over to one side, a block of wood could be fitted in and a bolt driven in diagonally through it and the rudder, the end of the bolt being left exposed so that it could be backed out and the block removed at any time when it became necessary to un-ship the rudder (Fig. 230). Yet, with this block in, the rudder could not raise and unship itself. And as ships often sailed in ballast, when the rudder was so far out of water that it did not float its own weight and so would cause undue wear between the edges of the pintles and gudgeons, a dumb-brace, a metal cleat, was fastened under the third pintle, which was fitted to rest on and wear on this dumb-brace and so keep the weight off the gudgeons (Fig. 231).

CHAPTER XIV

COPPER SHEATHING

BARNACLES and grass that fouled the ship's planking have always been the bane of a sailor's life. In the time of Henry VIII a coating of pitch or tar and pitch was applied over the charred wood, after breaming, as the process of burning or scorching the marine growth on a ship's bottom to kill it and make it easy to remove, was called, and the bottom was then covered with loose, animal hair obtained from the tanneries where hair was scraped off in tanning leather.

The ship *Josiah,* built in 1694 and sunk in 1715, was so treated, and long years after, when the hull was raised, the hair was found to be in a perfect state of preservation, though inch board sheathing, put over all to hold the hair in place, was badly eaten and decayed. Hair, used in caulking the seams of the frigate *Golden Horse,* was also found to be in good condition when all the oakum had rotted away.

Breaming and then coating the charred wood with either tar, rosin, tallow, soot, pulverized charcoal, brimstone, or other substance poisonous to worms, was the old method of preserving a ship's bottom. Vegetable tar was used until 1764, when coal tar was manufactured and found good.

In 1670, thin, milled lead was manufactured and tried on the bottom of the frigate *Phœnix,* but criticism arose as to its virtue and to test it out in 1768, the *Marlborough,* 68 guns, was covered and when hauled out in 1770, was found covered with weeds. In 1761, copper sheathing was first tried on the 32-gun frigate *Alarm* and found to be a success; so by 1783, its use became general in the British navy. The British East India Company found that a coppered bottom shortened the voyage of their ships by two months over ships with nailed-filled bottoms, which was the means they had previously adopted of preserving ship's bottoms. Black iron nails were studded all over the planking, an inch or less apart, so that the rust from these nails permeated the wood and resisted the teredo's attacks.

New ships were not generally coppered until they had made a voyage or two to work them into shape and squeeze down on the new caulking. They were then hauled out and the bottom planking seams were all carefully searched and recaulked. The seams were then payed with hot pitch to fill them and hold the oakum in and then a sheathing of felt, about a quarter of an inch thick, was laid on and the sheets of copper were nailed down over this felt.

This coating of copper extended over the whole immersed portion of the bottom. It was formed of sheets of copper four feet in length and fourteen inches in breadth, the lower edges of the upper sheets lapping over the upper edges of those below and the after end of each sheet lapping over the forward end of the one immediately following it.

Sheathing copper and yellow metal sheathing was made in a number of different thicknesses but always in the same size of sheets: fourteen inches wide and four feet long.

14 ounce copper per sheet weighed 4 lb. 1 oz.
16 ounce copper per sheet weighed 4 lb. 10 oz.
18 ounce copper per sheet weighed 5 lb. 4 oz.
20 ounce copper per sheet weighed 5 lb. 13 oz.

22 ounce copper per sheet weighed 6 lb. 7 oz.
24 ounce copper per sheet weighed 7 lb. 0 oz.
26 ounce copper per sheet weighed 7 lb. 9 oz.
28 ounce copper per sheet weighed 8 lb. 3 oz.
30 ounce copper per sheet weighed 8 lb. 12 oz.
32 ounce copper per sheet weighed 9 lb. 5 oz.

The composition nails used in putting it on were a chisel-pointed cut nail with large flat head, the head bevelled on the underside.

There were 230 nails, $\frac{7}{8}$ inch   long, to a pound.
There were 190 nails, 1   inch   long, to a pound.
There were 186 nails, 1 $\frac{1}{8}$ inches long, to a pound.
There were 169 nails, 1 $\frac{1}{4}$ inches long, to a pound.
There were 112 nails, 1 $\frac{3}{8}$ inches long, to a pound.
There were 107 nails, 1 $\frac{1}{2}$ inches long, to a pound.

Yellow sheathing metal has been generally used of late, it being less expensive than copper. Zinc sheathing, manufactured by La Veille Montague Zinc Mining Company, of Liege, France, has been introduced for sheathing vessels. It is said to be considerably cheaper than copper or yellow metal, lasts longer, and many shipmasters certify that it continues as clean as yellow metal.

The copper or metal, used in sheathing vessels, is divided into three thicknesses, consisting of twenty, twenty-four and twenty-eight ounces; but more often it is equally divided into four thicknesses of twenty-two, twenty-four, twenty-six, and twenty-eight ounce, and is applied in the following manner:—the twenty-eight ounce should cover the bows, diagonally from the foremast, at load line, to the heel of the forefoot. The twenty-six ounce should run parallel from the heel of the foremast to the mainmast, at the load line. The twenty-four ounce should run from the heel of the mainmast to the load line at the mizzenmast; and the twenty-two ounce should cover all abaft the mizzenmast, except the rudder, which should be sheathed with twenty-six ounce, the beardings with twenty-eight ounce, and the keel with twenty-six ounce.

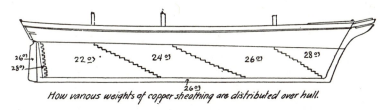

How various weights of copper sheathing are distributed over hull.

Fig. 232

The sheets are laid on so that the joint of the two lower sheets comes in the middle of the upper sheet, just as bricks are laid.

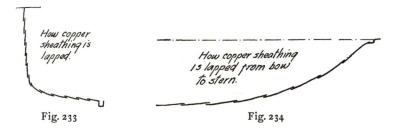

Fig. 233   Fig. 234

Beginning at the keel they form parallel bands on the ship's bottom, almost horizontal amidships, but rolling over at the ends, due to the shape of the ship, until they are vertical at the ends. This causes the copper to climb up higher at the ends and after eight or ten belts of copper are laid on, a diagonal line along the ship's bilge is struck with a chalk line and when this is reached the plates forward and aft are shaped into wedges along this line.

Beginning with a belt along this diagonal line, the sheathing is then carried up in belts parallel with the water-line. Under the bow and stern ends, these plates are shaped off into triangles, the same as below, and then a belt, one plate wide, is worked fore and aft along the top edge (Fig. 235).

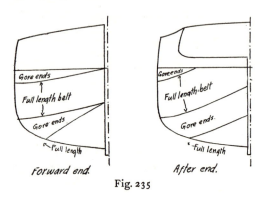

Fig. 235

On a ⅛ inch scale model it is impossible to make a good job of coppering. The best that can be done is to paint the bottom a dull yellow and imitate the green

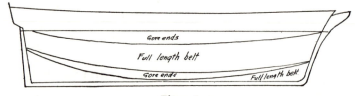

Fig. 236

and red patches that usually appear in sheathing, just as new white patches show in the sails. To copper a ¼ inch scale model, use shim copper or brass and small bank pins. It is an interminable job to attempt each plate individually, so take a strip long enough to make a belt of copper and crimp or fold it back on itself to imitate the laps, for the beauty of the job is in getting fair lines along the edges of the belts of plating and a strip helps to accomplish this. Drill or punch for the pins and do not drive the heads in too hard. It is better to file them down flush, later, with a fine cut smooth file.

How gore end look aft.

Fig. 237

CHAPTER XV

The Ground Tackle

GROUND tackle" is a generic term used to denote such paraphernalia as anchors and chains or rope cables used to hook into the ground, under water, and hold the ship stationary.

To "break out" an anchor that was hooked deep into the thick mud bottom required more power than human hands, so capstans were fitted vertically to ship's decks and when fitted horizontally were called a windlass. Even in Columbus' time these appliances existed in crude forms.

The capstan consisted of a wooden spindle or round spar that went down through the deck, with its lower end stepped into a heavy block in which it turned. The part above deck was padded out with cleats to make it larger in diameter and give it a slight taper so that the rope could be "fleeted," the sailors' name for the process of slacking the rope slightly so that the upper turns can slip up and make room for the new turns below. This capstan had no automatic ratchet to hold the strain and the men held with the bars until no more cable could be hove in. The capstan was then locked by a chock of wood pivoted at one end to the deck, which a man at the bars could push in with his feet so that it engaged behind one of the vertical cleats (Fig. 238). A chock of wood bolted on deck

Fig. 238

butted against this chock or ratchet-like piece to hold it in place.

The early windlass was equally crude and consisted of a round spar held horizontally, a few inches off the deck, by stanchions at each end and turned by heaving-bars fitted into holes cut at irregular intervals around the spar (Fig. 239). As in the case of the capstan, it was necessary to fleet the cable to prevent its riding along until it got jammed at the end of the barrel of the windlass, and cleats, tapered so that the cable could be pushed down to prevent riding one turn over the other, were fastened to the windlass.

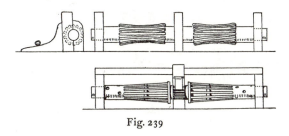

Fig. 239

At first a bar was left to hold the windlass from turning back, but a wooden dog or toggle, fastened to a heavy post and dropping into a series of notches cut around the center of the windlass barrel, seems to have come into use in the seventeenth century. The old style of turning the windlass with heavers existed until long afterwards and was found on many small coasters as late as 1820.

The use of chain cables called for heavier cleats on the windlass barrel than had previously been used for rope. A timber was also fastened across the top of the windlass so that the chain could be slacked on one side and the links of the three turns of chain about the wind-lass hung up clear of it while the chain on the other side was being hove in, for the windlass had to serve both sides of the ship.

The so-called pump-brake windlass was the next improvement. On each side of the central samson post, the windlass was built up with two narrow collars of wood on whose edge an iron-toothed rim was fastened. On the forward side, an iron ratchet gripped the smooth edges of this iron rim and it had a tongue or dog, as it was called, pivoted to engage in the toothed rim. An iron arm stuck out rigidly from this ratchet to engage

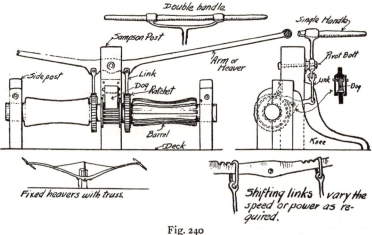

Fig. 240

with vertical links forward of the samson post on whose forward edge was pivoted a long rocker arm that stuck off each side over the ship's forward deck giving considerable leverage as the arms were pumped up and down to turn the windlass barrel (Fig. 240).

The early ships had fixed arms, but an improvement was soon invented, making the arms or windlass heavers, as they were called, a separate piece that fitted into a socket in the end of the arms close in by the samson post (Fig. 241). The heavers could then be unshipped to clear the forward deck.

While all these windlasses hove in the cables there was no way of letting them run out. The several turns of cable around the barrel of the windlass had to be overhauled and pulled around by hand until there was length enough of chain to reach bottom where the ship was to anchor. This process was called "ranging" the cable, that is, laying it out on the deck in long loops so that it would run clear and not get fouled.

Fig. 241

The log windlass was next made with an iron shaft through it and the greatest improvement of all followed—a means of releasing that part of the windlass barrel that held the chain. The chain links fitted into a socket wheel, cast to fit the links of the chain, that was free to revolve on the iron shaft until a disc wheel was screwed up, on a worm thread, until lugs on this disc engaged with other lugs on a similar disc attached to the socket wheel. When both were locked and revolved as one, the chain could be wound back inboard again.

The first Hyde windlass was fitted on the ship *Gatherer,* built by A. Hathorne, at Bath, Maine, in 1874. It

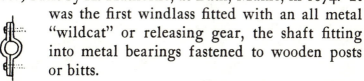

was the first windlass fitted with an all metal "wildcat" or releasing gear, the shaft fitting into metal bearings fastened to wooden posts or bitts.

Bearings
Fig. 242

Instead of the ratchet gear these later windlasses had a spiral gear in the center with double ratchet rims, one on each side. This spiral gear engaged in a gear wheel at the lower end of a vertical shaft that went up through the forecastle head deck and was the spindle of a geared iron capstan by which the windlass was operated. When this capstan was turned clockwise, it had great leverage on the windlass; but by shipping the capstan bars into an upper row of holes, in the upper part of the capstan head and going around

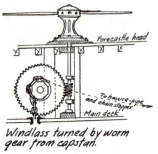

Windlass turned by worm gear from capstan.

Fig. 243

the reverse way, more than double the power was obtained, as both turned the windlass in the same direction. The upper head of the capstan operated through a set of small gears that multiplied the power but slowed the speed proportionally and it was only used for the last final pull in breaking out the anchor when the chain was up and down.

Men-of-war did not use windlasses. They hove their anchors with a capstan, as they were strongly manned and it was a quicker process. The cable was not, as many suppose, brought around the capstan, for it was too thick a rope to bend and handle it around the barrel of a capstan. On a line-of-battle ship this cable was eight inches thick. A special rope termed a "messenger," formed in a long loop, with many small, short ropes spliced into it, went around the capstan, and was laid alongside of the cable. As many of the small ropes as could

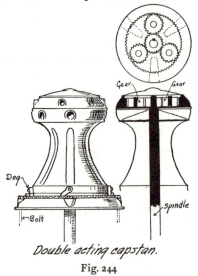

Double acting capstan.

Fig. 244

be were wrapped about the cable and the messenger
pulled the cable in; the stop or small ropes were cast
off as it came near the capstan and others behind were
made fast (Fig. 245). As the cable was hove in, it was
passed down the main hatch to be coiled away in the

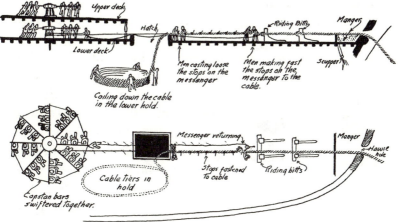

Diagram showing how cables are hove in with a capstan and messenger

Fig. 245

cable tier, down in the bottom of the ship, on each side
abreast of the mainmast. The messenger went round
and round, in an endless loop.

On large ships where the cables came in on the main
deck, the capstans were double, one
above the other, on the same shaft or
spindle (Fig. 246). The lower capstan operated the cables and the
upper one was used for mastheading topsails and hoisting the lower

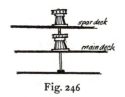

Fig. 246

yards by their jeer tackles. These capstans were abaft
the mainmast. There was also a single capstan abaft
the foremast and used for handling the foreyard jeer
tackles.

On the smaller ships, sloops-of-war, brigs, etc., the process of heaving in the cable was the same only it was done with a single capstan. Merchantmen, in the days of the packets when rope anchor-cables were used, handled their ground tackle in the same way. At the same time (in the 1830's) doubtless there were many small ships and brigs still using the old log windlass.

There is nothing about a ship more picturesque than an old-style wooden capstan, the kind on which the ship's fiddler used to squat and fiddle a lively tune to

Fig. 247

put enthusiasm and unity of effort into the hard-straining gang of seamen, three and four on each capstan bar, working like cart horses. Those were the days when chanties and capstan songs were a reality; when some little glib-tongued rat of a man, who couldn't pull a pound, was worth his weight in gold aboard a ship, for the songs he could chant and the kick and merriment he could put into the thirty-odd men who then became as strong as oxen. Once get them enthused and bellowing out the chorus of the tunes of that little packet rat and the anchors came home as if it were a steam-windlass that was heaving. And such a chorus once heard over the still waters in some foreign harbor, as a homeward-bounder was heaving anchor, will live in one's memory forever.

In making a ship model, though everything is meas-ured and made to a scale, I always carve a small figure of a man about five feet nine inches high and mount him on a small disc or square of tin and when a capstan is made, I set this man in position to see if the capstan bars are just the proper height for him to heave on (Fig.

247). Capstan bars should come breast-high and by using this little dummy of a man I sometimes catch errors. The bars will often come too high, up level with his head, and though the capstan looks good, when lowered it looks very much better.

Fig. 248

If you can spin it up in a lathe it is an easy matter to turn out a capstan in profile and then carve out between the cleats with a pen knife; but if no lathe is available it is difficult to get the wood rounded to a true circle. On ⅛ inch scale models, two copper rivets with a disc of wood between, the bar holes bored into it, make a very good capstan head (Fig. 248).

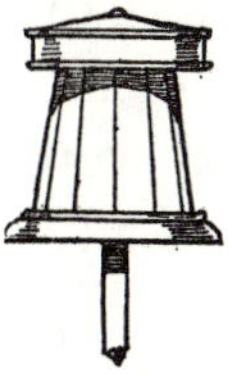

The barrel of the capstan is then cut out, octagonal in shape, and another rivet makes the base. A round-headed nail holds the parts together and fastens it to the deck (Fig. 249).

Fig. 249

If on a larger scale than one-eighth, the capstan can be built up on a wooden barrel. First turn out the head and barrel in one piece leaving the top with a very slight round and not perfectly flat (Fig. 250). Then make the vertical cleats and glue them in place, eight of them, and fit the short chocks that brace the cleats just above the shoulder on the cleats and just above the base. Below the cleats fit a circular ratchet-piece on to which, at each cleat, pin a dog that engages in a ratchet or cogged rim on top of a base just below

Fig. 250

the ratchet piece. This base is bolted to the deck or more usually to a pad of wood built a couple of inches high to level off the slight crown or round in the deck (Fig. 251).

An iron capstan is more easily turned up on a lathe. The barrel is the same but the heads are either single or double, the latter being a later improvement that came out in the 1860's (Fig. 252). The slight raised pads or cleats can be painted and so can the reenforcing ridges around the capstan bar holes, but if carved out in relief they look more real. From about 1860 on there was a crank-turned, geared capstan, largely in use on sailing ships whose decks were pretty well filled up with hatches and houses (Fig.

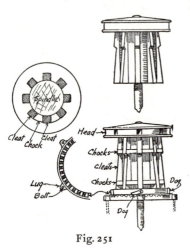

Fig. 251

253). This capstan was similar to the single-gear type, but out on each side of the head protruded a short shaft on which could be fitted a crank by which to turn it. Bars also could be used in the regular way.

Do not fail to provide, adjacent to the capstan, proper stowing places for the capstan bars. On

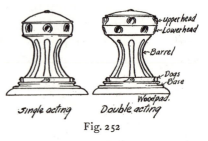

Fig. 252

the forecastle head they were generally stowed horizontally in racks inside the rail (Fig. 254). The heavy

Crank capstan.

Fig. 253

Capstan bar rack on inside of forecastle head bulwark.

Fig. 254

tapered end of the bar that fitted the
holes in the capstan lay aft. The holes
in the thin handle end being large
enough made it possible to push forward and get the butt end into the
after cleat where the bar jammed snug.

Around the mainmast, just above the
deck, the capstan bars were stowed
vertically in cleats; either in a ring,
three-quarters of the way around the
mast, or in two half cleats, on each side
only (Fig. 255).

On the forward side of the booby
hatch, that little box-like house, about
four feet high, lashed over the after

Capstan bars stowed
on the mast.

Fig. 255

Capstan bars stowed on
end of booby-hatch.

Fig. 256

hatch, was another favorite place to
stow the bars horizontally (Fig.
256). On the ships from 1850 on,
this was just aft of the capstan on the
poop deck.

The large clippers carried four
capstans, one on each side, on the
poop, and two on the forecastle head. Some also had
one away aft on the stern, abaft the wheel box. In
docking ships the capstans
on the extreme ends were
used in heaving in the bow
and stern lines. They were
also useful at sea.

Until shortly after 1800,
ships that carried no deck-
house abaft the foremast,
carried a capstan just aft of
the foremast. The crews in

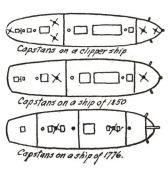

Capstans on a clipper ship

Capstans on a ship of 1850

Capstans on a ship of 1776.

Fig. 257

those days lived down under the main deck up in the
bows of the ships.

One of the most dangerous and difficult jobs in
anchoring a ship was to make fast the huge cables so
as to hold the strain of the ship and yet do it so that
they would not get jammed. Chain around a wild cat,
on a modern windlass with
its chain stopper, is easy
to handle. A dog or pawl
lowered until it fetches up
on a shoulder of a link
in the chain as it runs
through an iron chain
stopper (an iron trough-

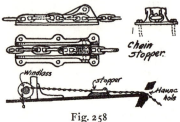

Fig. 258

like box bolted on deck between the windlass and the
hawse pipes) and the cable is soon locked fast (Fig.
258). It is released in a moment by heaving slightly on
the windlass, to pull the chain an inch back and ease
the strain on the pawl so that it can be lifted. A small
rope made fast to an eye in the top of the pawl serves
to tie it up so that the
chain runs free when
not wanted.

But a hawser, eight
inches in diameter, is
quite another matter to
hold when a thousand-
ton ship is jerking at it

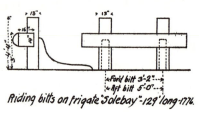

Riding bitts on frigate 'Solebay'-129'long-1776.

Fig. 259

in a gale of wind and every sea that tosses the ship
multiplies the strain. Old wooden ships had riding
bitts, immense, wooden posts built and braced to the
deck frame of the ship. They were of the toughest oak
obtainable and generally of live oak. One bitt was a
little in advance of the other and there were two on

each side of the ship. The big cable was twisted around
the forward bitt, brought aft and hitched about the
after one.

To give the actual dimensions of these bitts, we may
take, for example, the
frigate *Solebay,* 32 guns,
of the year 1776. She
had two pairs of bitts
that were 13 inches
square and stood 4 feet
4 inches above the deck.
The forward bitts were
18 feet aft of the stem
and spaced 3 feet 2 inches
apart. The after bitts
were 15 feet 10 inches aft
of the forward bitts and
spaced 5 feet apart (Fig.
259). The rule for de-

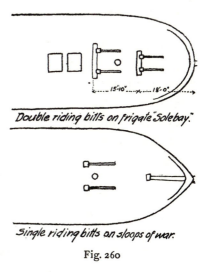

Double riding bitts on frigate "Solebay."

Single riding bitts on sloops of war.

Fig. 260

termining the size of these bitts was to multiply the
beam of the ship by .45, the product being in inches.
The *Solebay* was 129 feet long, 35 feet 4 inches beam,
12 feet 7 inches depth of hold.

Across the after side of each pair of these bitts, a
bolster piece, about 14 by 16 inches in size, was jogged
over them, the after edge being rounded out with a
hardwood facing to take the wear and crushing strain
of the cable. Each upright was strengthened by a
heavy knee bolted to the deck, for-
ward of it.

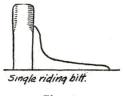

Single riding bitt.

Fig. 261

On small ships,—sloops-of-war,
brigs and small merchant ships,—
the riding bitts were a pair of single
posts (Fig. 261), one each side,

kneed to the deck, more like a snubbing post than a bitt, a round turn about which took the strain and the end of the cable was lashed to ringbolts in the deck.

In the 1860's, at the time of the Civil War, men-of-war had cast iron riding bitts with a shoulder cast on that went halfway around spirally, just as the rope would be wound around the bitt.

A better realization of what the old-time sailors had to contend with may be arrived at when we read of the weight of the anchors that they handled. Anchors of over four tons weight were carried on a line-of-battle ship and frigates had anchors weighing 7720 pounds. These ships carried large crews, but they needed them to handle gear of such unwieldy proportions.

The rule for determining the size of cables and anchors is as follows:—hemp cables should be one inch in circumference for each foot of the ship's beam, that is, her greatest width. The weight of the ship's bower anchor, the heaviest one in pounds, is found by adding the ship's beam and depth of hold and multiplying this sum by 100. The stream anchor should be one-third the weight of the bower anchor. Vessels smaller than frigates had anchors of 500 pounds per hundred tons of their tonnage. A first-class United States line-of-battle ship carried three chains of 2¼ inch diameter and 180 fathoms length and anchors of 9000 pounds weight. In the merchant service, fewer and shorter chains were used than in the navy, hence heavier chains were needed. A clipper-built ship required chains and anchors of less weight than the full-built ship of the same tonnage.

The following will give some idea of anchors and cables as carried on old ships:—

Schooner of 16 guns, built in 1794, 62 feet keel, 23

feet beam, 11 feet depth of hold; 3 anchors, 1100 lbs.; 1 anchor, 350 lbs.; 1 kedge, 100 lbs.; 1 grapnel, 21 lbs.; 3 cables (rope) 10 inch circumference, 120 fathoms; 1 cable (rope) 4 inch circumference, 120 fathoms.

Brig of 18 guns, built in 1794, 75 feet keel, 27 feet beam, 11½ feet depth of hold; 3 anchors, 1500 lbs.; 1 stream, 600 lbs.; 1 kedge, 300 lbs.; 1 kedge, 112 lbs.; 1 grapnel, 28 lbs.; 3 cables (rope) 12 inch circumference, 120 fathoms; 1 cable (rope) 6 inch circumference, 120 fathoms; 1 cable (rope) 4 inch circumference, 120 fathoms.

Ship of 74 guns, built in 1800, 210 feet knight head to taffrail, 53 feet 6 inches beam, 22 feet hold; 2 sheet anchors, 10,000 lbs.; 2 bowers, 10,000 lbs.; 1 stream, 3000 lbs.; 1 kedge, 1400 lbs.; 1 kedge, 1300 lbs.; 1 kedge, 1100 lbs.; 1 kedge, 900 lbs.; 1 kedge, 700 lbs.; 1 grapnel, 1500 lbs.; 1 grapnel, 80 lbs.

An English first-rate, of 120 guns, 2609 tons, had three cables of 25 inch circumference and four chain cables of 2¼ inch diameter links and four anchors of 4 tons, 19 hundredweight. An 84-gun ship, of 2284 tons, had three cables of 23½ inch circumference and four 2⅛ inch chains and four anchors of 4 tons 5 hundredweight each. A 50-gun frigate of 2082 tons, had three 21½ inch circumference cables, four 2 inch diameter chains and four anchors of 3 tons, 10 hundredweight each. A 42-gun ship of 1084 tons, had three 18½ inch cables, three 1¾ inch diameter chains and four anchors of 47 hundredweight each. A 26-gun ship of 913 tons, had three 17 inch cables, three 1⅝ inch diameter chains and four anchors of 38 hundredweight each. An 18-gun ship of 462 tons, had one 14 inch diameter cable, three 1⅜ inch diameter chains and four anchors of 23 hundredweight each.

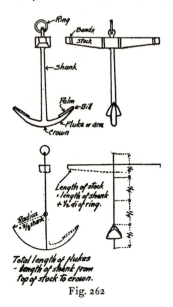

Fig. 262

There are several ways of making anchors but before you begin, be sure that you have the right proportions. The flukes are as long as the shank from the crown to the top of the stock. The stock, across it, is equal to the shank, plus one-half the diameter of the ring. The palm is half the length of one fluke on its top edge from shank to bill, as the point of the fluke is termed. The palms are as wide as they are long (Fig. 263), and the curve on each edge is a section of a parabola rather than an arc of a circle.

The stock is square, in size one inch for every foot of length of the shank. An anchor with a nine-foot shank would have a nine-inch square stock. This stock is straight across the top and also across the bottom for one quarter its length which then has a straight taper to the ends which are one-half the size at the middle (Fig.

Palm

Fig. 263

264). The stock is made of two pieces, notched in the middle to take the shank, but they do not quite come wood-to-wood in the middle. Four square, iron bands are driven on that clamp the two sides of the stock tightly to the square shank.

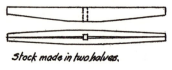

Stock made in two halves.

Fig. 264

Bend or shape the flukes, so that their outer ends are even across from bill to bill, with a mark one-third up the shank (Fig. 265). The outer end of each arm or fluke, for half its length, is tapered almost to a point ending in a square nib end that sticks out just a trifle beyond the palm. The shank and flukes are of square iron with the sharp edges or corners slightly rounded and the shank tapers slightly being about one-third smaller at the stock than it is at the point where it joins the flukes.

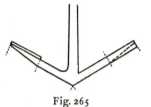

Fig. 265

One method of making model anchors is to saw the shank and flukes out of heavy sheet copper or brass, with a metal jigsaw. Then rivet or solder on the palms. Anchors made in this way are generally left unpainted to show the workmanship, just as the box-wood planked models are varnished to show off the details of construction.

Another way is to cut out of thick lead the shape of the anchor desired and hammer and file this to the exact shape desired, gluing the palms onto the flukes. Then mix up a solution of dental, fast drying plaster and press the greased lead model of the anchor, half way

Fig. 266

down into the face of the plaster and allow it to harden. Then make several dowel holes in the face of the plaster around the anchor and after greasing the surface thoroughly, dowel holes and all, pour some more plaster to cover the anchor.

When this has hardened and become thoroughly dry, for if moist it may explode with the sudden generation of steam, separate the two plaster molds and remove the anchor. After cutting a channel in both pieces of plaster, from the tip of the impression to the edge, put the molds together and pour in melted Babbitt metal. Allow some time for it to cool and harden before you separate the mold and you will have a smooth finished anchor and a mold in which you can cast others (Fig. 266).

Still another way to make an anchor is to file copper wire to the required shape for flukes, using another piece for the shank and leaving a small dowel projection on the lower end of the shank. After bending the flukes to their proper angle, drill a hole and insert the dowel on the end of the shank into this hole and rivet the end over. Then heat this junction of the two pieces and run solder to fillet out the corners.

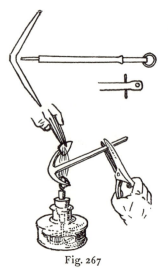

Fig. 267

A small inkbottle, with a piece of copper or brass tube through the cork and a round wick to feed the wood alcohol, gives an excellent flame to do this bit of soldering. Heat the palms, touch with soldering fluid, put on a drop of solder, and with tweezers hold for a few seconds in the flame, and the palm will soon be securely soldered to the fluke (Fig. 267). Then file off the little surplus solder and you will have a finished anchor. The greatest mistake is in using too much solder.

The stock will not turn if it is well fitted and clamped tight with bands made of a small strip of shim brass soldered together. I have found it good practice, however, to drill a hole and solder a short piece of wire that stands in the same direction as the stock and prevents its being knocked out of place. Real anchors have a slight shoulder on the shank just under the stock to hold it in place.

If one has no facilities for soldering metal, the anchors can all be made out of wood, glued or pinned together and when painted and stowed on a model's bows, if made in correct proportions, they look as well as the metal ones. The only trouble with them is that curious admirers are continually feeling of everything they can get hold of on a model and wooden anchors are easily broken.

The following table supplying the size of anchors and chains on ships in the 1850's, will be found useful:—

Tonnage of ship in tons	Weight of anchors in pounds	Size of chain in inches	Weight per fathom (6 ft.) in pounds
30	150	$\frac{1}{2}$	14
50	200	$\frac{9}{16}$	18
75	300	$\frac{5}{8}$	22
100	400	$1\frac{1}{16}$	27
120	500	$\frac{3}{4}$	32
140	600	$1\frac{3}{16}$	38
160	700	$\frac{7}{8}$	44
180	800	$1\frac{5}{16}$	50
200	900	1	56
240	1100	$1\frac{1}{16}$	63
280	1300	$1\frac{1}{8}$	70
320	1450	$1\frac{3}{16}$	78
360	1600	$1\frac{1}{4}$	86
400	1750	$1\frac{5}{16}$	95
440	1900	$1\frac{3}{8}$	105
500	2100	$1\frac{7}{16}$	115
550	2300	$1\frac{1}{2}$	125
600	2500	$1\frac{9}{16}$	136
700	2700	$1\frac{5}{8}$	145

To find the weight, per foot, of cable-laid rope, multiply the square of the circumference by .036.

To find the weight, per foot, of tarred ropes and cables, multiply the square of the circumference by .04.

CHAPTER XVI

GUN PORTS

THE following rule will help ship model builders who are reproducing old-time English men-of-war ships of about 1750. The dimensions of the ports and parts of the gun carriages are in proportion to the diameter of the shot and are easily figured.

> 1 lb. shot 1.923 inches in diameter
> 2 lb. shot 2.423 inches in diameter
> 3 lb. shot 2.793 inches in diameter
> 4 lb. shot 3.053 inches in diameter
> 6 lb. shot 3.494 inches in diameter
> 9 lb. shot 4.   inches in diameter
> 12 lb. shot 4.403 inches in diameter
> 18 lb. shot 5.040 inches in diameter
> 24 lb. shot 5.546 inches in diameter
> 32 lb. shot 6.106 inches in diameter
> 36 lb. shot 6.350 inches in diameter
> 42 lb. shot 6.684 inches in diameter

Gun ports, from center to center, should be 25 times the diameter of the shot. Gun port's length, fore and aft, should be $6\frac{1}{2}$ times the diameter of the shot. Gun ports' height should be six times the diameter of the shot. The sills of the gun ports should be $3\frac{1}{2}$ times the diameter of the shot above the deck.

The thickness of the sides or brackets, as they were called, of the gun carriages, should be the same as the diameter of the shot, and the axletrees the same size. The bolts should be $\frac{1}{5}$ of the diameter of the shot.

The diameter of a shot or cannon ball may be found

by its weight:—subtract ⅛ of the weight and multiply the remainder by 8, and extract the cube root of the product.

To find the weight by its diameter: cube the diameter and divide by 8 and add ⅛ of the product for weight of ball in pounds.

The size of gun ports as used in the American Navy, in 1850, was somewhat larger than those of the older type of ships, being as follows:—

Cannon	Height of sill above deck	Height of port	Breadth of port fore and aft
24 pounders	28 inches	34 inches	40 inches
18 pounders	26 inches	31 inches	36 inches
12 pounders	24 inches	28 inches	33 inches
8 pounders	22 inches	25 inches	30 inches
6 pounders	20 inches	22 inches	27 inches
4 pounders	18 inches	19 inches	24 inches
3 pounders	16 inches	17 inches	21 inches

CHAPTER XVII

BOATS

THE stowage of ship's boats often confounds the landsman who does not see ships off soundings when everything is properly stowed for sea. As he sees them and as most artists depict them, they have boats hung out on davits ready for lowering into the water.

Whalers, the old blubber-hunters, were the only ships that carried boats in readiness for lowering away, but that was their business and they could reduce sail and drift along where a packet that was trying her best to make a quick passage would be carrying so much sail that her boats would be swept away by a sea and lost.

The only ships that carried boats on davits, at sea, in the 1890's, were the big 'Frisco ships. They carried a pair of quarter boats, generally a light-built whale boat, just forward of the mizzen rigging, on a pair of iron davits, in case of a man overboard. On most ships off soundings all boats were taken in and turned upside down on skids and then lashed securely to ring bolts in the deck. The two big long boats were similarly stowed on top of the forward house just abaft the foremast. In those days but little dependence was put in the small boats. Planks were laid fore and aft on the thwarts of the upturned long boats and four or five barrels of potatoes were usually spread out to air and prevent rotting as would be the case if left packed in barrels. The strain of this load of potatoes would soon open the top seams of these boats wide enough to stick a pencil through them. Government regulations required so many cubic feet of boat space per man and these boats had to be carried to comply with the law.

When I was seagoing, in the 1890's, we only carried the two long boats on top of the forecastle and a light rowing yawl boat lashed across the forward end of the poop deck. After we anchored at Valparaiso, Chili, a pair of davits for the yawl boat were got out of the half deck and shipped into their sockets just forward of the starboard mizzen rigging, and the gangway and side ladder was shipped just forward of the boat, a davit and tackle holding the lower platform just clear of the water which permitted the ladder to be hoisted each night so that no one could sneak aboard easily. A night watch was always kept by one man on the forecastle-head. The yawl boat was hoisted each night to prevent its being lost or stolen, and dropped astern during the day for the captain's use.

In the 1850's and 1860's, ships had bigger crews and

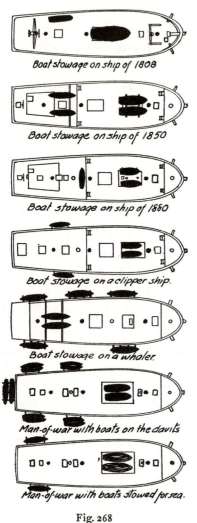

Boat stowage on ship of 1808

Boat stowage on ship of 1850

Boat stowage on ship of 1860

Boat stowage on a clipper ship.

Boat stowage on a whaler.

Man-of-war with boats on the davits

Man-of-war with boats stowed for sea.

Fig. 268

besides the two long boats on top of the forward house, carried two whale boats, stowed bottom up; their after ends on top of the after house, and their forward ends reaching forward over the poop deck. They were supported on a "skid-beam," an arched beam reaching from rail to rail across the ship at the main rigging.

The small ships of 1800 carried one long boat, and as there were no deck houses to prevent it, this was stowed in chocks, right side up, between the foremast and the main hatch. A small, square, cooking caboose was usually lashed fast on top of the main hatch after it was battened down when the cargo was all stowed. In addition to the long boat there was always a small, light boat of some kind, round bottomed, flat bottomed, or a canoe, that was lashed to port on deck just forward of the mizzen rigging and when nearing land it was hoisted on davits at the stern.

Men-of-war carried more boats than merchantmen and some idea of their size is handed down to us in the following old navy rule:—

To find the length of the first launch, multiply the square root of the length of the ship by 2.6; the breadth is ¼ the length so found. The first and second cutters of ships-of-the-line and the first cutters of sloops-of-war to be .9 of the launch. The third and fourth cutters of ships-of-the-line, and the second cutters of sloops-of-war to be .9 of the first cutter. Quarter, waist or stern boats to be the same dimensions as the third and fourth cutters of ships-of-the-line, or second cutters of sloops-of-war, only built lighter. Gigs are the same dimensions as third and fourth cutters.

A ship-of-the-line carries twelve boats.

A frigate carries nine boats.

A sloop-of-war carries six boats.

A brig-of-war carries five boats.

To determine the siding of a boat's keel multiply the breadth of beam in feet by .4, which gives the size in inches.   Frames sided .5 of keel.   Molding of frames at heel 1.5 of the siding; head .5 of heel.   Thickness of planking is boat's breadth in feet multiplied by .10.

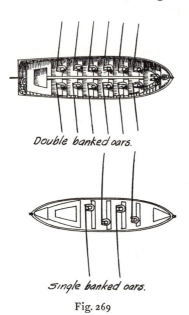

Double banked oars.

Single banked oars.

Fig. 269

The proportional length of boat's oars, outboard; for double banked boats 1.25 of beam of launch, 1.30 for first cutter, 1.40 for second cutter, 1.45 for third cutter. For single banked boats their breadth multiplied by 2.20 for fourth cutter, and whale boats; for gigs multiply by 2.5.

The second-class line-of-battle ship *North Carolina,* 209 feet long on her spar deck, 53 feet 6 inches beam, built at Philadelphia in 1820, carried twelve boats as follows:

1st launch	40 ft. long,	10 ft. 8 in. beam,	4 ft. 6 in. depth,	anchor 300 lbs.
2d launch	40 ft. long,	10 ft. 8 in. beam,	4 ft. 6 in. depth,	anchor 200 lbs.
1st cutter	36 ft. long,	9 ft. 6 in. beam,	3 ft. 6 in. depth,	anchor 150 lbs.
2d cutter	36 ft. long,	9 ft. 6 in. beam,	3 ft. 6 in. depth,	anchor 100 lbs.
3d cutter	33 ft. long,	8 ft. 5 in. beam,	3 ft. 2 in. depth,	anchor 75 lbs.
4th cutter	33 ft. long,	8 ft. 5 in. beam,	3 ft. 2 in. depth.	
5th cutter	30 ft. long,	7 ft. 6 in. beam,	2 ft. 7 in. depth.	
6th cutter	30 ft. long,	7 ft. 6 in. beam,	2 ft. 7 in. depth.	
1st whale boat	30 ft. long,	7 ft. 8 in. beam,	2 ft. 8 in. depth.	
2d whale boat	30 ft. long,	7 ft. 8 in. beam,	2 ft. 8 in. depth.	
Barge	38 ft. long,	7 ft. 2 in. beam,	2 ft. 8 in. depth.	
Gig	38 ft. long,	5 ft. 6 in. beam,	2 ft. 0 in. depth.	

The gig and barge both hung on the stern davits; the first whale boat and 5th cutter hung on the starboard quarter davits; the second whale boat and 6th cutter on the port quarter davits; the first and third cutters to starboard and the second and fourth cutters to port on the waist davits; the launches were only hoisted out when wanted for use. When stowed for sea, the odd numbered boats were stowed to starboard, the even numbered, 2, 4, 6, etc., to port. The launches were first hoisted in and stowed in their chocks on the gun deck

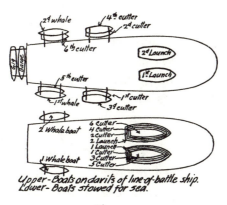

Upper-Boats on davits of line-of-battle ship.
Lower-Boats stowed for sea.

Fig. 270

in the well or opening left in the spar deck, the first and second cutters inside of the launches, the third and fourth cutters were just small enough to stow inside of them, and the fifth and sixth cutters again inside of these, all nesting together like fishermen's dories. The whale boats and stern davit boats were kept on the davits, the high sides keeping them out of water.

The steam sloop-of-war *Alliance,* of 1901, was 192 feet 6 inches long between perpendiculars and 35 feet beam, bark rigged, and carried the following boat equipment:—

4 cutters	26 ft. long,	30 men each,	120 men
1 sailing launch	28 ft. long,		36 men
1 steam cutter	28 ft. long,		35 men
2 whale boats	30 ft. long,	28 men each,	56 men
1 whale boat	28 ft. long,		23 men
1 gig (whale boat)	28 ft. 2 in. long,		16 men
1 dinghy	18 ft. long,		10 men
2 life rafts	22 ft. long,	25 men each,	50 men
			346 total

The *Alliance's* complement consisted of 15 officers, 101 apprentices and 224 in the crew, a total of 340 persons.

Navy boats are well standardized in design and have been for years. There is a book published by the United States Government called "Standard Boats of the U. S. Navy," that gives the lines, construction plans and detail drawings of every item, nail and screw in them. In one of the six volumes of ship's plans, published in France and compiled by Admiral de Paris, there is a set of plans showing the shape of each sized boat used in the French navy at that time.

Don't retain the idea that the boats of a hundred years ago were crude affairs. Human vision is so limited and each one of us sees so little of all there is to see and know that we are apt to judge by the few specimens that have come under our observation. My impression of ship's boats naturally goes back to the boats on the old Hudson River sloops that I saw so much of in my youth. I was severely and agreeably shocked one day when a man-of-war anchored up off Poughkeepsie and I saw the beautiful cutters and gig that came ashore, and had I been alive in Nelson's time, I have no doubt the boats then in use were as handsome as any today,—possibly

Boats on stern davits

Fig. 271

handsomer,—for people in those days took delight in embellishing their buildings and ships with much hand carving. There were crude boats then, just as now, among the class of poor people who have to practice economy. Crudeness belongs to a class, not to an age.

CHAPTER XVIII

DAVITS

THERE are two kinds of davits that were in use in the days of sailing ships but now, in the age of steamships, there are a dozen or more different types. Iron davits and wooden davits are the two kinds we are mostly concerned with. The iron davits were a round, tapered bar with its head bent over

Fig. 272

in an arc of a circle ending in an eye, or flattened and bored to take an eye-bolt, into which the tackle that hoists the boats could be hooked (Fig. 272).

Davits should not be made out of a parallel piece of wire. To look right, they should be tapered, particularly at the upper end. Just back of the eye the metal should be one-half of what it is at the largest part where it wears in the upper socket and at the lower end it should only be about two-thirds as big as at the upper socket.

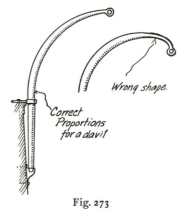

Fig. 273

Davits are made of varying heights and reach to suit the size of the boat to be hoisted, but the general character of the curve is the same. So many model makers bend the outer end of their davits down too far (Fig. 273). They look more like the ornamental street lamp posts than davits.

Everything above the height of the eye is wasted material and sailors are economical.

The eye should reach out from the center of the davit far enough to overhang the center of the boat when its side is just clear of the davit and high enough to lift the boat so that when it is swung in-board, its keel will clear the top of the ship's rail. The davit should hold the boat so that a boom (padded where it touches the boat's side) lashed from davit to davit just under where the boat's gunwale comes, will just touch the boat's side.

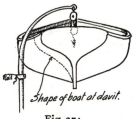

Shape of boat at davit.

Fig. 274

This boom prevents the boat from swinging on the davits and permits lashings to be passed around the boat to hold it steady (Fig. 275). These lashings are termed gripes and are made of several thicknesses of heavy canvas folded and sewed so

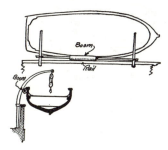

Fig. 275

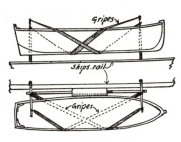

Fig. 276

as to make a flat belt about 4 or 5 inches wide, with a large iron ring in each end (Fig. 276). One end is lashed to the outer end of the davit, and is passed over, around, and brought up under the boat and made fast to the opposite davit, so that the two make an X-shaped lashing to hold the boat steady.

The davit tackles or boat falls, are rove with a various number of turns depending on the weight of the boat to be raised, but are always rove athwartships so that the hauling end leads inboard over a leader,—a

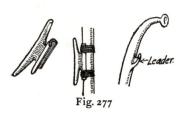

Fig. 277

flat, hook-like projection welded on to the davit to keep the rope clear of the boat's gunwale; and it belays to a cleat on the back of the davit.

A davit, with the weight of a boat hanging upon it, should not be weakened by drilling holes to rake rivets for the cleat. Some davits have the cleats welded onto them, but on most ships these cleats were made with a pad shaped to fit the round davit and these pad ends were lashed to the davit (Fig. 277).

Iron stern davits were not used until about the year 1850. In shape they were somewhat different from ship's side davits in that the bend was more sudden and the outer end straighter. A stout plank about 2 x 6 inches, was generally lashed across from one end of the davit

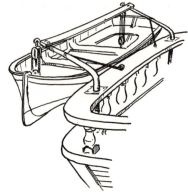

Fig. 278

to the other and iron rod braces, hooked into eyes on the side of the davits, about half-way out, were also hooked into eye-bolts in the taffrail to prevent the davits swinging as the ship heeled over (Fig. 278).

Small craft and coasters, in later years, used an iron davit that, instead of having an eye in its outer end, had two sheaves like a pulley, but the old deep-water ships carried the eye and hooked the davit fall-blocks into it (Fig. 279).

Davit guys of wire rope, or hemp, were fitted to the quarter and waist boat davits to hold them steady. One span between the two davits and one from the forward davit forward and the after davit aft, were lashed to eye-bolts in the ship's rail.

Eyesplices, with thimbles in the ends of each guy, were seized fast to the neck of the davit just inside of the eye, so they could be cast loose when the davits were lifted out and stowed away.

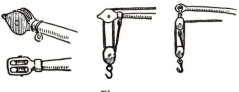

Fig. 279

Wooden davits are instantly recognizable by their clumsiness. Whalers, in particular, look so ungainly with five pairs of wooden davits sticking up in the air; but whalers cared little for looks; theirs was a dirty, homely calling and required that kind of gear. They were made extra strong, to meet all contingencies, and were about a foot square where they were bolted fast against the outside of the ship's planking and ten inches square at the top. The top or head stuck out from the ship's side at an angle of forty-five degrees.

Three sets of davits were fitted along the port side of the whaler and two on the starboard side, one aft on the quarter and one abreast of the fore rigging. The waist, amidships, on the starboard side was left clear for rigging out the cutting-in staging and hoisting in of the blubber as it was cut off in strips from the whale's carcass alongside.

Except for the small boat carried on the wooden stern davits, merchant ships, prior to 1800, carried their boats or boat stowed amidships, for most of them were small ships and only had one long boat.

Men-of-war carried the stern boat and quarter boats on wooden davits, but most of their boats were stowed "nested," one inside the other, amidships in the waist and were hoisted out by tackles from the mastheads and yard-arms.

The big, high-sided line-of-battle ships had straight timbers for davits hinged to the side just above the channels and supported by a rope span that led up to the mizzenmast just under the tops. Tackles to hoist two boats, one outside of the other, were hooked to these davits.

APPENDIX

WITH TABLES

DIMENSIONS OF THE SPARS OF A 200-TON ENGLISH MERCHANT BRIG OF 1750

| | Mast | | Yard | |
	Length ft.	Diameter in.	Length ft.	Diameter in.
Main	56	19	42	9¾
Maintop	31	10	31½	8¼
Main-topgallant	23½	6¼	23½	5
Main-royal			15¾	3½
Fore	49	17	42	9¾
Foretop	31	10	31½	7
Fore-topgallant	23½	6¼	23½	5
Fore-royal			15	3½
Bowsprit	34	17	31½	7
Jib-boom	24	7	23½	5
Main boom	45	10½		
Main gaff	28	7¼		
Lower studding-sail boom . .	23½	4¾	13½	2¾
Main-topsail studding boom . .	21	4⅛	12	2½
Main-topgallant studding boom .	11¾	2¼	6¾	2
Fore-topsail studding boom . .	21	4⅛	12	2½
Fore-topgallant studding boom .	11¾	2¼	6¾	2

The depth of hold is added to the length and breadth of the ship and ½ = the length of the mainmast.

DIMENSIONS OF SPARS ON TWO ENGLISH SHIPS OF ABOUT 1750

Size of spars on Captain Bowman's ship.

Length, 76 ft. 6 in. on lower deck; 22 ft. 6 in. beam. Tonnage, 162.

	Length ft.	Diameter in.	Yard-length ft.
Main	60	16	41
Maintop . . .	32	10	31
Main-topgallant . .	17	5	24
Fore	54	15½	36
Foretop . . .	28½	9½	28
Fore-topgallant . .	15	4½	22
Mizzen	50	11	20
Mizzentop . . .	25	6	25
Bowsprit . . .	34½	16½	30
Crossjack yard . .			30

Size of spars on Captain Kennedy's ship.

Length, 81 ft. 8 in. on lower deck; 23 ft. beam. Tonnage, 182.

	Length ft.	Diameter in.	Yard-length ft.
Main	62	16½	44
Maintop . . .	33	10	32
Main-topgallant . .	18	5½	24
Fore	56	16½	39
Foretop . . .	30	9½	30
Fore-topgallant . .	16	5	22
Mizzen	53	11	40
Mizzentop . . .	28	6½	24
Bowsprit . . .	36	16½	

Crossjack yard and spritsail yard, 32 ft.
Spritsail-topsail yard, 24 ft.

DIMENSIONS OF SPARS OF MERCHANT SHIP OF 400 TONS, YEAR 1800

	Length ft.	Diameter in.		Length ft.	Diameter in.
Mainmast	72	22	Main yard	52	13
Maintopmast . . .	43	14	Main-topsail yard . .	41	10½
Main-topgallant mast .	23	8	Main-topgallant yard .	31	7
Main-royal mast . . .	15	5	Main-royal yard . . .	20	5
Foremast	67	22	Fore yard	52	12⅛
Foretopmast . . .	41	14	Fore-topsail yard . .	41	10½
Fore-topgallant mast .	22	8	Fore-topgallant yard .	28	6½
Fore-royal mast . . .	14	5	Fore-royal yard . . .	19	5
Mizzenmast	63	15	Mizzen yard (crossjack) .	44	19
Mizzentopmast . . .	30	10	Mizzen-topsail yard . .	32	8
Mizzen-topgallant mast .	17	5½	Mizzen-topgallant yard .	21	5
Bowsprit	48	23	Spritsail yard . . .	39	8½
Jib-boom	35	10	Mizzen gaff	32	8
Driver boom	46	9			

UNITED STATES SPARRING SYSTEM, OF 1840, FOR SCHOONERS

Divide length between perpendiculars into 756 parts. From forward perpendicular to foremast = 192 parts; foremast to mainmast = 258 parts. Masts rake ⅝ to ⅞ inch to foot.

Hoist of sails = 2⅔ times the beam.

Foot of foresail = 336 parts.

Foot of mainsail = 408 parts.

One half the foot of mainsail = length for both fore and main gaffs.

Foot of jibs = 348 parts.

This applies to fast sailing coasting vessels, but wide flat centerboard schooners have greater sails.

UNITED STATES SPARRING SYSTEM, OF 1840, FOR SLOOPS

Hoist of mainsail = 2½ beams.
Foot of mainsail = 3 beams + depth of hold.
After leech of mainsail = 3 beams + 3 times the depth of hold.
Jibstay the same length as after leech of mainsail.
After leech of jib same as hoist of mainsail.
Gaff = beam + 3 times the depth of hold.
Foot of jib same as after leech of jib.
Mast ¾ of the sloop's beam from forward part of the deck and to rake aft ½ inch to the foot.
For masting brigs the foremast is put ⅖ of the vessel's length from forward perpendicular; mainmast ⅗ or ½ the distance from foremast to after perpendicular.

UNITED STATES SPARRING SYSTEM, OF 1840, FOR SHIPS

Divide length between perpendiculars into 760 parts. From forward perpendicular to foremast = 150 parts; foremast to mainmast = 264 parts; mainmast to mizzenmast = 211 parts; mizzenmast to after perpendicular = 135 parts. This gives you the spacing of the masts fore and aft on the ship.
Mainmast = $11\frac{1}{20}$ of the length.
Foremast = $18\frac{}{19}$ of the mainmast.
Mizzenmast = $17\frac{}{19}$ of the mainmast.
Maintopmast = $10\frac{}{19}$ of the mainmast.
Main-topgallant mast = $12\frac{2}{23}$ of the main topmast.
Main-royal = $14\frac{}{20}$ of the main-topgallant mast.
Main-skysail = $10\frac{}{14}$ of the main-royal mast.
All other masts on foremast are $18\frac{}{19}$ that on the mainmast.
All other masts on mizzenmast are $17\frac{}{19}$ that on the mainmast.
Main yard = ⅞ of the length of mainmast.
Main-topsail yard = $14\frac{}{17}$ of main yard.
Main-topgallant yard = $37\frac{}{49}$ of main-topsail yard.
Main-royal yard = $28\frac{}{37}$ of main-topgallant yard.
Main-skysail yard = $20\frac{}{28}$ of main-royal yard.
All other yards on foremast are $18\frac{}{19}$ that on the mainmast.
All other yards on mizzenmast are $17\frac{}{19}$ that on the mainmast.
Crossjack = $17\frac{}{19}$ of main yard.
Mizzen-topsail yard = $14\frac{}{17}$ of crossjack.
Bowsprit outboard = ⅛ foremast.
Jib-boom = $18\frac{}{24}$ of outboard part of bowsprit.
Spanker boom = ½ length of foremast.
Spanker gaff = $25\frac{}{36}$ length of spanker boom.

DIMENSIONS OF MASTS AND SPARS OF THE FRIGATE *ESSEX*

Taken from the original manuscript given the Peabody Museum, Salem, February, 1892, by Mrs. George P. Farrington, granddaughter of Enos Briggs, the builder of the Essex, *in Salem, Mass., in 1797.*

Dimensions of the *Essex* frigate, viz.: 118 feet keel, 37 feet beam; 27 inches deadrising; 850²⁹⁄₉₅ tons; gun deck, 141 feet; depth of hold, 12 feet 3 inches; height between gun deck and lower deck, 5 feet 9 inches; depth of waist (bulwarks), 6 feet; height under quarter-deck, 6 feet 3 inches.

	Length ft.	Head ft.	Diameter in.
Mainmast	85	12	27
Foremast	75½	11½	26
Mizzenmast	71½	10	21
Maintopmast	55	7½	18½
Foretopmast	51	7	18½
Mizzentopmast	40	6	14
Bowsprit	54		26
Jib-boom	40		14
		Royal	
Main-topgallant mast	40	15	12
Fore-topgallant mast	37	14	11½
Mizzen-topgallant mast	33	12	9½
Main yard	80		20
Fore yard	72		19
Crossjack yard	52		14
Main-topsail yard	58		14
Fore-topsail yard	52		13½
Mizzen-topsail yard	40		10½
Spritsail yard	52		13½
Spritsail topsail yard	35		10
Main-topgallant sail yard	37		10
Fore-topgallant sail yard	35		9½
Mizzen-topgallant sail yard	28		7½
Main-royal yard	30		7
Fore-royal yard	27		6
Mizzen royal yard	20		5
Mizzen boom	57		14
Mizzen gaff	46		11

DIMENSIONS OF SPARS ON BRIG *HASSAN-BASHAW*

*Designed and built by J. Humphreys in 1794—presented by the United States
to the Dey of Algiers as tribute to permit American merchant
ships to pass unmolested.*

To have 4½ ft. waist, fitted with gangway, light quarter-deck, fo'csle head
and light orlop deck. Brig, 75 ft. keel; 27 ft. beam; to carry 18 six-
pound cannon.

	Length ft. in.		Head ft. in.		Yard ft.	Diameter ft. in.	
Foremast	56	8	8	3	48	2	3
Foretopmast	36	0	5	0	36	2	3
Fore-topgallant mast . . .	29	0	10	0	25		12
Mainmast	73	0	8	0	42	1	8
Maintopmast	33	0	4	9	33	2	0
Main-topgallant mast . . .	27	0	9	0	22		12
Fore-royal yard	20	0					12
Main-royal yard . . .	17	0					

Boom, 12 ft. over the stern. Gaff, 30 ft. long.
Bowsprit, 27 ft. outside stem.
Jib-boom, 29 ft.
Foretop to be 13½ ft.
Maintop to be 12 ft.

DIMENSIONS OF SPARS ON SCHOONER *SKJOLDEBRAND*

*Carrying 16 four-pound cannon. Designed by J. Humphreys and built by
Nathaniel Hutton, in 1794. Presented by the United States
to the Dey of Algiers as tribute.*

Dimensions: 62 ft. keel, 23 ft. beam, 11 ft. hold; to have 4 ft. 3 in. solid waist
(bulwarks) and to have quarter-deck and roundhouse.

Mainmast	76 ft. long	7 ft. head	34 ft. topmast	11 ft. head
Foremast	70 ft. long	8 ft. head	37 ft. topmast	13 ft. head
Fore-crossjack yard		35 ft. arms 12 in.		
Fore-topsail yard		24 ft. arms 12 in.		
Fore-topgallant yard		17 ft. arms 9 in.		
Main-crossjack yard		32 ft. arms 12 in.		
Main-topsail yard		22 ft. arms 9 ft.		
Main-topgallant yard		15 ft. arms 6 in.		

Fore gaff   24 ft. long.   Main gaff   20 ft. long.
Bowsprit   21 ft. outboard.   Jib-boom   23 ft.
Main boom   10 ft. over the stern.

Designed by Daniel Westervelt, built by his father, Jacob Westervelt, of New York.

Length of keel, 216 ft.; length on deck, 228 ft.; beam, 41 ft. 6 in.; depth of hold, 21 ft. 6 in.

	Length					
Foremast	86 ft.	dia. 3 ft.	head 15 ft.	yard 78 ft.	arm 5 ft.	dia. 1 ft. 9 in.
Foretopmast	49 ft.	dia. 1 ft. 6 in.	head 8 ft. 7 in.	yard 62 ft. 6 in.	arm 5 ft. 6 in.	dia. 1 ft. 5 in.
Fore-topgallant	32 ft. 6 in.	dia. 1 ft. ½ in.	head 5 ft. 3 in.	yard 43 ft. 6 in.	arm 2 ft. 9 in.	dia. 11½ in.
Fore-royal	20 ft.			yard 33 ft.	arm 2 ft.	dia. 9½ in.
Fore-skysail	12 ft.		pole 7 ft. 6 in.	yard 27 ft.	arm 1 ft. 6 in.	dia. 6 in.
Mainmast	90 ft.	dia. 3 ft. in.	head 15 ft.	yard 83 ft.	arm 5 ft.	dia. 1 ft. 10 in.
Maintopmast	51 ft.	dia. 1 ft. 6½ in.	head 9 ft.	yard 67 ft.	arm 5 ft. 6 in.	dia. 1 ft. 5 in.
Main-topgallant	34 ft.	dia. 1 ft. 1 in.	head 5 ft. 6 in.	yard 48 ft.	arm 2 ft. 9 in.	dia. 1 ft.
Main-royal	21 ft.			yard 38 ft.	arm 2 ft.	dia. 9½ in.
Main-skysail	13 ft.	dia. 10½ in.	pole 9 ft.	yard 31 ft.	arm 1 ft. 6 in.	dia. 7½ in.
Mizzenmast	82 ft.	dia. 2 ft. 5 in.	head 13 ft.	yard 65 ft.	arm 3 ft. 10 in.	dia. 1 ft. 5½ in.
Mizzentopmast	42 ft.	dia. 1 ft. 3 in.	head 8 ft.	yard 50 ft. 3 in.	arm 4 ft.	dia. 1 ft.
Mizzen-topgallant	29 ft.	dia. 11 in.	head 4 ft. 6 in.	yard 35 ft. 3 in.	arm 2 ft. 3 in.	dia. 9 in.
Mizzen-royal	16 ft.			yard 26 ft. 6 in.	arm 1 ft.	dia. 6 in.
Mizzen-skysail	10 ft.		pole 6 ft.	yard 21 ft.	arm 1 ft.	dia. 5 in.
Bowsprit outboard	26 ft.	square 2 ft. 9 in.				
Inner jib-boom	16 ft.					
Outer jib-boom	15 ft. 3 in.					
Flying jib-boom	50 ft.	dia. 10 in.	outboard 10 ft.	pole 5 ft.		
Spanker boom	56 ft.					
Spanker gaff	47 ft.	dia. 10 in.				
Swinging booms	49 ft.	dia. 10 in.				
Topmast-studding-sail boom	50 ft. 11 in.					
Topgallant-studding-sail boom	42 ft.					
Royal-studding-sail boom	34 ft.					

Foremast 47 ft. abaft the knight-heads on main deck.

Mainmast 67 ft. abaft foremast.

Mizzenmast 60 ft. abaft mainmast and 50 ft. to stern.

Width abreast the foremast on the main rail outside of bulwarks	38 ft.
Width abreast the mainmast on the main rail outside of bulwarks	41 ft.
Width abreast the mizzenmast on the main rail outside of bulwarks	33 ft.
Width across the stern	27 ft.

DIMENSIONS OF UNITED STATES 44-GUN FRIGATES

	Constitution	United States	Guerrière
	1576	1576	1507
Tonnage	1576	1576	1507
Length on gun deck from rabbet of stem to rabbet of stern-post	174 ft. 10½ in.	175 ft.	175 ft.
Length of keel	145 ft.		145 ft.
Extreme beam (molded)	43 ft. 6 in.	43 ft. 6 in.	44 ft. 6 in.
Extreme beam over all			
Height of wing transom above rabbet of keel	25 ft. 8½ in.		
Height of lower deck transom	20 ft. 9 in.		
Height between gun deck and lower deck	6 ft. 4 in.		
Depth of hold	14 ft. 3 in.		
Fore side knight-heads to center foremast			29 ft. 7 in.
Center of foremast to center mainmast			78 ft. 1¼ in.
Center of mainmast to center of mizzen			44 ft. 5 in.
Center of mizzen to taffrail			31 ft. 10 in.
Beam at foremast			40 ft. 10½ in.
Depth top of keelson to spar deck at foremast			26 ft.
Width of channel			3 ft. 2 in.
Length of channel			36 ft. 6 in.
Width of foretop			20 ft. 6 in.
Length of foretop			12 ft. 11 in.
Beam at mainmast			41 ft. 2¼ in.
Depth top of keelson to spar deck at mainmast			27 ft. ¾ in.
Width of channel			2 ft. 10 in.
Length of channel			36 ft. 6 in.
Width of maintop			22 ft. 10 in.
Length of maintop			14 ft. 1 in.

DIMENSIONS OF UNITED STATES 44-GUN FRIGATES

	Constitution	United States	Guerrière
Beam at mizzenmast			35 ft. 6 in.
Depth top of poop deck to spar deck at mizzen .			20 ft.
Width of channel			2 ft. 7 in.
Length of channel			22 ft.
Width of mizzentop			17 ft. 2 in.
Length of mizzentop			11 ft. 5 in.
Depth at mizzen of breast from top of channel to the rail .			3 ft. 6 in.
Rake foremast			square with deck
Mainmast rakes			½ in. in 3 ft.
Mizzenmast rakes			1¾ in. in 3 ft.
Height gun deck to upper deck . . .	7 ft.		
Depth at mainmast top of keelson to spar deck .			27 ft. ¾ in.

DIMENSIONS OF UNITED STATES 44-GUN FRIGATE'S SPARS IN 1815

Copied from letter book of Commander T. Macdonough of the Constitution.

	Constitution						*United States*						*Guerrière*					
	Length		Dia.		Head Arm		Length		Dia.		Head Arm		Length		Dia.		Head Arm	
	ft.	in.	ft.	in.	ft.	in.	ft.	in.	ft.	in.	ft.	in.	ft.	in.	ft.	in.	ft.	in.
Foremast	94		2	7	16		89	9½	2	6½	11	6	93				16	
Foretopmast	56				10		59		1	6¾	8	9	58				9	4
Fore-topgallant	31						32	11		10½	5	1½	28					
Fore-royal	20	6					19	11		7½			20	8				
Fore-skysail pole	36						17	1		6			36					
Mainmast	104		2	10	18	6	101	6½	3		17		104				18	
Maintopmast	62				10	4	63	2	1	6¾	9		62				10	
Main-topgallant	33						35	10		11	5		31					
Main-royal	22						22			7½			23					
Main-skysail pole	39						18			6			40					
Mizzenmast	81		1	11	13	2							83	3			14	
Mizzentopmast	48				8		45	9	1	2¼	6	7	48	6			7	9
Mizzen-topgallant	26						26	8½		7¼	3	5	22					
Mizzen-royal	17						16	2		4½			17					
Mizzen-skysail pole	30						13			4			30					
Fore yard	81				4		81	6	1	9			81	8	1	¼	4	9
Fore-topsail	62	2			6	3	65	6	1	2	5	6	61	3	1	3¼	5	
Fore-topgallant	45				2	3	41	6		8¾	2		40			10	2	
Fore-royal	28						29	2		6¼	1		27			6⅛	1	1
Fore-skysail							24			4			18	1		4¼		8
Main yard	95				4	6	92	2	1	11¾	4		94		1	11½	4	9
Main-topsail	70	6			6	6	69	9	1	2½	5	6	69	6	1	5¼	5	10
Main-topgallant	46				2	3	48	6		9	2		45			11¼	2	6
Main-royal	30						33			6¾	1	2	30			7¼	1	7

DIMENSIONS OF UNITED STATES 44-GUN FRIGATE'S SPARS IN 1815

Copied from letter book of Commander T. Macdonough of the Constitution.

All dimensions given as ft. in. (Head–Arm measured in ft. in.; diameters in ft. in. or in. only.)

Spar	Constitution			United States			Guerrière		
	Length	Dia.	Head Arm	Length	Dia.	Head Arm	Length	Dia.	Head Arm
Main-skysail				24	4¼		20	5	10
Mizzen yard	75 3		6 6	69 6	1 ¾	4 6	72	1 6	4 3
Mizzen-topsail	49		5	52	9	3	46	11½	3 2
Mizzen-topgallant	32		3	30 6	8	1 6	30	7¼	1 6
Mizzen-royal	20			22	5	9½	17 5	4¾	10
Mizzen-skysail				16 4	3¾		12 4	3¼	5
Bowsprit	65 3			65	2 8		65		
Spritsail yard				60			61		
Spanker boom	62			66	1 10	4 6	62	1 5¼	5
Spanker gaff	40			46 9			30		
Jib-boom	53			48 6	1 1½	1 2	43		
Flying jib boom				58	9		53		
Lower studding sail boom				54 2	10¼	10	51 3		
Jib of jib-booms				42	8¼	4		10	
Ringtail boom							30		
Foretopmast stud boom							35		*Yard*
Main							42	8¾	25 9
Mizzen							47	11	20
Fore-topgallant stud boom									
Main							30 7	6½	18 6
Mizzen							34 9	7½	20
Fore-royal stud boom							23		
Main							22		
Mizzen							15		

DIMENSIONS OF THE MASTS AND SPARS OF THE 74-GUN UNITED STATES SHIP *WASHINGTON*

Copied from 1815 letter book of Commander T. Macdonough.

	Length ft.	in.	Diameter in. and 10th.	Mast head ft.	in.
Bowsprit*	75				
Foremast†	104	4	32.8	17	4
Mainmast	116		36.6	19	4
Mizzenmast‡	96		26.	16	
Foretopmast (exclusive of heel block) .	62	6	20.	10	4
Maintopmast (exclusive of heel block) .	69	7	21.	11	7
Mizzentopmast (exclusive of heel block) .	56		16.	9	2
Fore-topgallant mast (exclusive of pole) .	31	2	11.8		
Main-topgallant mast (exclusive of pole) .	34	7	12.7		
Mizzen-topgallant mast (exclusive of pole)	27	6	9.2		
Fore-royal mast	24		8.8		
Main-royal mast	26	11	9.5		
Mizzen-royal mast	20	10	7.		
Fore-skysail mast 16					
Royal mast 24	40		5.9		
Main-skysail mast 18					
Royal mast 26	11	44	11	6.	
Mizzen-skysail mast . . . 14					
Royal mast 20	10	34	10	4.7	

	Length ft.	in.	Diameter in. and 10th.	Yard arm ft.	in.
Spritsail yard§	69	10	4.7	7	
Fore yard	93	7	20.	4	2
Main yard	104	1	21.9	5	3
Mizzen (crossjack) yard	78		16.	7	9
Fore-topsail yard	69	10	16.2	7	
Main-topsail yard	78		18.	7	9
Mizzen-topsail yard	53	7	12.4	5	9
Fore-topgallant yard	44		10.1	2	2
Main-topgallant yard	49		11.2	2	6

* To house ⅛ its length.

† The diameters of lower masts are calculated for yellow pine, with oak cheeks to extend down to receive the wedges of the berth or lower gun deck. Consequently if white pine be used, the masts ought to be ⅟₁₅ more in diameter.

‡ It is calculated that the mizzenmast is to step on the orlop deck.

§ Lower yards in the slings to be the same size as topmasts in the caps, if made of white pine, but if made of yellow pine to be 1 inch for every 5 feet the yards are long.

DIMENSIONS OF THE MASTS AND SPARS OF THE 74-GUN UNITED STATES SHIP *WASHINGTON*

Copied from 1815 letter book of Commander T. Macdonough by C. G. Davis in 1922.

	Length		Diameter	Mast head	
	ft.	in.	in. and 10th.	ft.	in.
Mizzen-topgallant yard	34		7.6	1	7
Fore-royal yard	31	4	7.2	1	3
Main-royal yard	35		8.	1	5
Mizzen-royal yard	24	3	5.5		11
Fore-skysail yard	22	2	5.		
Main-skysail yard	25		5.9		
Mizzen-skysail yard	15	10	3.9		
Jib-boom	56	3	16.9		
Flying jib boom	56	3	11.3		
Spanker boom	70	6	14.1		
Spanker gaff	49	4	8.8		
Lightning conductors—foremast . . .	200	4			
Mainmast	224	2			
Mizzenmast	185	2			

Shrouds to foremast   10 each side, topmast 6, topgallant 3.
Shrouds to mainmast   11 each side, topmast 7, topgallant 3.
Shrouds to mizzenmast   7 each side, topmast 5, topgallant 3.

AVERAGE PROPORTIONS OF THE SPARS OF MERCHANT VESSELS OF THE LARGEST CLASS AS FORMERLY BUILT

From Seaman's Manual (American), 1840.

Mainmast = 2½ times ship's beam; diameter, 1¼ in. per 3 ft. at deck; middle, 9/10; hounds, ⅔.
Foremast = 8/9 of mainmast.
Mizzenmast = 5/6 of mainmast.
Bowsprit = ⅔ of mainmast.
Topmasts = ⅗ of lower masts.
Topgallant masts = ½ of topmasts.
Main yard = 2 beams; diameter 1 in. at slings per 4 ft. (½ in. within squares).
Fore yard = ⅞ main yard.
Main-topsail yard = ⅔ main yard.
Fore-topsail yard = ⅔ fore yard.
Crossjack yard = main-topsail yard.

Topgallant yards = ⅔ topsail yards.
Mizzen-topsail yard = main-topgallant yard.
Royal yards = ⅔ topgallant yards.
Spritsail yard = ⅚ fore-topsail yard.
Spanker boom = main-topsail yard.
Spanker gaff = ⅔ spanker boom.
Breadth of maintop = ½ beam of ship.
Breadth of foretop = ⅚ maintop.

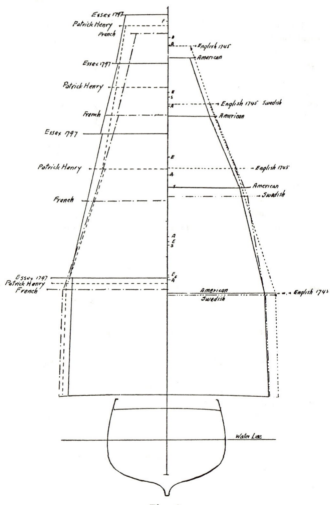

Fig. 280

SWEDISH SYSTEM OF SPARRING SHIPS

Mainmast height $= 2.23 \times$ beam, $^{11}\!/_{12}$ of this for merchant ship; head, $^{5}\!/_{36}$. Foremast is lower than the mainmast by $2.22 \times \frac{1}{8}$ of the head for frigates, $2 \times \frac{1}{8}$ head for merchant ships.

Maintopmast (top of crosstrees to top of maintop), $\dfrac{^{11}\!/_{10} \text{ mainmast}}{2.73}$ for frigates, $\dfrac{^{11}\!/_{10} \text{ mainmast}}{2.84}$ for trading ship.

Bowsprit (outboard), beam $\times 1.15$ for frigates; beam $\times 1.1$ for trading ship.

Mizzentopmast $= 1.3 \times \frac{6}{7}$ of maintopmast for frigates; $1.316 \times \frac{6}{7}$ of maintopmast for trading ship.

Head of foremast $= \frac{9}{10}$ of mainmasthead; mizzenhead $= \frac{3}{4}$ of mainmasthead.

Foretopmast $= \frac{9}{10}$ of maintopmast; head $\frac{1}{9}$ or $\frac{9}{17}$ of their length.

Fore-topgallant mast $= .54 \times$ topmast.

Length of main yard $=$ length of ship (post to post) $\times .52$ for frigate; $.6 \times \frac{20}{21}$ of length for trader.

Length of main-topsail yard $= .79$ of main yard for frigate; $.81$ of main yard for trader.

Length of main-topgallant yard $= .7$ of main-topsail yard.

All yards on the foremast are $\frac{9}{10}$ of those on the mainmast.

Mizzen-topsail yard is same per cent of its mast as main-topsail yard is to maintopmast.

Crossjack yard $= 1.22 \times$ mizzen-topsail yard for frigate; $1.18 \times$ mizzen-topsail yard for trader.

Spritsail yard $=$ fore-topsail yard.

Sprit-topsail yard $=$ foretopgallant yard.

Yardarms of lower and topgallant yards $= \frac{1}{11}$ their length; topsail yard arms $= \frac{1}{7}$.

Foremast $= \frac{4}{31}$ aft of perpendicular at stem; mainmast $= \frac{2}{31}$ aft of middle of ship; mizzenmast $= .182 \times$ length of the ship forward of after perpendicular.

Mainmast to rake aft, 1 ft. in 30 ft.; mizzenmast to rake double that of main; foremast to stand perpendicular.

Steeve of bowsprit $= 4$ ft. up in 7 ft. for frigates; 3 ft. up in 7 ft. for traders.

Diameter of mainmast $=$ length of mast $\times \frac{1}{8}$ length of main yard $\div 13$.

Diameter of maintopmast $= ^{11}\!/_{10}$ mainmast $\div 4.68$.

Diameter of foremast $\frac{1}{20}$ less than mainmast.

Diameter of foretopmast $\frac{1}{20}$ less than maintopmast.

Diameter of topgallant masts $= .3$ their length.

Diameter of bowsprit $=$ the mean between diameter of main- and foremasts.

Diameter of jib-boom $= \frac{3}{4}$ that of the maintopmast.

Diameter of mizzenmast $= \frac{2}{3}$ that of the mainmast.

Diameter of mizzentopmast $= \frac{2}{3}$ that of the maintopmast.

Diameter of main and fore yards in inches $= .25 \times$ length of the yards.

Diameter of topsail yards $= .23 \times$ length of yards.

Diameter of topgallant yards = 1/6 their length.
Diameter of crossjack and spritsail yard = .21 × their length.
Diameter of sprit-topsail yard = diameter of main-topgallant yard.
Diameter of mizzen gaff = 1 in. for every 4 ft. in length.
Studding-sail booms have 2 ft. more length than 1/2 the yard and their diameter in inches is 1/5 or 1/6 their length.
Depth of main trestle-trees in inches = 1/4 topmast in feet less 1/2 in.
Depth of fore trestle-trees = 1/15 less than main.
Depth of mizzen trestle-trees = 3/5 of the main.
Thickness of topmast crosstrees = 3/7 that of trestle-trees of respective tops.
Breadth of topmast crosstrees = 5/7 or 3/4 of their depth.
Thickness of caps = 4/5 the diameter of topmasts.
Lower masts taper 1/8 smaller at trestle-trees than at deck.
Topmasts taper 1/5 smaller at crosstress than at cap of lower masts.
Bowsprits taper 1/2 at cap to what it is at gammoning.
Schooners—masts to hounds = 3 × beam.
Sloops—whole mast = 3 × beam.
East India ships: mainmast = 2.43 × beam; maintopmast = .586 × mainmast.
Cap of foremast = 2/5 of mainmasthead lower than cap on mainmast; main yard = .54 × length of ship; topsail yard = .8 × main yard; topgallant yard = .7 topsail yard; mizzentopmast = 3/4 foretopmast. Other masts and yards same as for frigates given.

DANISH RULE FOR MASTING

Ships: center of foremast 1/8 to 1/9 LWL aft, to rake 1/2° to 1°.
Center of mainmast 1/14 to 1/15 aft of center of LWL, to rake 3/4° to 2°.
Center of mizzenmast 1/6 to 4/25 forward of aft end of LWL, to rake 2° to 5°.
Steeve of bowsprit 20° to 25°.
Bark: center of foremast 1/6 to 1/7 LWL aft.
Center of mainmast 1/12 aft of center of LWL.
Center of mizzenmast 1/6 to 4/25 forward of aft end of LWL.
Brigs: center of foremast 1/6 to 1/7 LWL aft, to rake 1° to 3°.
Center of mainmast 1/8 to 1/9 aft of center of LWL, to rake 3° to 5°.
Steeve of bowsprit 15° to 25°.
Schooners: center of foremast 1/4 to 1/5 LWL aft, to rake 4° to 10°.
Center of mainmast 1/8 to 1/9 aft of center of LWL, to rake 6° to 10°.
Steeve of bowsprit 8° to 10°.
Sloops: center of mast 1/3 to 3/8 aft of forward perpendicular, to rake 0° to 4°.
Steeve of bowsprit 6° to 8°.
Ships: mast whole length = beam × 2 + depth of hold; head, 1/8 to 1/9; diameter = 1 in. every 3½ ft.
Topmast = beam + depth; head 1/6; diameter = 1 in. every 3 ft.
Topgallant mast = 1/2 to 2/3 topmast; diameter = 1 in. every 3 ft.
Royal = 1/2 to 2/3 topgallant; pole = 1/2.

Main yard, whole length = beam × 2 or 1⅝; arms 1/16 long; diameter = 1 in. every 4 ft.

Topsail yard = ¾ main yard; arms ⅛ long; diameter = 1 in. every 4 ft.

Topgallant yard = ⅔ of topsail yard; diameter = 1 in. to 4 ft.

Royal = ½ to ⅔ of topgallant yard; diameter = 1 in. to 5 ft.

Foremast = ⅖ of length of main masthead shorter than main. Other diameters are 8/9 or 9/10 that of the main; mizzenmast, ⅔ to ¾ of the mainmast.

Barks: mainmast same as ship; mizzen same length as main; masthead = 1/7 its length; diameter = 1 in. to 4½ ft.

Spanker boom = ⅕ its length outboard; diameter = 1 in. to 4 ft.

Gaff = ⅔ or ¾ length of boom; diameter = 1 in. to 3½ ft.

Bowsprit outboard = ⅘ to ⅚ molded beam; diameter same as foremast.

Jib-boom outboard = 8/9 of bowsprit.

Schooners: whole length of mainmast = 3 to 3¼ times extreme beam.

Diameter, 1 in. to 4 ft. length; masthead = ⅛ to 1/9 length.

Foremast = 8/9 to 9/10 mainmast; diameter = 1 in. to 4 ft.; head = ⅛ to 1/9 length.

Bowsprit outboard = ½ to ⅔ beam; diameter same as foremast.

Jib-boom outboard = ¾ of beam; diameter = 1 in. to 5 ft.

Main boom = ⅓ distance main to stern outboard; diameter = 1 in. to 5 ft.

Gaff = ⅔ to ¾ boom; diameter = 1 in. to 4 ft.

Fore gaff = 4 ft. to 6 ft. shorter than main.

Maintopmast = 2 or 3 ft. longer than ½ the lower mast.

Foretopmast = 8/9 or 9/10 of maintopmast.

Lower yard = 1¾ to 1⅚ times the beam.

Topsail yard = ¾ of lower yard.

Topgallant yard = ⅔ of topsail yard.

Sloops (if able): mast = LWL, if ordinary stability 3 × beam; head = ⅛ length; diameter = 1 in. to 4 ft.

Topmast length = deck to trestle-trees.

Bowsprit outboard = 2 ft. to 3 ft. more than beam.

Jib-boom = ⅔ to ¾ length outboard part of bowsprit.

Boom = 2 ft. to 6 ft. over the stern.

Gaff is ⅔ to ¾ beam.

ENGLISH SYSTEM OF SPARRING SHIPS

(L = length between stem and stern post on deck. B = breadth outside wales.)

Mainmast (whole length) = $\frac{L + B}{2}$; diameter = ⅞ in. to 3 ft.

Foremast = 8/9 of mainmast.

Mizzenmast = ¾ of mainmast; diameter = ⅔ main.

Maintopmast = ⅗ of mainmast; diameter = 1 in. to 3 ft.

Foretopmast = 8/9 of maintopmast.

Mizzentopmast = 5/7 of maintopmast; diameter = 7/10 of maintopmast.

Topgallantmast = ½ topmast; diameter = 1 in. to 3 ft.

Royal mast = ¾ of topgallantmast; diameter = ⅔ of topgallantmast.

Whole length bowsprit = 3/7 of mainmast; outboard = 3/4 its length; diameter = foremast.
Jib-boom outboard = same as bowsprit outboard; diameter = 1 in. to 2½ ft.
Flying jib boom outboard = 5/7 of jib-boom; diameter = 7/8 in. to 3 ft.
Main yard length = 7/8 of mainmast; diameter = .7 in. to 3 ft.
Fore yard length = 7/8 of mainmast.
Crossjack yard = same as foretopsail yard; diameter = 5/8 in. to 3 ft.
Maintopsail yard = 5/7 of main yard; diameter = 5/8 in. to 3 ft.
Foretopsail yard = 7/8 of maintopsail yard.
Mizzentopsail yard = 2/3 of maintopsail yard.
Topgallant yard = 3/5 of topsail yard.
Royal yard = ½ of topsail yard.
Mizzen (spanker) boom = same as maintopsail yard.
Mizzen gaff = 5/8 of boom; diameter = 5/8 in. to 3 ft.

FRENCH RULE FOR MASTING SHIPS

Center of foremast = .29 × length of ship forward of middle, rake 1/16 in. to 1 ft.
Center of mainmast = .155 × length of ship aft of middle, rake 1/12 in. to 1 ft.
Center of mizzenmast = .365 × length of ship aft of middle, rake 1/8 in. to 1 ft.
Whole length of mainmast = 2.33 × beam; diameter = 1 in. to 3½ ft.; head = 1/7 length.
Whole length of foremast = 2.25 × beam; diameter = 1 in. to 3½ ft.; head = 1/7 length.
Whole length of mizzenmast = 2.22 × beam; diameter = 1 in. to 4 ft.; head = 1/8 length.
Bowsprit length (outboard) = .75 × beam; diameter same as foremast.
Jib-boom length (outboard) = .66 × beam; diameter = ½ diameter of bowsprit.
Flying jib boom of outboard part of jib-boom = .5 × beam; diameter = 2/3 diameter of jib-boom.
Main yard = .5 × length of ship; diameter = 1 in. to 4 ft.; yardarms = 1/9.
Fore yard = .5 × length of ship; diameter = 1 in. to 4 ft.; yardarms = 1/9.
Topsail yards = .375 × length of ship; diameter = 1 in. to 4 ft.; yardarms = 1/7.
Topgallant yards = .25 × length of ship; diameter = 1 in. to 4 ft.; yardarms = 1/8.
Royal yards = .184 × length of ship; diameter = 1 in. to 3½ ft.; yardarms = 1/8.
Length of topmasts = 1.25 × beam; diameter = 1 in. to 3 ft.; head = 1/8 length.
Length of topgallant mast = .66 × beam; diameter = 1 in. to 3 ft.
Length of royal mast = .66 × beam; diameter = 1 in. to 5 ft.; pole = ¼ length.

Length of mizzentopmast = 1.7 × beam; diameter = 1 in. to 5 ft.; pole = 1/5 length.

Fore spencer gaff = .2 × length; diameter = 1 in. to 4 ft.

Main spencer gaff = .25 × length; diameter = 1 in. to 4 ft.

Spanker boom = .25 × length; diameter = 1 in. to 4 ft.

Spanker gaff = .154 × length; diameter = 1 in. to 3½ ft.

HERMAPHRODITE BRIG (SCHOONER BRIG)

Center of foremast = .25 × length of ship forward of center; rake = .083 ft. per ft.

Center of mainmast = .125 × length of ship aft of center; rake = .25 ft. per ft.

Mainmast, whole length = 2.895 × beam; diameter = 1/48 length of mast; head = 1/12 length.

Foremast, whole length = 2.25 × beam; diameter = 1/36 length of mast; head = 1/6 length.

Bowsprit (outboard) = .75 × beam; diameter = same as foremast.

Jib-boom (outboard) = 1.15 × beam; diameter = ½ bowsprit diameter.

Flying jib boom (outboard) = .5 × beam; diameter = 2/3 jib-boom diameter.

Maintopmast = 1.8 × beam; diameter = 1/48 length; pole = 1/5 length.

Foretopmast = 1.25 × beam; diameter = 1/36 length; pole = 1/7 length.

Fore-topgallant mast = .666 × beam; diameter = 1 in. to 3 ft.

Fore-royal mast = .68 × beam; diameter = 1 in. to 4 ft.; pole = 1/3 length.

Fore yard = .53 × length; diameter = 1/48 length; arms = 1/10 length.

Foretopsail yard = .39 × length; diameter = 1/48 length; arms = 1/6 length.

Fore-topgallant yard = .25 × length; diameter = .02 length; arms = 1/7 length.

Fore-royal yard = .184 × length; diameter = .02 length; arms = 1/7 length.

Fore gaff = .25 × length; diameter = 1 in. to 3½ ft. of length.

Main gaff = .3 × length; diameter = 1 in. to 3½ ft. of length.

Main boom = .535 × length; diameter = 1 in. to 4 ft. of length.

Steeve of bowsprit from horizontal line = .42 ft. per ft.

DIMENSIONS OF THE SAILS ON AN ENGLISH MERCHANT BRIG OF ABOUT 1750

	Head yards	Foot yards	Depth yards
Main course	13½	19	{ 9 in middle { 13½ at edges
Fore course	18	18	6½ at both
Main topsail	12½	19	{ 9¾ in middle { 10¼ at edges
Fore topsail	12½	19	{ 9½ in middle { 10 at edges
Main-topgallant sail . . .	10	14	5 at both
Fore-topgallant sail . . .	9	13	4½ at both
Main-royal	6	10	3½ at both
Fore-royal	5	9	3 at both
Main staysail		15	8½
Fore staysail		11	7
Maintopmast staysail . . .	12	14	{ 4 at luff { 12 at aft leech
Foretopmast staysail . . .		11	9½
Middle staysail	13	13	{ 4 at luff { 10 at leech
Main-topgallant staysail . .	12	12	{ 2½ at luff { 9½ at leech
Main studding sail	11	11	11 at both
Fore studding sail	10	10	9 at both
Maintopmast studding sail . .	8	11	12 at both
Foretopmast studding sail . .	7	10	11 at both
Main-topgallant studding sail .	5	8	6¼ at both
Fore-topgallant studding sail .	4	7	5¾ at both
Flying jib		16	15
Sprit sail	16	16	5 at both
Sprit topsail	10	17	5¾ at both
Driver	12	16	{ 7 at luff { 15 at leech

DIMENSIONS OF SAILS ON FRIGATE *CONSTITUTION*

(From log of Commander Thomas Macdonough, 1815)

	Head ft.	in.	Foot ft.	in.	Hoist ft.	in.	ft.	in.
Mainsail	78	6	84	6	47	6		
Main topsail	55	6	82	6	53			
Main topgallant	38		54		29	5		
Main royal	29	6	38	9	17			
Foresail	59		69		40			
Foretopsail	46		71		46			
Fore topgallant	32	6	46		29			
Fore royal	26	6	34		15	4		
Mizzen								
Mizzen topsail	36	4	56	4	42			
Mizzen topgallant	24	6	37	6	22	4		
Mizzen royal	16	6	25		15			

	Leech		Foot		Stay		Tack	
Main storm staysail	45		61		66			
Fore storm staysail	36		29		40			
Fore-topmast staysail	47	6	28	6	53	8		
Main-topmast staysail	71		54		58		30	
Main-topgallant staysail	36		40	6	44	6	11	6
Main-royal staysail	26		41	6	42		9	6
Mizzen staysail	22		28		27		12	
Mizzen-topgallant staysail	22	6	27		27		12	
Spindle staysail	30		25	8	32	6	14	6
							Hoist	
Spanker	52		58		42		34	
Jib	77		47				94	
Flying jib	70		35				84	
					Tack			
Gaff topsail	56		36	6	54	9		
Upper gaff topsail	21	3	10	6	25	9		
					Head			
Lower studding sail	42		45		45			
Foretopmast studding sail	46	6	31	6	21			
Fore-topgallant studding sail	26		25	9	17			
Fore-royal studding sail	21		16		10			
Maintopmast studding sail	52	6	35		23	6		
Main-topgallant studding sail	28		29	4	18	6		
Main-royal studding sail	21	4	16	4	10			

DIMENSIONS OF SAILS OF UNITED STATES FRIGATE *UNITED STATES*

(From letter book of Commander T. Macdonough of 1815)

	Head ft. in.	Hoist ft. in.	Foot ft. in.	ft.
Main course	81	48	97	
Main topsail	55	54 6	82	
Main topgallant	40	31 6	57	
Main royal	30	21	40	
Main skysail	22	18 6	30 6	
Fore course	74	42	74	
Fore topsail	50 10	50	75	
Fore topgallant	36	28	52 10	
Fore royal	26	19	35	
Fore skysail	20	15	25 6	
Mizzen topsail	42	39	57	
Mizzen topgallant	26	22 6	44	
Mizzen royal	19	15 6	26	
Mizzen skysail	14	11 6	19 6	
Maintopmast studding sail . . .	22	54	36	
Main-topgallant studding sail . .	19	35	30	
Main-royal studding sail . . .	12	21	17	
Foretopmast studding sail . . .	20	50	33	
Fore-topgallant studding sail . .	17	33	28	
Fore-royal studding sail . . .	11 6	19	16	

	Leech	Foot	Stay	Square tack
Maintopmast staysail	48	48	54	30
Main-topgallant staysail . . .	47	38	39	10
Main-royal staysail	35	28	39	10
Foretopmast staysail	48	27	51	
Mizzen-topgallant staysail . . .	41	29	30	9
Mizzen-royal staysail	22	27	28	
Middle staysail	44	39	40	20
Standing jib	72	47	98	
Flying jib	70	34	90	
			Head	
Spanker	52	64	44	34
Main storm stay	49	55	75	
Fore storm stay	35	33	45	
Mizzen storm stay	36	35	50	

DIMENSIONS OF THE SAILS OF UNITED STATES 74-GUN SHIP
WASHINGTON

(*From record of Thos. B. Kendall, sailmaker.*)

	Head ft. in.	Leech ft. in.	Foot ft. in.	Hoist ft. in.
Foresail	78	42 6	78	
Fore-topsail	50	52	77	
Fore-topgallant sail	37	31	48	
Fore royal	26	23 6	36	
Fore skysail	19	14	25	
Mainsail	86 6	49	98	
Main topsail	57	59	87	
Main-topgallant sail	39	34	56	
Main royal	29 6	26	40 6	
Main skysail	21	15	27	
Mizzen topsail	37 6	48	55 6	
Mizzen topgallant sail	28	26 6	38 5	
Mizzen royal	20	20	28	
Mizzen skysail	12	18	13	
Spanker	45	54	66	36 6
Fore-topmast staysail		55	31 6	60
Jib		82	60	105
Flying jib		73	34	87
Jib of jibs		62	27	72
Main-topmast staysail	73 6	56	64 6	31 6
Middle staysail	32	36	39	19 6
Main-topgallant staysail	33	34	38	12
Main-topgallant upper staysail	27 6	30	33	14
Mizzen staysail	39	38	38	32
Mizzen-topmast staysail	36	33	36	12
Fore storm staysail		44 6	31	51
Main storm staysail		49	67	82
Mizzen storm staysail		36	37	51
Fore lower studding sail	57	47 6	57	
Fore-topmast studding sail	22	49 inner / 54 outer	38	
Fore-topgallant studding sail	17	29 inner / 33 outer	33	
Main-topmast studding sail	26	57 inner / 62 outer	41	
Main-topgallant studding sail	19	34 inner / 35 outer	34	
Ring tail	13	59 inner / 51 outer	24	
Gaff topsail		69	43	Stay 65

DIMENSIONS OF STANDING RIGGING OF 74-GUN SHIP-OF-THE-LINE *WASHINGTON*, 1815

	Circumference: in.	Pair
Fore shrouds	11½	10
Main shrouds	11½	11
Mizzen shrouds	8	7
Fore stay	17	
Main stay	18	
Mizzen stay	12	
Fore spring stay	12¾	
Main spring stay	14	
Fore-topmast shrouds	6¾	6
Main-topmast shrouds	6¾	7
Mizzen-topmast shrouds	5⅛	5
Fore-topmast stay	10¼	
Main-topmast stay	10¼	
Mizzen-topmast stay	7¼	
Fore-topmast spring stay	7½	
Main-topmast spring stay	7½	
Mizzen-topmast spring stay	5½	
Fore-topmast back stay	9¼	
Main-topmast back stay	10	
Mizzen-topmast back stay	7	
Fore-topmast breast back stay	8	
Main-topmast breast back stay	8¾	
Mizzen-topmast breast back stay	6	
Fore-topgallant shrouds	5	3
Main-topgallant shrouds	5½	3
Mizzen-topgallant shrouds	4	3
Fore-topgallant backstays	6½	
Main-topgallant backstays	7	
Mizzen-topgallant backstays	5¼	
Fore-topgallant breast backstay	5½	
Main-topgallant breast backstay	6	
Mizzen-topgallant breast backstay	4	

TABLE SHOWING THE NUMBER OF SHROUDS TO EACH MAST FOR EVERY CLASS OF VESSEL IN THE UNITED STATES NAVY, 1844

Shrouds	Ship-of-the-Line			Razee	Frigates		Sloop of War			Brig	Schooner	Mace-donian
	120-gun	74-gun 1st class	74-gun 2d class		44-gun	36-gun	1st class	2d class	3d class			
Fore	10	10	10	10	9	8	6	6	5	5	4	7
Foretop	6	6	6	6	5	5	4	4	3	3	2	4
Fore-topgallant	2	2	2	2	2	2	2	2	2	2	1	3
Fore-royal	1	1	1	1	1	1	1	1	1	1		2
Main	11	10	10	10	10	9	7	7	6	5	3	7
Main-top	6	6	6	6	5	5	4	4	3	3	2	4
Main-topgallant	2	2	2	2	2	2	2	2	2	2	1	3
Main-royal	1	1	1	1	1	1	1	1	1	1		2
Mizzen	6	6	6	6	6	5	5	5	5	1		5
Mizzentop	4	4	4	4	4	4	3	3	3			3
Mizzen-topgallant	2	2	2	2	2	2	2	2	2			2
Mizzen-royal	1	1	1	1	1	1	1	1	1			2

RULE FOR DETERMINING THE SIZE OF ROPE RIGGING

From Ship Builder's Assistant, *by Wm. Sutherland, 1755.*

Fore shrouds: circumference = $\frac{2}{7}$ diameter of mast at partners; pendants = the same; runners of tackle = $\frac{11}{12}$ of pendant; tackle falls = $\frac{1}{2}$ pendants.

Forestay: circumference = $\frac{1}{2}$ diameter of foremast; lanyard = $\frac{7}{12}$ of the stay; lifts and braces = $\frac{1}{2}$ shrouds.

Fore-topmast shrouds: circumference = $\frac{1}{8}$ diameter of topmast; futtock shrouds = $\frac{7}{12}$ of shrouds; standing backstays = shrouds.

Fore-topmast stay: circumference = $\frac{9}{25}$ of diameter of fore-topmast; staysail stay = $\frac{7}{9}$ stay; lifts = $\frac{5}{9}$ stay; braces = same as lifts.

Fore-topgallant shrouds: circumference = $\frac{2}{5}$ diameter of mast; stay = $\frac{3}{4}$ shrouds; lifts and braces = $\frac{1}{2}$ shrouds.

Mainmast shrouds: circumference = $\frac{9}{22}$ of diameter of mast at partners; lifts = $\frac{7}{16}$ of the shrouds; braces = $\frac{6}{7}$ of the lifts; stay = $\frac{1}{2}$ diameter of mast.

Main-topmast shrouds: circumference = $\frac{9}{29}$ diameter mast in the cap; ratlines = $\frac{2}{9}$ shrouds; stay = same as shrouds: staysail stay = $\frac{1}{8}$ stay.

Runners for topsail halliards: circumference = $\frac{1}{2}$ diameter of topsail yard; halliards = $\frac{3}{5}$ runners; lifts = $\frac{5}{9}$ stays; runners and braces = same as lifts.

Main-topgallant shrouds: circumference = $\frac{5}{9}$ topmast shrouds; futtocks = the same; stay = $\frac{3}{4}$ shrouds; tye = shrouds; halliards = $\frac{3}{5}$ tye; braces = $\frac{2}{3}$ lifts; lifts = halliards.

Mizzenmast shrouds: circumference = $\frac{2}{29}$ diameter mast at partners; stay = shrouds.

Mizzen-topmast shrouds = main-topgallant mast; stay = shrouds.

LIST OF BLOCKS REQUIRED TO RIG MAINMAST OF 74-GUN UNITED STATES SHIP-OF-THE-LINE *WASHINGTON*

(From letter book of Commander T. Macdonough, 1815.)

	Kind	Number	Size: in.	Rope: in.
Jeers	Treble	2	30	8
Yard tackles	D	2	18	3½
	S	2	18	3½
Stay tackles	D	2	18	3½
	S	2	20	3½
Mainbrace	S	4	16	4½
Lifts	S	6	16	4½
Clew garnets	S	4	15	4
Tack and sheet	S	6	20	7
Tackles	D	6	18	3½
	S	6	18	3½
Backstays, iron strop . . .	Treble	6	16	3½
Backstays, rope strop . . .	Treble	4	16	3½
Top block, brass sheave . .	S	3	24	9
Top block, iron strop . .	Treble	4	24	5
Topsail tye	D	1	24	7
	S	2	24	7
Topsail halliard	D	2	26	3½
	S	2	26	3½
Foresail brace	S	4	14	4
Clewlines	D	2	14	4
	S	2	14	4
Foresheet shoulder . . .	S	2	24	7
Quarter blocks	S	2	26	7
	S	100	8 to 12	2 to 4 various
	D	60	8 to 12	2 to 4 various

INDEX

A CATALOG OF SELECTED
DOVER BOOKS
IN ALL FIELDS OF INTEREST

A CATALOG OF SELECTED DOVER
BOOKS IN ALL FIELDS OF INTEREST

DRAWINGS OF REMBRANDT, edited by Seymour Slive. Updated Lippmann, Hofstede de Groot edition, with definitive scholarly apparatus. All portraits, biblical sketches, landscapes, nudes. Oriental figures, classical studies, together with selection of work by followers. 550 illustrations. Total of 630pp. 9⅛ × 12¼.
21485-0, 21486-9 Pa., Two-vol. set $25.00

GHOST AND HORROR STORIES OF AMBROSE BIERCE, Ambrose Bierce. 24 tales vividly imagined, strangely prophetic, and decades ahead of their time in technical skill: "The Damned Thing," "An Inhabitant of Carcosa," "The Eyes of the Panther," "Moxon's Master," and 20 more. 199pp. 5⅜ × 8½. 20767-6 Pa. $3.95

ETHICAL WRITINGS OF MAIMONIDES, Maimonides. Most significant ethical works of great medieval sage, newly translated for utmost precision, readability. Laws Concerning Character Traits, Eight Chapters, more. 192pp. 5⅜ × 8½.
24522-5 Pa. $4.50

THE EXPLORATION OF THE COLORADO RIVER AND ITS CANYONS, J. W. Powell. Full text of Powell's 1,000-mile expedition down the fabled Colorado in 1869. Superb account of terrain, geology, vegetation, Indians, famine, mutiny, treacherous rapids, mighty canyons, during exploration of last unknown part of continental U.S. 400pp. 5⅜ × 8½. 20094-9 Pa. $6.95

HISTORY OF PHILOSOPHY, Julián Marías. Clearest one-volume history on the market. Every major philosopher and dozens of others, to Existentialism and later. 505pp. 5⅜ × 8½. 21739-6 Pa. $8.50

ALL ABOUT LIGHTNING, Martin A. Uman. Highly readable non-technical survey of nature and causes of lightning, thunderstorms, ball lightning, St. Elmo's Fire, much more. Illustrated. 192pp. 5⅜ × 8½. 25237-X Pa. $5.95

SAILING ALONE AROUND THE WORLD, Captain Joshua Slocum. First man to sail around the world, alone, in small boat. One of great feats of seamanship told in delightful manner. 67 illustrations. 294pp. 5⅜ × 8½. 20326-3 Pa. $4.95

LETTERS AND NOTES ON THE MANNERS, CUSTOMS AND CONDITIONS OF THE NORTH AMERICAN INDIANS, George Catlin. Classic account of life among Plains Indians: ceremonies, hunt, warfare, etc. 312 plates. 572pp. of text. 6⅛ × 9¼. 22118-0, 22119-9 Pa. Two-vol. set $15.90

ALASKA: The Harriman Expedition, 1899, John Burroughs, John Muir, et al. Informative, engrossing accounts of two-month, 9,000-mile expedition. Native peoples, wildlife, forests, geography, salmon industry, glaciers, more. Profusely illustrated. 240 black-and-white line drawings. 124 black-and-white photographs. 3 maps. Index. 576pp. 5⅜ × 8½. 25109-8 Pa. $11.95

THE BOOK OF BEASTS: Being a Translation from a Latin Bestiary of the Twelfth Century, T. H. White. Wonderful catalog real and fanciful beasts: manticore, griffin, phoenix, amphivius, jaculus, many more. White's witty erudite commentary on scientific, historical aspects. Fascinating glimpse of medieval mind. Illustrated. 296pp. 5⅜ × 8¼. (Available in U.S. only) 24609-4 Pa. $5.95

FRANK LLOYD WRIGHT: ARCHITECTURE AND NATURE With 160 Illustrations, Donald Hoffmann. Profusely illustrated study of influence of nature—especially prairie—on Wright's designs for Fallingwater, Robie House, Guggenheim Museum, other masterpieces. 96pp. 9¼ × 10¾. 25098-9 Pa. $7.95

FRANK LLOYD WRIGHT'S FALLINGWATER, Donald Hoffmann. Wright's famous waterfall house: planning and construction of organic idea. History of site, owners, Wright's personal involvement. Photographs of various stages of building. Preface by Edgar Kaufmann, Jr. 100 illustrations. 112pp. 9¼ × 10. 23671-4 Pa. $7.95

YEARS WITH FRANK LLOYD WRIGHT: Apprentice to Genius, Edgar Tafel. Insightful memoir by a former apprentice presents a revealing portrait of Wright the man, the inspired teacher, the greatest American architect. 372 black-and-white illustrations. Preface. Index. vi + 228pp. 8¼ × 11. 24801-1 Pa. $9.95

THE STORY OF KING ARTHUR AND HIS KNIGHTS, Howard Pyle. Enchanting version of King Arthur fable has delighted generations with imaginative narratives of exciting adventures and unforgettable illustrations by the author. 41 illustrations. xviii + 313pp. 6⅛ × 9¼. 21445-1 Pa. $6.50

THE GODS OF THE EGYPTIANS, E. A. Wallis Budge. Thorough coverage of numerous gods of ancient Egypt by foremost Egyptologist. Information on evolution of cults, rites and gods; the cult of Osiris; the Book of the Dead and its rites; the sacred animals and birds; Heaven and Hell; and more. 956pp. 6⅛ × 9¼. 22055-9, 22056-7 Pa., Two-vol. set $20.00

A THEOLOGICO-POLITICAL TREATISE, Benedict Spinoza. Also contains unfinished *Political Treatise*. Great classic on religious liberty, theory of government on common consent. R. Elwes translation. Total of 421pp. 5⅜ × 8½. 20249-6 Pa. $6.95

INCIDENTS OF TRAVEL IN CENTRAL AMERICA, CHIAPAS, AND YUCATAN, John L. Stephens. Almost single-handed discovery of Maya culture; exploration of ruined cities, monuments, temples; customs of Indians. 115 drawings. 892pp. 5⅜ × 8½. 22404-X, 22405-8 Pa., Two-vol. set $15.90

LOS CAPRICHOS, Francisco Goya. 80 plates of wild, grotesque monsters and caricatures. Prado manuscript included. 183pp. 6⅝ × 9⅝. 22384-1 Pa. $4.95

AUTOBIOGRAPHY: The Story of My Experiments with Truth, Mohandas K. Gandhi. Not hagiography, but Gandhi in his own words. Boyhood, legal studies, purification, the growth of the Satyagraha (nonviolent protest) movement. Critical, inspiring work of the man who freed India. 480pp. 5⅜ × 8½. (Available in U.S. only) 24593-4 Pa. $6.95

ILLUSTRATED DICTIONARY OF HISTORIC ARCHITECTURE, edited by Cyril M. Harris. Extraordinary compendium of clear, concise definitions for over 5,000 important architectural terms complemented by over 2,000 line drawings. Covers full spectrum of architecture from ancient ruins to 20th-century Modernism. Preface. 592pp. 7½ × 9⅜. 24444-X Pa. $14.95

THE NIGHT BEFORE CHRISTMAS, Clement Moore. Full text, and woodcuts from original 1848 book. Also critical, historical material. 19 illustrations. 40pp. 4⅝ × 6. 22797-9 Pa. $2.25

THE LESSON OF JAPANESE ARCHITECTURE: 165 Photographs, Jiro Harada. Memorable gallery of 165 photographs taken in the 1930's of exquisite Japanese homes of the well-to-do and historic buildings. 13 line diagrams. 192pp. 8⅜ × 11¼. 24778-3 Pa. $8.95

THE AUTOBIOGRAPHY OF CHARLES DARWIN AND SELECTED LETTERS, edited by Francis Darwin. The fascinating life of eccentric genius composed of an intimate memoir by Darwin (intended for his children); commentary by his son, Francis; hundreds of fragments from notebooks, journals, papers; and letters to and from Lyell, Hooker, Huxley, Wallace and Henslow. xi + 365pp. 5⅜ × 8. 20479-0 Pa. $6.95

WONDERS OF THE SKY: Observing Rainbows, Comets, Eclipses, the Stars and Other Phenomena, Fred Schaaf. Charming, easy-to-read poetic guide to all manner of celestial events visible to the naked eye. Mock suns, glories, Belt of Venus, more. Illustrated. 299pp. 5¼ × 8¼. 24402-4 Pa. $7.95

BURNHAM'S CELESTIAL HANDBOOK, Robert Burnham, Jr. Thorough guide to the stars beyond our solar system. Exhaustive treatment. Alphabetical by constellation: Andromeda to Cetus in Vol. 1; Chamaeleon to Orion in Vol. 2; and Pavo to Vulpecula in Vol. 3. Hundreds of illustrations. Index in Vol. 3. 2,000pp. 6⅛ × 9¼. 23567-X, 23568-8, 23673-0 Pa., Three-vol. set $38.85

STAR NAMES: Their Lore and Meaning, Richard Hinckley Allen. Fascinating history of names various cultures have given to constellations and literary and folkloristic uses that have been made of stars. Indexes to subjects. Arabic and Greek names. Biblical references. Bibliography. 563pp. 5⅜ × 8½. 21079-0 Pa. $7.95

THIRTY YEARS THAT SHOOK PHYSICS: The Story of Quantum Theory, George Gamow. Lucid, accessible introduction to influential theory of energy and matter. Careful explanations of Dirac's anti-particles, Bohr's model of the atom, much more. 12 plates. Numerous drawings. 240pp. 5⅜ × 8½. 24895-X Pa. $4.95

CHINESE DOMESTIC FURNITURE IN PHOTOGRAPHS AND MEASURED DRAWINGS, Gustav Ecke. A rare volume, now affordably priced for antique collectors, furniture buffs and art historians. Detailed review of styles ranging from early Shang to late Ming. Unabridged republication. 161 black-and-white drawings, photos. Total of 224pp. 8⅜ × 11¼. (Available in U.S. only) 25171-3 Pa. $12.95

VINCENT VAN GOGH: A Biography, Julius Meier-Graefe. Dynamic, penetrating study of artist's life, relationship with brother, Theo, painting techniques, travels, more. Readable, engrossing. 160pp. 5⅜ × 8½. (Available in U.S. only) 25253-1 Pa. $3.95

HOW TO WRITE, Gertrude Stein. Gertrude Stein claimed anyone could understand her unconventional writing—here are clues to help. Fascinating improvisations, language experiments, explanations illuminate Stein's craft and the art of writing. Total of 414pp. 4⅝ × 6⅜. 23144-5 Pa. $5.95

ADVENTURES AT SEA IN THE GREAT AGE OF SAIL: Five Firsthand Narratives, edited by Elliot Snow. Rare true accounts of exploration, whaling, shipwreck, fierce natives, trade, shipboard life, more. 33 illustrations. Introduction. 353pp. 5⅜ × 8½. 25177-2 Pa. $7.95

THE HERBAL OR GENERAL HISTORY OF PLANTS, John Gerard. Classic descriptions of about 2,850 plants—with over 2,700 illustrations—includes Latin and English names, physical descriptions, varieties, time and place of growth, more. 2,706 illustrations. xlv + 1,678pp. 8½ × 12¼. 23147-X Cloth. $75.00

DOROTHY AND THE WIZARD IN OZ, L. Frank Baum. Dorothy and the Wizard visit the center of the Earth, where people are vegetables, glass houses grow and Oz characters reappear. Classic sequel to *Wizard of Oz*. 256pp. 5⅜ × 8.
24714-7 Pa. $4.95

SONGS OF EXPERIENCE: Facsimile Reproduction with 26 Plates in Full Color, William Blake. This facsimile of Blake's original "Illuminated Book" reproduces 26 full-color plates from a rare 1826 edition. Includes "The Tyger," "London," "Holy Thursday," and other immortal poems. 26 color plates. Printed text of poems. 48pp. 5¼ × 7. 24636-1 Pa. $3.50

SONGS OF INNOCENCE, William Blake. The first and most popular of Blake's famous "Illuminated Books," in a facsimile edition reproducing all 31 brightly colored plates. Additional printed text of each poem. 64pp. 5¼ × 7.
22764-2 Pa. $3.50

PRECIOUS STONES, Max Bauer. Classic, thorough study of diamonds, rubies, emeralds, garnets, etc.: physical character, occurrence, properties, use, similar topics. 20 plates, 8 in color. 94 figures. 659pp. 6⅛ × 9¼.
21910-0, 21911-9 Pa., Two-vol. set $15.90

ENCYCLOPEDIA OF VICTORIAN NEEDLEWORK, S. F. A. Caulfeild and Blanche Saward. Full, precise descriptions of stitches, techniques for dozens of needlecrafts—most exhaustive reference of its kind. Over 800 figures. Total of 679pp. 8⅛ × 11. Two volumes. Vol. 1 22800-2 Pa. $11.95
Vol. 2 22801-0 Pa. $11.95

THE MARVELOUS LAND OF OZ, L. Frank Baum. Second Oz book, the Scarecrow and Tin Woodman are back with hero named Tip, Oz magic. 136 illustrations. 287pp. 5⅜ × 8½. 20692-0 Pa. $5.95

WILD FOWL DECOYS, Joel Barber. Basic book on the subject, by foremost authority and collector. Reveals history of decoy making and rigging, place in American culture, different kinds of decoys, how to make them, and how to use them. 140 plates. 156pp. 7⅞ × 10¾. 20011-6 Pa. $8.95

HISTORY OF LACE, Mrs. Bury Palliser. Definitive, profusely illustrated chronicle of lace from earliest times to late 19th century. Laces of Italy, Greece, England, France, Belgium, etc. Landmark of needlework scholarship. 266 illustrations. 672pp. 6⅛ × 9¼. 24742-2 Pa. $14.95

ILLUSTRATED GUIDE TO SHAKER FURNITURE, Robert Meader. All furniture and appurtenances, with much on unknown local styles. 235 photos. 146pp. 9 × 12. 22819-3 Pa. $7.95

WHALE SHIPS AND WHALING: A Pictorial Survey, George Francis Dow. Over 200 vintage engravings, drawings, photographs of barks, brigs, cutters, other vessels. Also harpoons, lances, whaling guns, many other artifacts. Comprehensive text by foremost authority. 207 black-and-white illustrations. 288pp. 6 × 9. 24808-9 Pa. $8.95

THE BERTRAMS, Anthony Trollope. Powerful portrayal of blind self-will and thwarted ambition includes one of Trollope's most heartrending love stories. 497pp. 5⅜ × 8½. 25119-5 Pa. $8.95

ADVENTURES WITH A HAND LENS, Richard Headstrom. Clearly written guide to observing and studying flowers and grasses, fish scales, moth and insect wings, egg cases, buds, feathers, seeds, leaf scars, moss, molds, ferns, common crystals, etc.—all with an ordinary, inexpensive magnifying glass. 209 exact line drawings aid in your discoveries. 220pp. 5⅜ × 8½. 23330-8 Pa. $3.95

RODIN ON ART AND ARTISTS, Auguste Rodin. Great sculptor's candid, wide-ranging comments on meaning of art; great artists; relation of sculpture to poetry, painting, music; philosophy of life, more. 76 superb black-and-white illustrations of Rodin's sculpture, drawings and prints. 119pp. 8⅜ × 11¼. 24487-3 Pa. $6.95

FIFTY CLASSIC FRENCH FILMS, 1912-1982: A Pictorial Record, Anthony Slide. Memorable stills from Grand Illusion, Beauty and the Beast, Hiroshima, Mon Amour, many more. Credits, plot synopses, reviews, etc. 160pp. 8¼ × 11. 25256-6 Pa. $11.95

THE PRINCIPLES OF PSYCHOLOGY, William James. Famous long course complete, unabridged. Stream of thought, time perception, memory, experimental methods; great work decades ahead of its time. 94 figures. 1,391pp. 5⅜ × 8½. 20381-6, 20382-4 Pa., Two-vol. set $19.90

BODIES IN A BOOKSHOP, R. T. Campbell. Challenging mystery of blackmail and murder with ingenious plot and superbly drawn characters. In the best tradition of British suspense fiction. 192pp. 5⅜ × 8½. 24720-1 Pa. $3.95

CALLAS: PORTRAIT OF A PRIMA DONNA, George Jellinek. Renowned commentator on the musical scene chronicles incredible career and life of the most controversial, fascinating, influential operatic personality of our time. 64 black-and-white photographs. 416pp. 5⅜ × 8¼. 25047-4 Pa. $7.95

GEOMETRY, RELATIVITY AND THE FOURTH DIMENSION, Rudolph Rucker. Exposition of fourth dimension, concepts of relativity as Flatland characters continue adventures. Popular, easily followed yet accurate, profound. 141 illustrations. 133pp. 5⅜ × 8½. 23400-2 Pa. $3.95

HOUSEHOLD STORIES BY THE BROTHERS GRIMM, with pictures by Walter Crane. 53 classic stories—Rumpelstiltskin, Rapunzel, Hansel and Gretel, the Fisherman and his Wife, Snow White, Tom Thumb, Sleeping Beauty, Cinderella, and so much more—lavishly illustrated with original 19th century drawings. 114 illustrations. x + 269pp. 5⅜ × 8½. 21080-4 Pa. $4.50

SUNDIALS, Albert Waugh. Far and away the best, most thorough coverage of ideas, mathematics concerned, types, construction, adjusting anywhere. Over 100 illustrations. 230pp. 5⅜ × 8½. 22947-5 Pa. $4.50

PICTURE HISTORY OF THE NORMANDIE: With 190 Illustrations, Frank O. Braynard. Full story of legendary French ocean liner: Art Deco interiors, design innovations, furnishings, celebrities, maiden voyage, tragic fire, much more. Extensive text. 144pp. 8⅜ × 11¾. 25257-4 Pa. $9.95

THE FIRST AMERICAN COOKBOOK: A Facsimile of "American Cookery," 1796, Amelia Simmons. Facsimile of the first American-written cookbook published in the United States contains authentic recipes for colonial favorites—pumpkin pudding, winter squash pudding, spruce beer, Indian slapjacks, and more. Introductory Essay and Glossary of colonial cooking terms. 80pp. 5⅜ × 8½. 24710-4 Pa. $3.50

101 PUZZLES IN THOUGHT AND LOGIC, C. R. Wylie, Jr. Solve murders and robberies, find out which fishermen are liars, how a blind man could possibly identify a color—purely by your own reasoning! 107pp. 5⅜ × 8½. 20367-0 Pa. $2.50

THE BOOK OF WORLD-FAMOUS MUSIC—CLASSICAL, POPULAR AND FOLK, James J. Fuld. Revised and enlarged republication of landmark work in musico-bibliography. Full information about nearly 1,000 songs and compositions including first lines of music and lyrics. New supplement. Index. 800pp. 5⅜ × 8¼. 24857-7 Pa. $14.95

ANTHROPOLOGY AND MODERN LIFE, Franz Boas. Great anthropologist's classic treatise on race and culture. Introduction by Ruth Bunzel. Only inexpensive paperback edition. 255pp. 5⅜ × 8½. 25245-0 Pa. $5.95

THE TALE OF PETER RABBIT, Beatrix Potter. The inimitable Peter's terrifying adventure in Mr. McGregor's garden, with all 27 wonderful, full-color Potter illustrations. 55pp. 4¼ × 5½. (Available in U.S. only) 22827-4 Pa. $1.75

THREE PROPHETIC SCIENCE FICTION NOVELS, H. G. Wells. *When the Sleeper Wakes, A Story of the Days to Come* and *The Time Machine* (full version). 335pp. 5⅜ × 8½. (Available in U.S. only) 20605-X Pa. $5.95

APICIUS COOKERY AND DINING IN IMPERIAL ROME, edited and translated by Joseph Dommers Vehling. Oldest known cookbook in existence offers readers a clear picture of what foods Romans ate, how they prepared them, etc. 49 illustrations. 301pp. 6⅛ × 9¼. 23563-7 Pa. $6.50

SHAKESPEARE LEXICON AND QUOTATION DICTIONARY, Alexander Schmidt. Full definitions, locations, shades of meaning of every word in plays and poems. More than 50,000 exact quotations. 1,485pp. 6½ × 9¼.
22726-X, 22727-8 Pa., Two-vol. set $27.90

THE WORLD'S GREAT SPEECHES, edited by Lewis Copeland and Lawrence W. Lamm. Vast collection of 278 speeches from Greeks to 1970. Powerful and effective models; unique look at history. 842pp. 5⅜ × 8½. 20468-5 Pa. $11.95

THE BLUE FAIRY BOOK, Andrew Lang. The first, most famous collection, with many familiar tales: Little Red Riding Hood, Aladdin and the Wonderful Lamp, Puss in Boots, Sleeping Beauty, Hansel and Gretel, Rumpelstiltskin; 37 in all. 138 illustrations. 390pp. 5⅜ × 8½. 21437-0 Pa. $5.95

THE STORY OF THE CHAMPIONS OF THE ROUND TABLE, Howard Pyle. Sir Launcelot, Sir Tristram and Sir Percival in spirited adventures of love and triumph retold in Pyle's inimitable style. 50 drawings, 31 full-page. xviii + 329pp. 6½ × 9¼. 21883-X Pa. $6.95

AUDUBON AND HIS JOURNALS, Maria Audubon. Unmatched two-volume portrait of the great artist, naturalist and author contains his journals, an excellent biography by his granddaughter, expert annotations by the noted ornithologist, Dr. Elliott Coues, and 37 superb illustrations. Total of 1,200pp. 5⅜ × 8.
Vol. I 25143-8 Pa. $8.95
Vol. II 25144-6 Pa. $8.95

GREAT DINOSAUR HUNTERS AND THEIR DISCOVERIES, Edwin H. Colbert. Fascinating, lavishly illustrated chronicle of dinosaur research, 1820's to 1960. Achievements of Cope, Marsh, Brown, Buckland, Mantell, Huxley, many others. 384pp. 5¼ × 8¼. 24701-5 Pa. $6.95

THE TASTEMAKERS, Russell Lynes. Informal, illustrated social history of American taste 1850's–1950's. First popularized categories Highbrow, Lowbrow, Middlebrow. 129 illustrations. New (1979) afterword. 384pp. 6 × 9.
23993-4 Pa. $6.95

DOUBLE CROSS PURPOSES, Ronald A. Knox. A treasure hunt in the Scottish Highlands, an old map, unidentified corpse, surprise discoveries keep reader guessing in this cleverly intricate tale of financial skullduggery. 2 black-and-white maps. 320pp. 5⅜ × 8½. (Available in U.S. only) 25032-6 Pa. $5.95

AUTHENTIC VICTORIAN DECORATION AND ORNAMENTATION IN FULL COLOR: 46 Plates from "Studies in Design," Christopher Dresser. Superb full-color lithographs reproduced from rare original portfolio of a major Victorian designer. 48pp. 9¼ × 12¼. 25083-0 Pa. $7.95

PRIMITIVE ART, Franz Boas. Remains the best text ever prepared on subject, thoroughly discussing Indian, African, Asian, Australian, and, especially, Northern American primitive art. Over 950 illustrations show ceramics, masks, totem poles, weapons, textiles, paintings, much more. 376pp. 5⅜ × 8. 20025-6 Pa. $6.95

SIDELIGHTS ON RELATIVITY, Albert Einstein. Unabridged republication of two lectures delivered by the great physicist in 1920–21. *Ether and Relativity* and *Geometry and Experience.* Elegant ideas in non-mathematical form, accessible to intelligent layman. vi + 56pp. 5⅜ × 8½. 24511-X Pa. $2.95

THE WIT AND HUMOR OF OSCAR WILDE, edited by Alvin Redman. More than 1,000 ripostes, paradoxes, wisecracks: Work is the curse of the drinking classes, I can resist everything except temptation, etc. 258pp. 5⅜ × 8½. 20602-5 Pa. $4.50

ADVENTURES WITH A MICROSCOPE, Richard Headstrom. 59 adventures with clothing fibers, protozoa, ferns and lichens, roots and leaves, much more. 142 illustrations. 232pp. 5⅜ × 8½. 23471-1 Pa. $3.95

PLANTS OF THE BIBLE, Harold N. Moldenke and Alma L. Moldenke. Standard reference to all 230 plants mentioned in Scriptures. Latin name, biblical reference, uses, modern identity, much more. Unsurpassed encyclopedic resource for scholars, botanists, nature lovers, students of Bible. Bibliography. Indexes. 123 black-and-white illustrations. 384pp. 6 × 9. 25069-5 Pa. $8.95

FAMOUS AMERICAN WOMEN: A Biographical Dictionary from Colonial Times to the Present, Robert McHenry, ed. From Pocahontas to Rosa Parks, 1,035 distinguished American women documented in separate biographical entries. Accurate, up-to-date data, numerous categories, spans 400 years. Indices. 493pp. 6½ × 9¼. 24523-3 Pa. $9.95

THE FABULOUS INTERIORS OF THE GREAT OCEAN LINERS IN HISTORIC PHOTOGRAPHS, William H. Miller, Jr. Some 200 superb photographs capture exquisite interiors of world's great "floating palaces"—1890's to 1980's: Titanic, Ile de France, Queen Elizabeth, United States, Europa, more. Approx. 200 black-and-white photographs. Captions. Text. Introduction. 160pp. 8⅜ × 11¼. 24756-2 Pa. $9.95

THE GREAT LUXURY LINERS, 1927–1954: A Photographic Record, William H. Miller, Jr. Nostalgic tribute to heyday of ocean liners. 186 photos of Ile de France, Normandie, Leviathan, Queen Elizabeth, United States, many others. Interior and exterior views. Introduction. Captions. 160pp. 9 × 12. 24056-8 Pa. $9.95

A NATURAL HISTORY OF THE DUCKS, John Charles Phillips. Great landmark of ornithology offers complete detailed coverage of nearly 200 species and subspecies of ducks: gadwall, sheldrake, merganser, pintail, many more. 74 full-color plates, 102 black-and-white. Bibliography. Total of 1,920pp. 8⅜ × 11¼. 25141-1, 25142-X Cloth. Two-vol. set $100.00

THE SEAWEED HANDBOOK: An Illustrated Guide to Seaweeds from North Carolina to Canada, Thomas F. Lee. Concise reference covers 78 species. Scientific and common names, habitat, distribution, more. Finding keys for easy identification. 224pp. 5⅜ × 8½. 25215-9 Pa. $5.95

THE TEN BOOKS OF ARCHITECTURE: The 1755 Leoni Edition, Leon Battista Alberti. Rare classic helped introduce the glories of ancient architecture to the Renaissance. 68 black-and-white plates. 336pp. 8⅜ × 11¼. 25239-6 Pa. $14.95

MISS MACKENZIE, Anthony Trollope. Minor masterpieces by Victorian master unmasks many truths about life in 19th-century England. First inexpensive edition in years. 392pp. 5⅜ × 8½. 25201-9 Pa. $7.95

THE RIME OF THE ANCIENT MARINER, Gustave Doré, Samuel Taylor Coleridge. Dramatic engravings considered by many to be his greatest work. The terrifying space of the open sea, the storms and whirlpools of an unknown ocean, the ice of Antarctica, more—all rendered in a powerful, chilling manner. Full text. 38 plates. 77pp. 9¼ × 12. 22305-1 Pa. $4.95

THE EXPEDITIONS OF ZEBULON MONTGOMERY PIKE, Zebulon Montgomery Pike. Fascinating first-hand accounts (1805-6) of exploration of Mississippi River, Indian wars, capture by Spanish dragoons, much more. 1,088pp. 5⅜ × 8½. 25254-X, 25255-8 Pa. Two-vol. set $23.90

A CONCISE HISTORY OF PHOTOGRAPHY: Third Revised Edition, Helmut Gernsheim. Best one-volume history—camera obscura, photochemistry, daguerreotypes, evolution of cameras, film, more. Also artistic aspects—landscape, portraits, fine art, etc. 281 black-and-white photographs. 26 in color. 176pp. 8⅜ × 11¼. 25128-4 Pa. $12.95

THE DORÉ BIBLE ILLUSTRATIONS, Gustave Doré. 241 detailed plates from the Bible: the Creation scenes, Adam and Eve, Flood, Babylon, battle sequences, life of Jesus, etc. Each plate is accompanied by the verses from the King James version of the Bible. 241pp. 9 × 12. 23004-X Pa. $8.95

HUGGER-MUGGER IN THE LOUVRE, Elliot Paul. Second Homer Evans mystery-comedy. Theft at the Louvre involves sleuth in hilarious, madcap caper. "A knockout."—Books. 336pp. 5⅜ × 8½. 25185-3 Pa. $5.95

FLATLAND, E. A. Abbott. Intriguing and enormously popular science-fiction classic explores the complexities of trying to survive as a two-dimensional being in a three-dimensional world. Amusingly illustrated by the author. 16 illustrations. 103pp. 5⅜ × 8½. 20001-9 Pa. $2.25

THE HISTORY OF THE LEWIS AND CLARK EXPEDITION, Meriwether Lewis and William Clark, edited by Elliott Coues. Classic edition of Lewis and Clark's day-by-day journals that later became the basis for U.S. claims to Oregon and the West. Accurate and invaluable geographical, botanical, biological, meteorological and anthropological material. Total of 1,508pp. 5⅜ × 8½.
21268-8, 21269-6, 21270-X Pa. Three-vol. set $25.50

LANGUAGE, TRUTH AND LOGIC, Alfred J. Ayer. Famous, clear introduction to Vienna, Cambridge schools of Logical Positivism. Role of philosophy, elimination of metaphysics, nature of analysis, etc. 160pp. 5⅜ × 8½. (Available in U.S. and Canada only) 20010-8 Pa. $2.95

MATHEMATICS FOR THE NONMATHEMATICIAN, Morris Kline. Detailed, college-level treatment of mathematics in cultural and historical context, with numerous exercises. For liberal arts students. Preface. Recommended Reading Lists. Tables. Index. Numerous black-and-white figures. xvi + 641pp. 5⅜ × 8½.
24823-2 Pa. $11.95

28 SCIENCE FICTION STORIES, H. G. Wells. Novels, *Star Begotten* and *Men Like Gods,* plus 26 short stories: "Empire of the Ants," "A Story of the Stone Age," "The Stolen Bacillus," "In the Abyss," etc. 915pp. 5⅜ × 8½. (Available in U.S. only)
20265-8 Cloth. $10.95

HANDBOOK OF PICTORIAL SYMBOLS, Rudolph Modley. 3,250 signs and symbols, many systems in full; official or heavy commercial use. Arranged by subject. Most in Pictorial Archive series. 143pp. 8⅛ × 11. 23357-X Pa. $5.95

INCIDENTS OF TRAVEL IN YUCATAN, John L. Stephens. Classic (1843) exploration of jungles of Yucatan, looking for evidences of Maya civilization. Travel adventures, Mexican and Indian culture, etc. Total of 669pp. 5⅜ × 8½.
20926-1, 20927-X Pa., Two-vol. set $9.90

DEGAS: An Intimate Portrait, Ambroise Vollard. Charming, anecdotal memoir by famous art dealer of one of the greatest 19th-century French painters. 14 black-and-white illustrations. Introduction by Harold L. Van Doren. 96pp. 5⅜ × 8½.
25131-4 Pa. $3.95

PERSONAL NARRATIVE OF A PILGRIMAGE TO ALMANDINAH AND MECCAH, Richard Burton. Great travel classic by remarkably colorful personality. Burton, disguised as a Moroccan, visited sacred shrines of Islam, narrowly escaping death. 47 illustrations. 959pp. 5⅜ × 8½.　21217-3, 21218-1 Pa., Two-vol. set $19.90

PHRASE AND WORD ORIGINS, A. H. Holt. Entertaining, reliable, modern study of more than 1,200 colorful words, phrases, origins and histories. Much unexpected information. 254pp. 5⅜ × 8½.
20758-7 Pa. $4.95

THE RED THUMB MARK, R. Austin Freeman. In this first Dr. Thorndyke case, the great scientific detective draws fascinating conclusions from the nature of a single fingerprint. Exciting story, authentic science. 320pp. 5⅜ × 8½. (Available in U.S. only)
25210-8 Pa. $5.95

AN EGYPTIAN HIEROGLYPHIC DICTIONARY, E. A. Wallis Budge. Monumental work containing about 25,000 words or terms that occur in texts ranging from 3000 B.C. to 600 A.D. Each entry consists of a transliteration of the word, the word in hieroglyphs, and the meaning in English. 1,314pp. 6⅜ × 10.
23615-3, 23616-1 Pa., Two-vol. set $27.90

THE COMPLEAT STRATEGYST: Being a Primer on the Theory of Games of Strategy, J. D. Williams. Highly entertaining classic describes, with many illustrated examples, how to select best strategies in conflict situations. Prefaces. Appendices. xvi + 268pp. 5⅜ × 8½.
25101-2 Pa. $5.95

THE ROAD TO OZ, L. Frank Baum. Dorothy meets the Shaggy Man, little Button-Bright and the Rainbow's beautiful daughter in this delightful trip to the magical Land of Oz. 272pp. 5⅜ × 8.
25208-6 Pa. $4.95

POINT AND LINE TO PLANE, Wassily Kandinsky. Seminal exposition of role of point, line, other elements in non-objective painting. Essential to understanding 20th-century art. 127 illustrations. 192pp. 6½ × 9¼.
23808-3 Pa. $4.50

LADY ANNA, Anthony Trollope. Moving chronicle of Countess Lovel's bitter struggle to win for herself and daughter Anna their rightful rank and fortune—perhaps at cost of sanity itself. 384pp. 5⅜ × 8½.
24669-8 Pa. $6.95

EGYPTIAN MAGIC, E. A. Wallis Budge. Sums up all that is known about magic in Ancient Egypt: the role of magic in controlling the gods, powerful amulets that warded off evil spirits, scarabs of immortality, use of wax images, formulas and spells, the secret name, much more. 253pp. 5⅜ × 8½.
22681-6 Pa. $4.00

THE DANCE OF SIVA, Ananda Coomaraswamy. Preeminent authority unfolds the vast metaphysic of India: the revelation of her art, conception of the universe, social organization, etc. 27 reproductions of art masterpieces. 192pp. 5⅜ × 8½.
24817-8 Pa. $5.95

CHRISTMAS CUSTOMS AND TRADITIONS, Clement A. Miles. Origin, evolution, significance of religious, secular practices. Caroling, gifts, yule logs, much more. Full, scholarly yet fascinating; non-sectarian. 400pp. 5⅜ × 8½.
23354-5 Pa. $6.50

THE HUMAN FIGURE IN MOTION, Eadweard Muybridge. More than 4,500 stopped-action photos, in action series, showing undraped men, women, children jumping, lying down, throwing, sitting, wrestling, carrying, etc. 390pp. 7⅞ × 10⅝.
20204-6 Cloth. $21.95

THE MAN WHO WAS THURSDAY, Gilbert Keith Chesterton. Witty, fast-paced novel about a club of anarchists in turn-of-the-century London. Brilliant social, religious, philosophical speculations. 128pp. 5⅜ × 8½.
25121-7 Pa. $3.95

A CEZANNE SKETCHBOOK: Figures, Portraits, Landscapes and Still Lifes, Paul Cezanne. Great artist experiments with tonal effects, light, mass, other qualities in over 100 drawings. A revealing view of developing master painter, precursor of Cubism. 102 black-and-white illustrations. 144pp. 8¾ × 6⅜.
24790-2 Pa. $5.95

AN ENCYCLOPEDIA OF BATTLES: Accounts of Over 1,560 Battles from 1479 B.C. to the Present, David Eggenberger. Presents essential details of every major battle in recorded history, from the first battle of Megiddo in 1479 B.C. to Grenada in 1984. List of Battle Maps. New Appendix covering the years 1967–1984. Index. 99 illustrations. 544pp. 6½ × 9¼.
24913-1 Pa. $14.95

AN ETYMOLOGICAL DICTIONARY OF MODERN ENGLISH, Ernest Weekley. Richest, fullest work, by foremost British lexicographer. Detailed word histories. Inexhaustible. Total of 856pp. 6½ × 9¼.
21873-2, 21874-0 Pa., Two-vol. set $17.00

WEBSTER'S AMERICAN MILITARY BIOGRAPHIES, edited by Robert McHenry. Over 1,000 figures who shaped 3 centuries of American military history. Detailed biographies of Nathan Hale, Douglas MacArthur, Mary Hallaren, others. Chronologies of engagements, more. Introduction. Addenda. 1,033 entries in alphabetical order. xi + 548pp. 6½ × 9¼. (Available in U.S. only)
24758-9 Pa. $11.95

LIFE IN ANCIENT EGYPT, Adolf Erman. Detailed older account, with much not in more recent books: domestic life, religion, magic, medicine, commerce, and whatever else needed for complete picture. Many illustrations. 597pp. 5⅜ × 8½.
22632-8 Pa. $8.50

HISTORIC COSTUME IN PICTURES, Braun & Schneider. Over 1,450 costumed figures shown, covering a wide variety of peoples: kings, emperors, nobles, priests, servants, soldiers, scholars, townsfolk, peasants, merchants, courtiers, cavaliers, and more. 256pp. 8⅜ × 11¼.
23150-X Pa. $7.95

THE NOTEBOOKS OF LEONARDO DA VINCI, edited by J. P. Richter. Extracts from manuscripts reveal great genius; on painting, sculpture, anatomy, sciences, geography, etc. Both Italian and English. 186 ms. pages reproduced, plus 500 additional drawings, including studies for *Last Supper, Sforza* monument, etc. 860pp. 7⅞ × 10¾. (Available in U.S. only) 22572-0, 22573-9 Pa., Two-vol. set $25.90

THE ART NOUVEAU STYLE BOOK OF ALPHONSE MUCHA: All 72 Plates from "Documents Decoratifs" in Original Color, Alphonse Mucha. Rare copyright-free design portfolio by high priest of Art Nouveau. Jewelry, wallpaper, stained glass, furniture, figure studies, plant and animal motifs, etc. Only complete one-volume edition. 80pp. 9⅜ × 12¼.   24044-4 Pa. $8.95

ANIMALS: 1,419 COPYRIGHT-FREE ILLUSTRATIONS OF MAMMALS, BIRDS, FISH, INSECTS, ETC., edited by Jim Harter. Clear wood engravings present, in extremely lifelike poses, over 1,000 species of animals. One of the most extensive pictorial sourcebooks of its kind. Captions. Index. 284pp. 9 × 12.
23766-4 Pa. $9.95

OBELISTS FLY HIGH, C. Daly King. Masterpiece of American detective fiction, long out of print, involves murder on a 1935 transcontinental flight—"a very thrilling story"—NY Times. Unabridged and unaltered republication of the edition published by William Collins Sons & Co. Ltd., London, 1935. 288pp. 5⅜ × 8½. (Available in U.S. only)   25036-9 Pa. $4.95

VICTORIAN AND EDWARDIAN FASHION: A Photographic Survey, Alison Gernsheim. First fashion history completely illustrated by contemporary photographs. Full text plus 235 photos, 1840–1914, in which many celebrities appear. 240pp. 6½ × 9¼.   24205-6 Pa. $6.00

THE ART OF THE FRENCH ILLUSTRATED BOOK, 1700–1914, Gordon N. Ray. Over 630 superb book illustrations by Fragonard, Delacroix, Daumier, Doré, Grandville, Manet, Mucha, Steinlen, Toulouse-Lautrec and many others. Preface. Introduction. 633 halftones. Indices of artists, authors & titles, binders and provenances. Appendices. Bibliography. 608pp. 8⅜ × 11¼.   25086-5 Pa. $24.95

THE WONDERFUL WIZARD OF OZ, L. Frank Baum. Facsimile in full color of America's finest children's classic. 143 illustrations by W. W. Denslow. 267pp. 5⅜ × 8½.   20691-2 Pa. $5.95

FRONTIERS OF MODERN PHYSICS: New Perspectives on Cosmology, Relativity, Black Holes and Extraterrestrial Intelligence, Tony Rothman, et al. For the intelligent layman. Subjects include: cosmological models of the universe; black holes; the neutrino; the search for extraterrestrial intelligence. Introduction. 46 black-and-white illustrations. 192pp. 5⅜ × 8½.   24587-X Pa. $6.95

THE FRIENDLY STARS, Martha Evans Martin & Donald Howard Menzel. Classic text marshalls the stars together in an engaging, non-technical survey, presenting them as sources of beauty in night sky. 23 illustrations. Foreword. 2 star charts. Index. 147pp. 5⅜ × 8½.   21099-5 Pa. $3.50

FADS AND FALLACIES IN THE NAME OF SCIENCE, Martin Gardner. Fair, witty appraisal of cranks, quacks, and quackeries of science and pseudoscience: hollow earth, Velikovsky, orgone energy, Dianetics, flying saucers, Bridey Murphy, food and medical fads, etc. Revised, expanded In the Name of Science. "A very able and even-tempered presentation."—The New Yorker. 363pp. 5⅜ × 8.
20394-8 Pa. $6.50

ANCIENT EGYPT: ITS CULTURE AND HISTORY, J. E Manchip White. From pre-dynastics through Ptolemies: society, history, political structure, religion, daily life, literature, cultural heritage. 48 plates. 217pp. 5⅜ × 8½.   22548-8 Pa. $4.95

SIR HARRY HOTSPUR OF HUMBLETHWAITE, Anthony Trollope. Incisive, unconventional psychological study of a conflict between a wealthy baronet, his idealistic daughter, and their scapegrace cousin. The 1870 novel in its first inexpensive edition in years. 250pp. 5⅜ × 8½. 24953-0 Pa. $5.95

LASERS AND HOLOGRAPHY, Winston E. Kock. Sound introduction to burgeoning field, expanded (1981) for second edition. Wave patterns, coherence, lasers, diffraction, zone plates, properties of holograms, recent advances. 84 illustrations. 160pp. 5⅜ × 8¼. (Except in United Kingdom) 24041-X Pa. $3.50

INTRODUCTION TO ARTIFICIAL INTELLIGENCE: SECOND, EN-LARGED EDITION, Philip C. Jackson, Jr. Comprehensive survey of artificial intelligence—the study of how machines (computers) can be made to act intelligently. Includes introductory and advanced material. Extensive notes updating the main text. 132 black-and-white illustrations. 512pp. 5⅜ × 8½. 24864-X Pa. $8.95

HISTORY OF INDIAN AND INDONESIAN ART, Ananda K. Coomaraswamy. Over 400 illustrations illuminate classic study of Indian art from earliest Harappa finds to early 20th century. Provides philosophical, religious and social insights. 304pp. 6⅜ × 9⅜. 25005-9 Pa. $8.95

THE GOLEM, Gustav Meyrink. Most famous supernatural novel in modern European literature, set in Ghetto of Old Prague around 1890. Compelling story of mystical experiences, strange transformations, profound terror. 13 black-and-white illustrations. 224pp. 5⅜ × 8½. (Available in U.S. only) 25025-3 Pa. $5.95

ARMADALE, Wilkie Collins. Third great mystery novel by the author of *The Woman in White* and *The Moonstone*. Original magazine version with 40 illustrations. 597pp. 5⅜ × 8½. 23429-0 Pa. $9.95

PICTORIAL ENCYCLOPEDIA OF HISTORIC ARCHITECTURAL PLANS, DETAILS AND ELEMENTS: With 1,880 Line Drawings of Arches, Domes, Doorways, Facades, Gables, Windows, etc., John Theodore Haneman. Sourcebook of inspiration for architects, designers, others. Bibliography. Captions. 141pp. 9 × 12. 24605-1 Pa. $6.95

BENCHLEY LOST AND FOUND, Robert Benchley. Finest humor from early 30's, about pet peeves, child psychologists, post office and others. Mostly unavailable elsewhere. 73 illustrations by Peter Arno and others. 183pp. 5⅜ × 8½. 22410-4 Pa. $3.95

ERTÉ GRAPHICS, Erté. Collection of striking color graphics: *Seasons, Alphabet, Numerals, Aces* and *Precious Stones*. 50 plates, including 4 on covers. 48pp. 9⅜ × 12¼. 23580-7 Pa. $6.95

THE JOURNAL OF HENRY D. THOREAU, edited by Bradford Torrey, F. H. Allen. Complete reprinting of 14 volumes, 1837–61, over two million words; the sourcebooks for *Walden*, etc. Definitive. All original sketches, plus 75 photographs. 1,804pp. 8½ × 12¼. 20312-3, 20313-1 Cloth., Two-vol. set $80.00

CASTLES: THEIR CONSTRUCTION AND HISTORY, Sidney Toy. Traces castle development from ancient roots. Nearly 200 photographs and drawings illustrate moats, keeps, baileys, many other features. Caernarvon, Dover Castles, Hadrian's Wall, Tower of London, dozens more. 256pp. 5⅜ × 8¼. 24898-4 Pa. $5.95

AMERICAN CLIPPER SHIPS: 1833–1858, Octavius T. Howe & Frederick C. Matthews. Fully-illustrated, encyclopedic review of 352 clipper ships from the period of America's greatest maritime supremacy. Introduction. 109 halftones. 5 black-and-white line illustrations. Index. Total of 928pp. 5⅜ × 8½.
25115-2, 25116-0 Pa., Two-vol. set $17.90

TOWARDS A NEW ARCHITECTURE, Le Corbusier. Pioneering manifesto by great architect, near legendary founder of "International School." Technical and aesthetic theories, views on industry, economics, relation of form to function, "mass-production spirit," much more. Profusely illustrated. Unabridged translation of 13th French edition. Introduction by Frederick Etchells. 320pp. 6⅛ × 9¼. (Available in U.S. only)
25023-7 Pa. $8.95

THE BOOK OF KELLS, edited by Blanche Cirker. Inexpensive collection of 32 full-color, full-page plates from the greatest illuminated manuscript of the Middle Ages, painstakingly reproduced from rare facsimile edition. Publisher's Note. Captions. 32pp. 9⅜ × 12¼.
24345-1 Pa. $4.95

BEST SCIENCE FICTION STORIES OF H. G. WELLS, H. G. Wells. Full novel *The Invisible Man,* plus 17 short stories: "The Crystal Egg," "Aepyornis Island," "The Strange Orchid," etc. 303pp. 5⅜ × 8½. (Available in U.S. only)
21531-8 Pa. $4.95

AMERICAN SAILING SHIPS: Their Plans and History, Charles G. Davis. Photos, construction details of schooners, frigates, clippers, other sailcraft of 18th to early 20th centuries—plus entertaining discourse on design, rigging, nautical lore, much more. 137 black-and-white illustrations. 240pp. 6⅛ × 9¼.
24658-2 Pa. $5.95

ENTERTAINING MATHEMATICAL PUZZLES, Martin Gardner. Selection of author's favorite conundrums involving arithmetic, money, speed, etc., with lively commentary. Complete solutions. 112pp. 5⅜ × 8½.
25211-6 Pa. $2.95

THE WILL TO BELIEVE, HUMAN IMMORTALITY, William James. Two books bound together. Effect of irrational on logical, and arguments for human immortality. 402pp. 5⅜ × 8½.
20291-7 Pa. $7.50

THE HAUNTED MONASTERY and THE CHINESE MAZE MURDERS, Robert Van Gulik. 2 full novels by Van Gulik continue adventures of Judge Dee and his companions. An evil Taoist monastery, seemingly supernatural events; overgrown topiary maze that hides strange crimes. Set in 7th-century China. 27 illustrations. 328pp. 5⅜ × 8½.
23502-5 Pa. $5.95

CELEBRATED CASES OF JUDGE DEE (DEE GOONG AN), translated by Robert Van Gulik. Authentic 18th-century Chinese detective novel; Dee and associates solve three interlocked cases. Led to Van Gulik's own stories with same characters. Extensive introduction. 9 illustrations. 237pp. 5⅜ × 8½.
23337-5 Pa. $4.95

Prices subject to change without notice.
Available at your book dealer or write for free catalog to Dept. GI, Dover Publications, Inc., 31 East 2nd St., Mineola, N.Y. 11501. Dover publishes more than 175 books each year on science, elementary and advanced mathematics, biology, music, art, literary history, social sciences and other areas.